Frederick County, Maryland
Church and Cemetery Records

Volume 6

Patricia A. Fogle

Heritage Books
2011

HERITAGE BOOKS
AN IMPRINT OF HERITAGE BOOKS, INC.

Books, CDs, and more—Worldwide

For our listing of thousands of titles see our website at
www.HeritageBooks.com

Published 2011 by
HERITAGE BOOKS, INC.
Publishing Division
100 Railroad Ave. #104
Westminster, Maryland 21157

Copyright © 1999 Patricia A. Fogle

Other books by the author:

Frederick County, Maryland Church and Cemetery Records, Volumes 1–6

Records of the Congregation of Trinity Reformed/United Church of Christ, Waynesboro, Franklin County, Pennsylvania, 1828–2003

Descendants of John and Mary (Miller) Cullers of Shenandoah County, Virginia

The Descendants of Michael Koller (Culler) and Elizabeth Schmid of Frederick County, Maryland

All rights reserved. No part of this book may be reproduced or transmitted in any form or by any means, electronic or mechanical, including photocopying, recording or by any information storage and retrieval system without written permission from the author, except for the inclusion of brief quotations in a review.

International Standard Book Numbers
Paperbound: 978-1-58549-640-2
Clothbound: 978-0-7884-8838-2

Deaths and Burials of Evangelical Reformed
United Church of Christ
Frederick, Frederick County, Maryland

Deaths and Burials

There are no death and burial records available at the church prior to 1788.

The following obituary notice was transcribed from a loose scrap of paper. It was written in German, in the hand-writing of Rev. William Runckel. (E. W. Reineke) It is interesting to note that he is not listed below.

25 Nov (1790)
Thomas **Schley**, first teacher in this congregation, born Aug. 31 1712 at Mertzheim(sic) in Germany, was married to Margaret **Wintz** (an. 1735- which latter died in June last. They lived in wedlock nearly 55 years, had nine children, of whom 8 are still living. He had been suffering for some time with asthma, but was confined to bed for one day only. He died yesterday morning, 10 o'clock, aged 78 years, 2 months and 3 days.

1788		Age
15 Apr	John, s/o Valentine **Schwartz**	27 years
3 May	John, of Thomas **Getzendanner**	0/2/0
28 Jul	Jacob, of Nicholas **Madery**	1/4/0
20 May	wife of Thomas **Beatty**	not given
not given	child of Peter **Bell**	not given
1789		
8 Mar	A. **Reitenauer**	not given
7 Mar	Stephen **Remsberg**	77/4/19
20 Mar	George **Wintz**	64/1/14
26 Mar	Susan, d\o Jacob **Schneider**	0/5/2
12 Apr	-------, child of Ad. **Wirtenbecher**	not given
4 May	Elizabeth, d/o Henry **Kempf**	not given
24 May	George, s/o Thomas **Ogle**	6/8/5
3 Jul	Jacob **Frosh**	1/4/15
20 Jul	John **Roth**	80/2/4
30 Jul	John **Kempf**	78/10/13
5 Aug	Elizabeth, d/o John **Faubel**	0/7/14
6 Aug	George **Jantz**	70/6/0
6 Aug	Catharine, d/o John **Paltzer**	1/2/14
6 Aug	William, s/o Jacob **Baltzel**	not given
9 Aug	George Frederick, s/o Andrew **Loh**	0/10/0
11 Aug	Anna Catharine, widow of Peter **Berg**	63/1/20
12 Aug	Margaret, w/o George **Roth**	32/5/24
16 Aug	Catharine, w/o Peter **Herget**	70/6/0
19 Aug	Susan, d/o John **Zimmerman**	3/1/0
7 Sep	Catharine, w/o Jacob **Beisser**	64/0/0
18 Sep	Michael, s/o John **Morgan**	0/9/10
26 Sep	William, s/o John **Hoffman**	0/8/3
3 Oct	Rebecca, d/o John **Beltz**	0/10/14
7 Oct	------- **Gottseelig**	68/0/0
21 Oct	Elizabeth, d/o Jacob **Aurand**	6/10/16
23 Oct	Catherine, d/o George **Reinhard**	1/1/21
29 Oct	Catharine, d/o Jacob **Aurand**	2/3/9
2 Nov	Elizabeth, d/o Andrew **Loh**	1/0/23

Deaths and Burials of Evangelical Reformed
United Church of Christ
Frederick, Frederick County, Maryland

11 Nov	Elizabeth, d/o David **Schultz**	4/3/6
17 Nov	Mary, d/o George **Hoffman**	0/10/0
24 Nov	Philip **Christ**	87/5/10
18 Nov	Peter, s/o Peter **Gebhardt**	12/9/3
1 Dec	Barbara, d/o John **Bockius**	3/2/9
4 Dec	Elizabeth, d/o John **Remsperger**	1/10/14
1790		
13 Jan	Blantina, w/o John **Holtz**	35/2/0
25 Jan	Mary, d/o Frantz **Kleinard**	0/11/0
27 Jan	Michael, s/o Nicholas **Deisz**	20/2/21
27 Jan	Caspar **Beckebach**	68/6/7
1 Feb	Christian, s/o Henry **Hartman** 11/8/1	
10 Feb	Christopher **Stoll**	48/1/9
20 Feb	Stephan, s/o Stephan **Brunner** 3/0/21	
23 Feb	Elizabeth **Keller**	14/0/0
28 Feb	Mary Ann, widow of Adam **Steckel**	47/2/9
2 Mar	Margaret, d/o Edward **Woodward**	6/0/3
8 Mar	Anna Catharine, w/o Sebastian **Doerr**	50/9/21
3 Apr	Anna Barbara, w/o Melchoir **Stehly**	63/3/8
3 Sep	Mary, d/o Jacob **Kast**	3/3/5
25 Sep	Daniel, s/o Elias **Brunner**	2/9/1
30 Sep	Jacob, s/o John **Schaefer**	12/10/27
31 Sep (sic)	Agnes, d/o Philip **Schmit**	5/1/0
11 Oct	William **Krum**	59/6/4
12 Oct	Valentine **Adam**	63/0/9
1791		
2 Jan	Anna Mary, d/o Lewis **Herm**	1/0/21
10 Jan	Catharine, w/o William **Crum** 49/0/0	
14 Jan	Jacob, s/o Joseph **Doll**	10/11/1
10 Feb	Anna Margaret, w/o Christoph **Eckhart**	56/4/6
1 Mar	Caspar **Mantz**	72/11/11
16 Mar	John, s/o John & Rebecca **Leshhorn**	0/8/15
20 Mar	Philip **Lehmer**	90/9/17
21 Mar	Melchior **Stehly**	71/9/16
2? Mar	Michael, s/o Jacob **Traut**	7/1/8
30 Mar	David, s/o Jacob & Sus. **Gombe**	1/0/27
31 Mar	Barbara, d/o Martin & Barbara **Tshudi**	7/11/23
8 Jun	Henry **Bruder**	46/3/3
12 Jul	Mary **Julianna**, consort of Balthasar Fuchs	42/2/21
3 Oct	Henry **Shober**, from Erlebach, Germany	74/6/0
11 Oct	Anna Barbara, widow of George **Josz**	nearly 67
13 Oct	Charlotte, w/o George **Gerlach**	30/5/27
10 Oct	George **Doffler**	not given
7 Nov	Jacob **Balzel**	80/2/0
16 Nov	Henry **Krass**	38/0/0
18 Nov	Michael **Christ**	55/2/0
2 Dec	Johanna Elenor, widow of George **Niecky**	78

Deaths and Burials of Evangelical Reformed
United Church of Christ
Frederick, Frederick County, Maryland

1792

Date	Name	Age
1 Jan	George Bernhardt **Kessler**	80/1/0
4 Jan	Mary Magdalen, widow of George **Dertzebach**	69
29 Jan	Catharine Elizabeth, w/o John **Steiner**	53/7/0
1 Feb	Barbara, widow of Conrad **Roth**	68/11
10 Feb	**Ott**'s child	not given
17 Mar	John, s/o John **Zimmerman**	11/1/16
4 Apr	John **Klein** (unmarried)	34/3/15
24 May	Benedict **Holtz**	75/2/2
27 Jun	Elizabeth, d/o John **Schaefer**	7/3/0
29 Jun	John, s/o Christian **Balzel**	4/6/8
30 Jun	Christian **Stauder**	68/5/8
1 Jul	Jacob **Hauck**	76
17 Jul	Conrad, s/o Jacob & Catharine **Schneider**	0/9/16
24 Jul	-------, **Bernesius** (an excommunicated Swiss minister. The funeral service was performed by the teacher)	
24 Jul	Daniel, s/o George & Mary **Hoffman**	age indistinct
31 Jul	Peter **Schaefer**	64
5 Aug	Elizabeth, widow of John **Heintz**	78/1/0
15 Aug	Jacob **Vollweiler**	57
24 Aug	Ann Elizabeth, d/o Daniel **Grim**	2/6/0
17 Sep	Elizabeth, d/o Frantz **Germayer**	1/5/0
20 Sep	John, s/o George **Bentz**	1/3/0
19 Oct	Valentine **May**	17/2/5
29 Oct	Jacob, s/o Balthasar **Getzedanner**	21/9
29 Oct	David, s/o John **Wallen**	1/1/21
12 Nov	Jacob **Roth**	52/1/1
3 De3c	Henry, s/o Adam **Klee**	16
17 Dec	Andrew **Dehaven**	22
19 Dec	Anna Catharine **Dofler**	67
30 Dec	Nicholas **Wollenschlager**	73

1793

Date	Name	Age
5 Jan	Peter, s/o Eckhardt **Gills**	0/7/0
19 Jan	George Michael **Beckebach**	63/10/0
22 Jan	Magdalen, d/o Benedict & Anna B. **Steiner**	13/11/0
23 Jan	the wife of Mr. **Cammel**, at Rocky Hill	not given
16 Feb	the widow **Hoffman** at the English Church	not given
11 Mar	Jacob, s/o Michael **Weber**	2
19 Apr	John, s/o Jacob **Keller**	2/3/23
8 May	George, s/o Jacob **Getzedanner**	5/2/4
13 May	Elizabeth, w/o John **Crum**	58/0/0
14 May	Eva, w/o Peter **Stimmel**	40/1/0
19 May	Adam **Schaefer**	60
15 Jun	Adam **Reeb**	50/1/0
26 Jun	William, s/o Jacob & Elizabeth **Steiner**	2/0/0
30 Jun	Mary, d/o Adam & Sybilla **Hausser**	1/2/0
12 Jul	Ann, w/o Balthasar **Getzedanner**	52/6/6
23 Jul	Mary, d/o Jacob & Elizabeth **Poley**	1/6/0
27 Jul	Mary Salome, w/o Michael **Veist**	51/3/2

Deaths and Burials of Evangelical Reformed
United Church of Christ
Frederick, Frederick County, Maryland

Date	Name	Age
31 Jul	Elizabeth **Hintzig**	12
2 Aug	Jacob **Christ**	54/4/1
2 Aug	w/o Jacob **Christ** (both buried in same grave)	51
5 Aug	William, s/o John and Gertrude **Heintz**	4/0/0
6 Aug	d/o Mr. **Campbel** at Rocky Hill	not given
6 Aug	Mary, w/o Joseph **Borckhardt** 26/0/0	
13 Aug	Lewis, s/o Lewis & Elizabeth **Kramer**	0/6/16
14 Aug	Peter, s/o Peter and Catharine **Wolf**	1/1/13
27 Aug	Michael, s/o Michael & Christina **Kern**	7/2/0
28 Aug	Elizabeth, d/o David & Sus. **Ehly**	12/0/1
2 Sep	Mary Catharine, w/o Peter **Engels**	65/4/0
9 Sep	Catharine, widow of Lewis **Wissinger**	74/0/0
13 Sep	Charles, s/o Michael & Margaret **Lingenfelder**	2/7/0
27 Sep	Mathew, s.o Jacob & Elizabeth **Traut**	7/0/0
27 Sep	Ann Barbara, w/o Jacob **Stehly**	40
28 Sep	Catharine, d/o Henry & Margaret **Kuhns**	1/1/16
29 Sep	Catharine, widow of G. **Jantz**	52/0/20
30 Sep	George, s/o John and Sus. **Morgan**	1/7/0
2 Oct	William, s/o Michael & Catharine **Weber**	5
2 Oct	Sybilla, widow of Valentine **Steckel**	73/0/16
9 Oct	Anna Mary, w/o Andrew **Derner**	35/8/0
10 Oct	Jacob, s/o John **Meyer**	10
10 Oct	David, s/o of John **Meyer**	5
19 Oct	Julianna, widow of John Diel **Berg**	69/1/23
21 Oct	Eva Mary, w/o Christian **Schryack**	54/9/13
24 Oct	George, s/o Sebastian **Doerr**	16/6/7
26 Oct	William, s/o Conrad & Sus. **Reitmay**	3/7/0
28 Oct	Elizabeth, d/o Peter & Catharine **Fleck**	2
5 Nov	Peter **Engels**	75
18 Nov	John **Rohr** (of, or from, Penn. Bucks)	22
28 Nov	Valentine, s/o Jacob **Traut**	9 weeks
27 Dec	Theobald **Kuhns**	71
31 Dec	George **Mertz**	50
1794		
8 Jan	William, s/o William **McClane**	1/0/24
13 Jan	William **Allbach**	70/10/5
14 Jan	Margaret, w/o Michael **Hafner**	31/11/0
16 Jan	Balthasar **Hemp**	73/10/0
19 Jan	Gabriel **Thomas**	73/7/12
30 Jan	Margaret, d/o Jacob & Catharine **Rohr**	1/11/6
31 Jan	Mary Catharine, w/o Frederick William **Handshu**	26/1/6
6 Feb	Jerome **Hildebrandt**	69/0/24
26 Feb	Jesse, a stranger, at J. Traut's	30
28 Feb	Jacob **Kempf**	29/2/19
7 Mar	Ann Margaret, widow of Henry **Hemp**	64/0/1
3 Apr	Adam **Knauf**	33
7 Apr	William, s/o John **Crum**	0/5/0
12 Apr	John **Schenkmayer** 71/9/0	

Deaths and Burials of Evangelical Reformed
United Church of Christ
Frederick, Frederick County, Maryland

Date	Name	Age
2 Jun	Peter **Slaethe**	79
6 Jun	Mary Elizabeth **Witmer**	77/9/0
15 Jul	Christina, d/o Mr. **Brine**	6/0/0
23 Jul	sister of Mrs. **Holliday**	not given
25 Jul	Anna, d/o Just. **Gerecht**	0/10/0
27 Jul	Mr. **Campbell**	not given
30 Jul	Barbara, d/o George **Daub**	19/7/3
31 Jul	George, s/o Henry **Smith**	6/6/0
3 Aug	d/o Mr. **Jacobs**	not given
6 Aug	Magdalen, w/o Conrad **Becker**	45/0/0
7 Aug	William, s/o Widow **Marshall**	not given
14 Aug	Susan, d/o George **Daub**	9/0/0
15 Aug	Elizabeth, d/o George **Lieblich**	0/11/0
16 Aug	Jacob, s/o Adam **Schaefer**	17/0/0
24 Aug	Jacob **Schmit**	69/2/0
5 Sep	Adam **Schaefer**	54/5/0
5 Sep	Christina, d/o John **Thomas**	1/1/0
5 Sep	Jacob, s/o George **Nichols**	2/8/0
18 Sep	Christina, d/o Bernard **Ott**	1/0/7
4 Oct	John **Dean**	45
5 Oct	Math. **Bucky**	66/5/18
5 Oct	Elizabeth, d/o Michael **Kern**	0/9/4
8 Oct	d/o William **Dewall** age unknown	
8 Oct	a man's wife (sic)	age unknown
9 Oct	Margaret, w/o ------- **Grafft**	50/0/0
22 Dec	Henry, s/o Henry **Fehling**	4/8/10
1795		
8 Jan	Dorothy, w/o John **Ried**	55/0/0
24 Jan	Jacob **Storm**	30/8/0
4 Feb	Charles, s/o Mat. **Ami**	22
5 Feb	Gabriel **Thomas**	42/9/21
15 Feb	Daniel **Mades**	75/8/18
16 Feb	Elizabeth, d/o Elias **Brunner**	0/2/14
16 Feb	Elizabeth, d/o Frederick **Häfner**	43/0/0
16 Mar	Elizabeth **Stehly**, widow	76/9/9
23 Mar	William, s/o John **Wallen**	1/6/0
20 Apr	Elizabeth, d/o Henry **Bantz**	0/7/0
22 Apr	Charles, s/o William **Springer**	1/7/0
9 May	Henry **Jung**	46
7 Jun	Anna Mary, widow of Peter **Baltzell**	83/3/0
20 Jun	John Adam **Eberly**	72/11/1
11 Jul	Joseph, s/o John **Getzendanner**	0/8/0
21 Jul	John **Schaefer**	85/10/27
8 Aug	Elizabeth **Dibuss**, widow	81/11/16
18 Aug	Margaret, widow of John **Schaefer**	70/0/0
22 Aug	Naomi, d/o Benjamin **Hull**	3/0/0
23 Aug	John, d/o Benjamin **Hull**	15/0/0
26 Aug	Valentine **Thomas**	70/1/4

Deaths and Burials of Evangelical Reformed
United Church of Christ
Frederick, Frederick County, Maryland

Date	Name	
31 Aug	Benjamin, s/o Benjamin **Hull**	10/0/0
5 Sep	Widow **Gottselig**	nearly 80
11 Sep	Elizabeth, w/o Jacob **Schaefer** 35/0/0	
12 Sep	Catharine, w/o Jacob **Getzedanner**	57/6/25
12 Sep	Julianna, d/o Jacob **Schaefer**	1/10/0
1 Oct	Mrs. **Tustin**	not given
5 Oct	Mr. **Tustin**	not given
7 Oct	George **Zimmerman**, Sr.	81/7/0
9 Oct	Henry, s/o Henry **Fehling**	0/7/0
22 Oct	Mary Elizabeth, widow of John **Chenkmeyer**	69
10 Dec	Margaret, w/o Adam **Wolff**, in Virginia	27/10/0
21 Dec	Charles **Hedge**	83
24 Dec	Ann Dorothy, w/o Paul **Leschhorn**	67

1796

Date	Name	
24 Mar	William Henry **Brandenburger**	73/7/0
6 Apr	John **Thomas**	38/10
12 Apr	Elizabeth, d/o John **Kramer**	0/5/0
24 May	John Peter, s/o John **Thomas**	5/2/21
14 Jun	Henry, s/o Henry **Kempf**	0/4/0
20 Jun	Abraham, s/o of Charles **Lang** 0/10/0	
2 Jul	Mary d/o Jacob **Eder**	5/2/1
23 Jul	Ann Catharine, w/o Balthasar **Reihm**	77/7
10 Aug	Mrs. **Linton**	70
1 Sep	George **Kramer**	58/3/0
19 Sep	Elizabeth **Huber**, widow	45/0/0
20 Sep	Mary **Huber**	22/0/0
21 Sep	Catharine, d/o Jacob **Wiest**	1/2/0
26 Sep	John Engelbert, s/o of Philip **Morgenstern**	13/0/0
6 Oct	Peter, s/o Peter **Stimmel**	20/0/0
9 Oct	Anna Barbara **Bergesser**	80/0/10
10 Oct	George Frederick **Draxel**	55/0/0
21 Nov	Esra, s/o Jacob **Kramer**	2/2/0
28 Nov	John **Ried**, Sr.	67/0/0
4 Dec	------ **McKinsey**	not given
15 Dec	John **Keller**	83/10/11
30 Dec	Valentine **Steckel**	23/11/0

1797

Date	Name	
19 Jan	Susan, d/o Ephriam **Crum**	not given
16 Apr	Susan, d/o John **Schaefer**	2
4 May	Eva, w/o John **Bockins**	47/5/0
12 May	George, s/o Andrew **Hedges**	not given
22 Jun	Elizabeth, d/o Valentine **Steckel**	0/9/21
29 Jun	John, s/o Peter **Stimmel**	9/8/0
4 Aug	Mary Ann Barbara, d/o David **Levig**	0/10/21
17 Auig	M. Magedalen, d/o Henry **Hemp**	5/9/11
22 Aug	Anna Mary, d/o John **Holtz**	3/8
29 Aug	Peter **Jauzy**	71/0/17
31 Aug	William s/o Henry **Otto**	3

Deaths and Burials of Evangelical Reformed
United Church of Christ
Frederick, Frederick County, Maryland

Date	Name	
5 Sep	A. Margaret, w/o George **Schneider**	68/9/2
7 Sep	Elizabeth, d/o John **Keplinger**	1/8/12
9 Sep	Frederick, s/o Henry **Otto**	0/5/8
9 Sep	John, s/o George **Briedy**	0/5/5
22 Sep	Frederick, a foundling	0/3/0
17 Oct	Elizabeth, d/o Andrew **Hedges**	2/6/4
15 Nov	Mary Elizabeth, w/o John **Breisz**	84/2/2
13 Dec	William s/o John **Crum**	11
17 Dec	a s/o Mr. **Marlow**	not given

(1798) Year not given in original records - original order observed.

Date	Name	
4 Feb	Philip **Weber**	58
14 Feb	James, s/o Mr. **Campbell**	not given
10 Mar	Widow **Morgenstern**	not given
19 Mar	Anne, w/o John **Farrin**	49/7/21
29 Mar	Mary Salome, w/o Elias **Lafeber**	49
8 Apr	Mary Magdalen, w/o Jacob **Levi**	24/3/0
11 Apr	Balthasar **Simmon**	75/2/21
13 Apr	Mrs. **Mackie**	not given
22 Apr	Lucas **Lukhorst**	44/0/5
20 May	Michael, s/o of Christian **Getzendanner**	6/11/8
31 May	Sus. Holtz, w/o William **Benedict**	76/3/28
7 Jun	Eva Elizabeth, d/o Michael **Eberhard**	7/4/23
27 Jun	Mary, widow of William **Crum**	51/0/0
28 Mun	Adam, s/o Adam **Knauf**	3/8/20
22 Jul	Peter **Hauck**	63/2/0
30 Jul	Willable, s/o George **Berg**	1/10/4
20 Aug	John Weiss, s/o Jacob **Beringer**	9/9/20
29 Aug	Mary, w/o George **Briedy**	38/1/24
5 Sep	Elizabeth, w/o David **Schreyer**	34/3/18
11 Sep	Elizabeth, d/o George **Beck**	0/7/0
21 Sep	Dorothy, w/o Philip **Stober**	41/9/0
13 Oct	Anna Mary, w/o Conrad **Doll**	53/7/0
20 Oct	Rebecca, d/o John **Rickert**	3/4/14
31 Oct	Lewis **Kramer**	50
11 Nov	Anna Susan **Dabler**	40/10/3
21 Nov	George **Daub**	66
24 Nov	Catharine, w/o Henry **Richter**	36/1/3

1799

Date	Name	
10 Feb	Melchior **Geisser**	110 yrs
6 Mar	Philip, s/o Conrad **Becker**	23/1/19
10 Apr	Andrew **Spannseiler**	77/0/0
14 May	Mrs. **Duwall**	not given
16 May	Magdalen, d/o John **Schaefer**	8/4/0
10 Jun	Daniel, s/o Simon **Schnook**	16
17 Jun	Mr. **Cample**	not given
18 Jun	Eva Catharine, w/o Jacob **Wiest**	44/0/0
21 Jun	Henry, s/o Henry **Kempf**	1
28 Jun	George **Elias**	57/3/11

Deaths and Burials of Evangelical Reformed
United Church of Christ
Frederick, Frederick County, Maryland

Date	Name	Age
11 Jul	Catharine, w/o George **Engel**	28/10/20
20 Jul	Daniel, s/o Jacob **Rohr**	0/4/0
24 Jul	Samuel, s/o of Jacob **Getzedanner**	1/0/11
3 Aug	Arthur, s/o Mr. **Dorsey**	0/8/0
23 Aug	John, s/o Adam **Koblenz**	3/6/21
13 Sep	Mary, d/o George **Briedy**	8/10/11
13 Sep	Sarah, w/o Peter **Schaun**	28/6/0
17 Sep	Margaret, widow of Balthasar **Simmon**	81/0/0
23 Sep	William **Umbach**	47
24 Oct	Margaret, w/o Frederick **Riehl** 31/9/7	
28 Oct	Mary Albertina, widow of Andrew **Bastian**	91
29 Oct	Nicholas **Deisz** (Tice)	57/0/17
11 Dec	Nicholas **Hauer**	66/4/3

1800

Date	Name	Age
15 Jan	Anna Mary **Bucky**, widow	62/1/22
16 Jan	Conrad **Miller**	33/8/13
11 Mar	Christina, w/o Andrew **Hedges**	24/11/3
25 Mar	Leonhard **Huber**	69/4/17
5 Apr	Catharine, d/o John **Reischwein**	1/8/0
8 Apr	Johanna M. Magdalen **Storm**, widow	81/10/5
15 Apr	Elizabeth **Spannseiler**, widow	79/7/0
17 Apr	Anna **Schober**, widow	76/7/0
20 Jun	Hubertus **Bayer**	71/7/0
20 Jun	Lewis **Hauer**	29/6/27
24 Jun	Jacob **Schneider**	67/0/20
7 Jul	Margaret, w/o Peter **Fuchs**	64
21 Jul	Jacob, s/o Jacob **Jung**	2/2/20
22 Jul	John, s/o Michael **Holtz**	5/0/22
8 Aug	Henry, s/o Henry **Herring**	19
24 Aug	Henry **Kempf**	41/2/1
31 Aug	Henry, s/o John **Hauck**	1/3/25
21 Oct	Mary, d/o John **Carny**	0/10
25 Oct	Jacob, s/o Michael **Holtz**	3/0/0
27 Oct	Catharine, w/o Peter **Berg**	32/10/7
28 Oct	John, s/o George **Schneider**	0/5/24
30 Oct	Anna Mary **Hildebrand**, widow	59/10/21
30 Oct	John **Breisz**	77/3/16
12 Nov	John **Spohn**	24/3/24
17 Nov	Henry **Wolff**	74
23 Nov	Jacob **Friederich**	27/3/14
29 Nov	Anna Mary, w/o John **Schamly**	68
9 Dec	Frantz **Becker**	57

1801

Date	Name	Age
1 Jan	Susan **Bayer**, widow	72
27 Feb	John, s/o Jacob **Steiner**	0/11/1
4 May	John Valentine **Schwartz**	76/1/6
22 Mar	Elizabeth **Ehhalt**, widow	63/0/0
23 Mar	Anna Mary, w/o Jacob **Steiner**	59/5/7

Deaths and Burials of Evangelical Reformed
United Church of Christ
Frederick, Frederick County, Maryland

Date	Name	Age
30 Mar	Anna Mary, d/o Peter **Degrange**	2/6/24
26 Apr	Anna Mary, w/o Leonhard **Storm**	67/2/22
10 May	George **Getzedanner**	42/6/7
16 Jun	Christina, d/o Jacob **Metzger**	2/2/26
27 Jun	Mary, d/o George **Josz**	3/8/9
1 Jul	John, s/o Henry **Jendes**	1 (and more)
3 Jul	Susanna Catharine Malvina, d/o Dr. **Runckel**	0/2/12
13 Jul	William, s/o George **Driszler**	0/7/19
10 Aug	Joseph **Maybury** of Penna.	22/8/0
10 Aug	Catharine, d/o Henry **Getzedanner**	0/6/4
14 Aug	Mary (Docts ?)	not given
19 Aug	Isaac, s/o Henry **Remsperger**	0/10/12
24 Aug	John s/o Conrad **Leschhorn**	0/11/17
1 Sep	Mary, d/o John **Faubel**	1/7/3
10 Sep	John **Beckebach**	31/10/24
24 Sep	Mary Eva, w/o William **Miller** 64/0/21	
26 Sep	Daniel, s/o Widow **Lehr**	11/11/14
4 Oct	Sarah, d/o Jacob **Bohley**	3/3/0
9 Oct	Elizabeth **Merckel** (single)	89/11/28
20 Oct	Abraham **Adams**	33/0/0
1 Nov	Elizabeth, d/o Widow **Graf**	1/8/1
2 Nov	Anna Mary, d/o Peter **Jung**	3/8/13
2 Nov	Mary Margaret, d/o Philip **Keller**	0/1/1
7 Nov	Dorothy, w/o Martin **Witterich**	83/2/0
28 Nov	Elizabeth, d/o George **Ehbrecht**	0/11/13
6 Dec	John George **Weil**	74/9/13
29 Dec	Paul **Leschhorn**	75
1802		
2 Feb	Elizabeth **Ried**	35/3/6
3 Feb	Adam **Wirtenbecher**	72

There are no death and burial records available between February 1802 and Jun 1874.

Deaths and burials recorded by Rev. Edmund Rishel Eschbach, DD

Name	Date of Death	Age	Place of Burial	Remarks
	1874			
Wolfe, Adam	22 Jun	74/7/25	Mt. Olivet	
Staley, Hester Ann	7 Jul	68/3/25	Doubs	paralysis
Albaugh, Charles Richardson	6 Aug	2/2/7	Mt. Olivet	dysentery
Grove, Maria	9 Aug	73/9/23	Mt. Olivet	
Rice, Harry Dennis	11 Aug	-/3/15	Mt. Olivet	cholera infantum
Kemp, Effie May	25 Aug	-/2/25	Mt Olivet	" "
Thomas, Elizabeth Ellen	29 Aug	-/11/20	Family grave yard	
Boetler, Henry	9 Sep	71/-/4	Mt. Olivet	concussion
Rupley, Frederick William	13 Sep	-/-/4	Mt. Olivet	
Staley, Alfred William	27 Sep	46/-/17	Mt. Olivet	typhoid fever
Shook, Edgar Haifew	1 Oct	-/4/1	Family grave yard	

Deaths and Burials of Evangelical Reformed
United Church of Christ
Frederick, Frederick County, Maryland

Name	Date	Age	Burial	Cause
Jarboe, Margaret	5 Oct	78/9/19	Middletown Reformed	
Schultz, George	8 Oct	87/4/20	Mt. Olivet	
Brengle, Lawrence J.	15 Oct	69/9/11	Mt. Olivet	heart disease
Brunner, James	21 Oct	66/9/8	Mt. Olivet	apoplexy
Gittinger, Annie Laurie	5 Nov	1/1/14	Mt. Olivet	croup
Brunner, Peter	23 Nov	65/9/23	Mt. Olivet	softening of brain

1875

Name	Date	Age	Burial	Cause
Hawman, Margaret	4 Jan	83/1/16	Mt. Olivet	consumption
Haller, Mrs. Ann L.	16 Feb	67/3/12	Mt. Olivet	consumption
Strailman, Mrs. Sarah	24 Feb	84	Mt. Olivet	old age
Ramsburg, Marion	2 Mar	1/5/14	Mt. Olivet	brain fever
Getzendanner, John J.	12 Mar	59/3/9	Mt. Olivet	died suddenly
Quynn, Allen G.	27 Mar	54	Mt. Olivet	hemorrhage
Hauer, George N.	10 Jun	44/7/16	Mt. Olivet	cramp cholic
Burkhart, Virginia	15 Jun	14/9/3	Reformed Grave Yard.	Consumption
Hildebrand, John	17 Jun	76/11/8	Doubs	gravel & age
Zellers, Charles C.	5 Jul	18/2/29	Mt. Olivet	drowned
Thomas, Mrs. Charlotte E.	25 Jul	54/-/24	Mt. Olivet	cancer
Gittinger, Maria Louisa, d/o of L.	27 Jul	-/7/18	Mt. Olivet	cholera infantum
Gerlach, Mollie A. G., d/o Christ.	5 Aug	-/5/10	Mt. Olivet	" "
Lease, infant d/o David	14 Sep	-/2/-	Reformed Grave Yard.	" "
Patterson, Charles Edison	6 Oct	7/10/15	Mt. Olivet	diphtheria
Stup, Mrs. Elizabeth	28 Oct	68	Mt. Olivet	rheumatism
Albaugh, Maurice	30 Oct	52	Reformed Grave Yard.	paralysis
Ellis, Mrs. Mary	16 Nov	75	Reformed Grave Yard.	cancer
Brengle, Charles A.	20 Nov	27/11/19	Mt. Olivet	Brights disease
Thomas, Christian	7 Dec	28/3/2	Mt. Olivet	suicide
Wilson, Charles	11 Dec	77/9/-	Shriver Grave Yard.	old age
Ramsburg, John	24 Dec	66/1/8	Mt. Olivet	heart disease

1876

Name	Date	Age	Burial	Cause
Detrick, Charles L.	1 Jan	8/10/-	Mt. Olivet	constipation
Stull, Joshua	1 Jan	58/11/5	Doubs	consumption
Shultz, Sophia	1 Jan	83	Mt. Olivet	
Roelky, Lucy M.	6 Jan	6/11/4	Mt. Olivet	croup
Pompell, Frederick	10 Jan	75/-/11	Reformed Grave Yard	died at Montevue
Flemming, Joseph P.	22 Jan	78/8/21	Reformed Grave Yard	paralysis
Fox, Jacob	31 Jan	76	Mt. Olivet	
Main, David	28 Feb	79/4/20	Mt. Olivet	cramps
Measel, Annie B., d/o of Charles	8 Mar	-/7/-	Mt. Olivet	pneumonia
Kennedy, Mrs. Ann Elizabeth	21 Mar	61/11/21	Reformed Grave Yard	dropsy
Gilbert, Harry C., s/o J. A.	24 Apr	3/7/9	Reformed Grave Yard	pneumonia
Hildebrand, Mrs. Lydia	7 Apr	76/-/25	Doubs	consumption
Baugher, Mrs. Ann E.	20 Apr	77/1/11	Mt. Olivet	
Miller, Edgar Lambert	24 Apr	1/10/24	Mt. Olivet	croup
Head, Mrs. Catharine	8 May	84/3/2	Reformed Grave Yard	asthma
Thomas, David O.	20 May	633/6/1	Mt. Olivet	heart disease
Shriver, Mrs. Louisa E.	24 May	78	Mt. Olivet	
Ricketts, Mrs. Mary Nannie T.	2 Jun	24/11/228	Mt. Olivet	consumption
Schley, Capt. Trench	26 Jun	38	Reformed Grave Yard	

Deaths and Burials of Evangelical Reformed
United Church of Christ
Frederick, Frederick County, Maryland

Name	Date	Age	Cemetery	Cause
Wolfe, Lewis Weltzheimer	27 Jun	49/7/24	Mt. Olivet	appoplexy
Wigle, Miss Polly	2 Jul	87	Reformed Grave Yard	old age
Akers, infant child of Abner	18 Jul	-/3/-	Reformed Grave Yard	cholera infantum
Neihoff, Mrs. Susan	27 Jul	62/9/10	Reformed Grave Yard	consumption
Kline, Frederick	30 Jul	87	Doubs	old age
Rice, Charles M.	16 Aug	23/9/17	Mt. Olivet	inflam. of bowels
Gilbert, George Mortimer	18 Aug	-/9/18	Reformed Grave Yard	cholera infantum
Hildebrand, Lewis Robert	20 Aug	-/5/4	Doubs	lung congestion
Brommett, Mrs. Ellen	6 Sep	69/5/20	Mt. Olivet	softening of brain
Cover, Mrs. Susan	5 Oct	79	Ref. Cem. Taneytown	stomach disorder
Staley, Mrs. Anna E.	6 Oct	79/7/-	Mt. Olivet	heart disease
Smith, Katie, d/o of D. M.	15 oct	-/11/3	Mt. Olivet	spasms
Himbury, J. B.	12 Nov	64/7/-	Mt. Olivet	heart disease
Pampell, Grace Irene	14 Nov	2/7/13	Mt. Olivet	pneumonia
Kemp, Charles Wesley	19 Nov	47	Mt. Olivet	Brights disease
Ebert, M. Lucretia	15 Dec	45	Mt. Olivet	stomach cancer
Hargate, Douglass Harry, s/o John E.	31 Dec	-/4/8	Mt. Olivet	pneumonia

1877

Name	Date	Age	Cemetery	Cause
Ramsburg, Peter	6 Jan	68/10/9	Mt. Olivet	paralysis
Keefer, Mrs. Elizabeth	9 Jan	61	Mt. Olivet	dysentery
Bentz, Miss Rebecca	10 Jan	78	Mt. Olivet	paralysis
Tabler, William Benjamin	13 Jan	2/7/12	Mt. Olivet	burned
Duvall, Mrs. Christiana R.	9 Feb	51/8/16	Reformed Grave Yard	pneumonia
Steiner, Ralph Denning Smith	19 Feb	2/5/7	Mt. Olivet	pneumonia
McDaniel, William A.	6 Mar	48	Mt. Olivet	heart disease
Davis, William D.	11 Mar	67/10/19	Mt. Olivet	gravel
Staley, Amanda Cordelia May	19 Mar	-/7/23	Doubs	inflam. of bowels
Mehrling, Florence Katie	2 Apr	13/3/23	Mt. Olivet	
Wills, Charles	11 Apr	70	York, PA	
Wilcoxon, Harry Jackson	23 Apr	8/3/21	Mt. Olivet	
Ramsburg, Edward F.	21 Apr	35/9/19	Mt. Olivet	drowned in river
Stup, Elijah Curtis	27 Apr	40/10/8	Mt. Zion Grave Yard	dropsy
Jenks, Dr. William D.	2 May	85/2/27	Mt. Olivet	heart disease
Hedges, John A.	5 May	61/9/23	Reformed Grave Yard	cancer
Keefer, Charles H.	12 Jun	41/9/23	Reformed Grave Yard	R.R. accident
Schley, Lewis H.	12 Jun	22/5/13	Mt. Olivet	R.R. accident
Lampe, Caroline A.	18 Jun	6 weeks	Mt. Olivet	
Houck, Samuel	19 Jul	25/10/8	Mt. Olivet	consumption
Smith, Daniel	20 Jul	76/8/27	Doubs	consumption
Cole, Williiam G.	26 Jul	63	Mt. Olivet	
Price, John E.	30 Jul	-/1/-	Mt. Olivet	cholera infantum
Hiteshew, Miss Elizabeth	3 Sep	75	Reformed Grave Yard	typhoid dysentery
Main, Mary R.	25 Sep	-/6/10	Mt. Olivet	consumption
Crum, Isaac	26 Sep	71/11/-	Mt. Olivet	consumption
Simmons, S. Cyrus	2 Oct	57/-/1	Mt. Olivet	cancer
Sechrist, Mrs. Sarah	7 Oct	63/9/23	Mt. Olivet	
Staley, Mrs. Kate E.	16 Oct	21/4/26	Mt. Olivet	consumption
Dutrow, Joseph L.	30 Oct	60/5/13	Buckeystown	paralysis
Dyer, Mrs. Rachel	5 Nov	77/4/5	Reformed Grave Yard	heart disease

Deaths and Burials of Evangelical Reformed
United Church of Christ
Frederick, Frederick County, Maryland

Name	Date	Age	Cemetery	Cause
Heck, John	7 Nov	64/9/12	Mt. Olivet	inflam. of bowels
Loehr, Miss Polly	19 Nov	83	Reformed Grave Yard	old age
Martz, Daisie Rebecca	19 Nov	3/11/1	Doubs	burned to death
Hilt, George Thomas	13 Dec	2/9/	Mt. Olivet	diphtheria
Feaga, Mrs. Susanna Maria	28 Dec	56/2/7	Mt. Olivet	pneumonia

1878

Name	Date	Age	Cemetery	Cause
Grove, Reuben D.	7 Feb	82/10/13	Mt. Olivet	found dead in bed
Barrick, Allen E.	24 Feb	-/6/27	Mt. Olivet	convulsions
Carmack, Miss Salome	21 Mar	59	Mt. Olivet	heart trouble
Winter, Frederick	25 Mar	66/-/20	Mt. Olivet	pneumonia
Houck, Ezra	8 Apr	76	Mt. Olivet	rheumatic gout
Lease, Mrs. Amelia	15 Apr	76/-/14	Reformed Grave Yard	pneumonia
Collum, Sanie	19 Apr	6	Mt. Olivet	scarlet fever
Finney, Robert Eugene	23 Apr	19/9/3	Mt. Olivet	consumption
Jones, Mary C.	25 Jun	21/5/1	Mt. Olivet	consumption
Gilbert, infant	26 Jun	-/5/17	Reformed Grave Yard	
Ginger, Frank	26 Jun	-/11/1	Mt. Olivet	consumption
Cutsail, Mrs. Susan	3 Jul	51/9/16	Mt. Olivet	paralysis
Dertzbaugh, George William	5 Jul	533/1/11	Mt. Olivet	lead poisoning
Getzendanner, Mrs. Martha V.	11 Jul	39/6/10	Mt. Olivet	fever
Trago, William	19 Jul	74	Mt. Olivet	weakness
Ott, John	2 Aug	79	Reformed Grave Yard	old age
Hedges, Mrs. Catharine	12 Aug	78/-/22	Mt. Olivet	
Stup, Harvey T., s/o Frances	25 Aug	2/11/1	Mt. Olivet	diphtheria
Ray, Nannie E., d/o of S.	26 Sep	2/7/-	Reformed Grave Yard	heart disease
Corey, Paris	9 Oct	54/-/21	Mt. Olivet	cancerous tumor
Duvall, Albert Justus, s/o James	29 Oct	3/7/7	Mt. Olivet	diphtheria
Starr, Mary Rosalie, d/o J. T.	12 Nov	3/3/21	Mt. Olivet	enysipelas (?)
Stull, Mrs. Susanna	27 Nov	77/8/22	Mt. Olivet	gangrene
Hagan, Miss Margaret	12 Dec	not given	Reformed Grave Yard	consumption
Titlow, Lewis Scholl	19 Dec	32/8/29	Mt. Olivet	typhoid fever
Seibert, Mrs. Anna Sophia	20 Dec	64	Lutheran Grave Yard	

1879

Name	Date	Age	Cemetery	Cause
Moberly, Daisy E.	1 Jan	3/8/7	Mt. Olivet	
Mantz, Mrs. Lucy Jane	9 Jan	58/1/-	Mt. Olivet	consumption
Mohler, Miss Bettie	10 Jan	54/8/25	Mt. Olivet	burned
Lutz, George Edward, s/o John	25 Jan	3/2/26	Mt. Olivet	chronic croup
Staley, Miss Agnes	1 Feb	67/7/15	Reformed Grave Yard	
Bragonier, Mrs. Ann	4 Feb	74/11/20	Mt. Olivet	old age
Starr, Mrs. Rebecca S.	23 Feb	35/2/28	Mt. Olivet	consumption
Brengle, Mrs. Eliza	5 Mar	79/11/11	Mt. Olivet	paralysis
Lamar, Mrs. Caroline J.	21 Mar	64/7/15	Mt. Olivet	paralysis of brain
Blumenauer, George	9 Apr	64/4/18	Mt. Olivet	consumption
Measell, Ellen R., d/o Charles T.	14 Apr	-/10/22	Mt. Olivet	pneumonia
Ott, Mrs. Mary A.	19 Apr	75/11/6	Reformed Grave Yard	pneumonia
Marble, Jesse H.	21 Apr	73	Mt. Olivet	
Hobbs, Mrs. Mary Margaret	29 Apr	47	Mt. Olivet	cancer in stomach
Bruner, Mrs. Susan M.	12 May	27/9/3	Reformed Grave Yard	lockjaw
Murphy, Philomen S.	30 May	78	Reformed Grave Yard	

Deaths and Burials of Evangelical Reformed
United Church of Christ
Frederick, Frederick County, Maryland

Name	Date	Age	Place	Cause
Blumenauer, George W.	5 Jun	29	Mt. Olivet	Brights disease
Lease, Jane Elizabeth	14 Jun	11/3/19	Reformed Grave Yard	
Mantz, Charles	28 Jun	71/6/19	Mt. Olivet	liver disease
Holtz, Mary Catharine	29 Jun	24/9/4	Glade Church	consumption
Ackerman, Mrs. Elizabeth	8 Jul	61/11/2	Mt. Olivet	cancer of stomach
Hoskins, George	12 Jul	74/6/7	Mt. Olivet	
Maynard, Lewis S.	12 Sep	22/2/24	Mt. Olivet	consumption
Nichols, Mrs. Elizabeth	17 Sep	60/1/16	Mt. Olivet	paralysis
Wilcoxon, Clarence Eugene	22 Sep	24/1/24	Mt. Olivet	consumption
Rigney, Miss Medora	5 Oct	38	Mt. Olivet	consumption
Hargate, Clara Emma	13 Oct	14/8/5	Mt. Olivet	typhoid fever
Bentz, Mrs. Catharine A.	23 Oct	54/8/18	Mt. Olivet	consumption
Lease, George W.	23 Oct	55/7/14	Reformed Grave Yard	
Galbraith, Mrs. G. L.	not given	not given	Mt. Olivet	
Brengle, Curtis	2 Nov	21	Reformed Grave Yard	consumption
Krantz, Mrs. Catharine Elizabeth	11 Nov	56/9/15	Mt. Olivet	pneumonia
Zeiler, Mrs. Emma M.	12 Nov	27/11/9	Mt. Olivet	consumption
Buckey, Miss Isabella W.	16 Nov	48	Mt. Olivet	Cancerous Con.
Brengle, Lewis A.	20 Nov	70/1/13	Reformed Grave Yard	nerv. prostration
Blumenauer, Grace, d/o G. W.	19 Dec	1/6/16	Mt. Olivet	whooping cough
Norris, Frank Albertis	22 Dec	2/9/-	Mt. Olivet	scarlet fever
Steven, Marion P.	26 Dec	13	Mt. Olivet	cancerous con.
1880				
English, James J.	23 Jan	60	Mt. Olivet	heart disease
Trago, Mrs. Eveline	28 Jan	75	Mt. Olivet	dropsy
Lease, Mrs. Ella	5 Feb	32/1/5	Reformed Grave Yard	consumption
Derr, Emma J.	18 Feb	18/10/14	Mt. Olivet	rheumatism
Best, David	27 Feb	76/1/10	Mt. Olivet	gangrene
Brooks, Mrs. Eleanor	2 Mar	85	Mt. Olivet	old age
Zumstein, Louis D.	22 Mar	30	Reformed Grave Yard	apoplexy
Brashears, J. Henry	20 Apr	47	Reformed Grave Yard	heart disease
Hargate, Harry M., s/o J. E.	23 Apr	-/9/15	Mt. Olivet	scarlet fever
Ramsburg, William H.	5 Jun	64/7/18	Mt. Olivet	heart disease
Epley, infant c/o of Frank	12 Jun	-/-/18	Reformed Grave Yard	
Hiteshew, Alick	19 Jun	3/7/2	Mt. Olivet	
Betzan, Mrs. Susan	28 Jul	75/5/20	Reformed Grave Yard	dropsy
Ebert, Samuel B.	35 Oct	45/1/28	Mt. Olivet	cancer
Peters, Charles Albert	28 Oct	-/9/26	Mt. Olivet	pneumonia
Knauff, Miss Deborah M.	3 Nov	79/2/11	Reformed Grave Yard	
Brunner, Isaac	29 Nov	65/9/14	Reformed Grave Yard	heart disease
Rohrback, Mrs. Ellen M.	14 Dec	47/6/9	Mt. Olivet	pleuro-pneumonia
Bruner, John H.	11 Dec	33/-/21	Mt. Olivet	typhoid fever
Thomas, Mary Eleanor, d/o Chewton	27 Dec	1/7/12	Mt. Olivet	diphtheria
Shawen, Mrs. Christianna	27 Dec	61/4/24	Mt. Olivet	Died Sandy Hook
Rhoderick, Mahlon	27 Dec	70/-/2	Mt. Olivet	paralysis
1881				
Fritchey, Miss Martha	1 Jan	45/2/14	Mechanicsburg, PA	consumption
Cramer, William McClellan	6 Jan	19/1/223	Mt. Olivet	typhoid fever
Yinger, Charles Lewis	14 Jan	1/2/5	Mt. Olivet	convulsions

Deaths and Burials of Evangelical Reformed
United Church of Christ
Frederick, Frederick County, Maryland

Name	Date	Age	Burial Place	Cause
Whaley, Mrs. Sophia	16 Jan	51	Mt. Olivet	softening of brain
Main, William	24 Jan	73/10/11	Mt. Olivet	paralysis
Metz, Mrs. Ann Phoebe	25 Jan	86/2/224	Reformed Grave Yard	old age
Lidie, Mrs. Mary Ann	6 Feb	86	Reformed Grave Yard	old age
Shue, Mrs. Sarah	7 Feb	82/11/21	Family ground	old age
Lease, Noah L.	28 Feb	8/2/23	Reformed Grave Yard	Lorflam rheum
Staley, Ezra	28 Feb	71/4/-	Reformed Grave Yard	heart disease
Bender, Emma Amelia	25 Apr	15/-/20	Reformed Grave Yard	consumption
Pyfer, Philip	7 May	57	Mt. Olivet	Bronchial inflam.
Clem, Mrs. Rhoda	24 May	66/10/2	Reformed Grave Yard	apoplexy
Stone, Mrs. Lydia A. E.	16 Jun	41/-/8	Reformed Grave Yard	cancer
Shipley, Blanche Catharine	5 Jul	-/6/20	Mt. Olivet	cholera infantum
Roelke, Margaret Walker	14 Jul	-/7/29	Mt. Olivet	" "
Brengle, Nicholas John	19 Jul	-/5/24	Mt. Olivet	" "
Gurlach, Jacob	25 Jul	25/55/28	Mt. Olivet	consumption
Kelletts, Mrs. Deborah	5 Aug	60	Reformed Grave Yard	Brights disease
Zimmerman, Barbara Alice	13 Sep	36/4/17	Mt. Oliver	hysteria mania
Renner, William A.	14 Sep	5/5/23	Mt. Olivet	diphtheria
Best, Frank Lawrence	16 Sep	1/7/1	Mt. Olivet	whooping cough
Shipley, Charles Nimrod	19 Sep	5/7/15	Reformed Grave Yard	diphtheria
Rhoderick, Williiam E.	26 Sep	26/4/27	Mt. Olivet	typhoid fever
Brish, Bessie J.	4 Oct	2/9/7	Mt. Olivet	diphtheria
Jones, Daisy Sophia	4 Oct	2/1/26	Episcopal Grave Yard	"
Shipley, Francis Key	4 Oct	-/3/4	Reformed Grave Yard	cholera infantum
Hodge, Mrs. Mary L. V.	9 Oct	30/10/6	Mt. Olivet	consumption
Brish, William H.	17 Oct	56	Mt. Olivet	internal hemmor.
Miller, Zoe Irene	29 Oct	2/6/23	Reformed Grave Yard	diphtheria
Markey, Bettie	8 Nov	2/-/14	Mt. Olivet	"
Measel, Willie Zacharias	23 Nov	13/6/11	Mt. Olivet	"
Titlow, Adie Ely	28 Nov	20/2/18	Mt. Olivet	"
Storm, Frank Winter	13 Dec	5/10/17	Mt. Olivet	"
Measell, Harry Victor	28 Dec	1/5/22	Mt. Olivet	"
Scholl, Louis V.	29 Dec	73/-/23	Mt. Olivet	
	1882			
Ebert, Frank Hill	1 Jan	4/1/11	Mt. Olivet	quinsy
Ebert, Elmer Clarence	4 Jan	1/7/3	Mt. Olivet	croup
Albaugh, Harry Lancaster	5 Jan	4/-/5	Mt. Olivet	diphtheria
Mussetter, Emma Catharine	9 Jan	2/8/11	Mt. Olivet	"
Albaugh, Justus Roy	14 Jan	1/1/24	Mt. Olivet	"
Clingan, Harry William	15 Jan	9/8/13	Mt. Olivet	brain fever
Albaugh, Frank Bertram	16 Jan	6/6/30	Mt. Olivet	diphtheria
Staley, Cora Phoebe	16 Jan	21/1/-	Mt. Olivet	"
Robinson, Mrs. Elizabeth A.	17 Jan	54/4/11	Reformed Grave Yard	pneumonia
Staley, Ida M.	19 Jan	27/- 29	Mt. Olivet	diphtheria
Renner, Florence Emma	28 Feb	8/1/21	Mt. Olivet	"
Metzger, George	5 Mar	78/1/-	Mt. Olivet	old age
Sturgis, Anna Eliza	10 Mar	9/6/24	Mt. Olivet	spine disease
Ramsburg, Mrs. Catharine A. R.	11 Mar	61/8/1	Mt. Olivet	consumption
Thomas, Lewis Michael	24 Mar	63	Mt. Olivet	apoplexy

Deaths and Burials of Evangelical Reformed
United Church of Christ
Frederick, Frederick County, Maryland

Name	Date	Age	Cemetery	Cause
Ellis, Daniel	1 Apr	86	Mt. Olivet	old age
Colliflower, Rev. William F.	30 Apr	69	Mt. Olivet	kidney disease
Houck, Mary E.	1 May	-/5/11	Mt. Olivet	whooping cough
Eckstein, Charles Louis	19 Jun	-/6/28	Mt. Olivet	
Carlin, Frank B.	29 Jun	47	Mt. Olivet	Brights disease
Ebert, Mrs. Fannie L.	6 Jul	32/4/-	Mt. Olivet	consumption
Betzan, John	10 Jul	78/1/21	Reformed Grave Yard	dropsy
Smith, Mrs. Jeannette J. S.	13 Jul	30	Mt. Olivet	congestive chill
Koester, Miss Mary	17 Jul	43	Mt. Olivet	consumption
Akers, Charles Marion	? Aug	-/3/15	Mt. Olivet	cholera infantum
Rohr, Miss Susan	11 Aug	73	Reformed Grave Yard	heart disease
Mohler, Mrs. Mary Catharine	25 Aug	88/2/11	Mt. Olivet	old age
Esterly, Mrs. Ann Rebecca	31 Aug	56/7/11	Mt. Olivet	cancer
Forrest, Minnie J.	11 Sep	2/2/6	Mt. Olivet	pneumonia
Wachter, Mrs. Catharine E. M.	7 Oct	38/7/5	Mt. Olivet	consumption
Hershperger, Mrs. Bettie	5 Nov	39	Mt. Olivet	pyaemia
Blumenauer, Nicholas	19 Nov	66/-/10	Mt. Olivet	inflam. bladder
Angivine, Hattie Sophia	27 Nov	12/6/24	Mt. Olivet	heart disease
Ely, James Arthur Garfield	29 Nov	1/6/-	Reformed Grave Yard	pneumonia
Rohr, Daniel	17 Dec	68	Reformed Grave Yard	gen. debility

1883

Name	Date	Age	Cemetery	Cause
Hargate, Mrs. Margaret Ann S.	2 Jan	54/3/17	Mt. Olivet	
Fauble, John	2 Jan	87/5/25	Mt. Olivet	old age
Metzger, Mrs. Sarah	25 Jan	77/4/22	Mt. Olivet	hernia
Shafer, Peter	1 Feb	84/5/18	Reformed Grave Yard	paralysis
Wilcoxon, John	4 Feb	75/1/6	Mt. Olivet	pyaemia
Adams, Abraham T.	5 Feb	55/11/12	Mt. Olivet	paralysis
Page, Calvin	9 Feb	78	Mt. Olivet	pneumonia
Bevan, Mrs. Sarah	17 Feb	67	Mt. Olivet	peritonitis
Shawen, Grafton	26 Feb	75/1/18	Mt. Olivet	paralysis
Staley, Cornelius A.	13 Mar	49/-/18	Mt. Olivet	consumption
Davis, Arthur Eugene	19 Mar	-/-/18	Mt. Olivet	
Byerly, Jacob	23 Mar	76/1/18	Reformed Grave Yard	heart disease
Thomas, William M.	28 mar	25	Mt. Olivet	suicide
Reese, Mrs. Louisa	1 Apr	47/7/5	Mt. Olivet	diabetes
Hobbs, Charles S.	3 Apr	45/3/-	Mt. Olivet	
Main, Eli R.	18 Apr	26/-/21	Mt. Olivet	Brights disease
Wachter, Catharine Ann	25 Apr	65/-/11	Mt. Olivet	paralysis
Miller, Ethel	26 Apr	1/10/19	Mt. Olivet	scarlet fever
Engle, Ezra M.	26 May	55	Mt. Olivet	cancer
Boetler, Miss Laura	2 Jun	50	Mt. Olivet	"
Chew, Charles Thomas Smith	6 Jun	-/-/6	Mt. Olivet	
Lerch, Charles	23 Jun	26	Mt. Olivet	consumption
Stauffer, Guy V.	23 Jun	10/6/13	Mt. Olivet	scarlet fever
Shipley, Frederick	24 Jun	64/1/10	Reformed Grave Yard	consumption
Clem, Mrs. Henrietta	7 Jul	72	Reformed Grave Yard	
Stauffer, Anna Rebecca	12 Jul	1/8/10	Mt. Olivet	scarlet fever
Roth, Donald A.	30 Jun	2/-/7	Mt. Olivet	"
Getzendanner, Mrs. Ann E.	6 Aug	82/4/8	Mt. Olivet	old age

Deaths and Burials of Evangelical Reformed
United Church of Christ
Frederick, Frederick County, Maryland

Name	Date	Age	Cemetery	Cause
Derr, Mrs. Elizabeth	7 Aug	75/6/23	Mt. Olivet	
Derr, Charles W.	9 Aug	34/5/23	Mt. Olivet	consumption
Hersperger, John Benjamin	9 Aug	-/10/-	Mt. Olivet	diphtheria
Miller, Bernice	30 Aug	-/10/8	Mt. Olivet	dropsy
Diehl, Philip August	15 Sep	27/1/1	Mt. Olivet	inflam of bowels
Nichols, Mrs. Catharine	30 Sep	63	Mt. Olivet	gangrene
Bartgis, James	6 Oct	63/11/4	Mt. Olivet	heart disease
Castle, John Jarboe	8 Oct	24/2/22	Mt. Olivet	consumption
Hanschew, Harriet C.	29 Oct	40/2/8	Mt. Olivet	"
Zimmerman, Jacob	6 Nov	83	Charlesville, Mt. Zion	paralysis
Fauble, Margaret R.	15 Nov	79	Mt. Olivet	old age
Schley, James M.	17 Nov	68	Mt. Olivet	paralysis

At this point all dates are listed as date of funeral instead of date of death. All burials are in Mt. Olivet Cemetery unless otherwise indicated.

1884

Name	Date	Age	Cemetery	Cause
Bender, Mrs. Eliza	3 Jan	75		cancer of stomach
Staley, David Levi	7 Jan	62/9/23		cancer of stomach
Albaugh, Charles Edward	28 Jan	49/10/29		consumption
Glaze, Mrs. Elizabeth	30 Jan	84/2/27		heart disease
Benton, Miss Ellen Elizabeth	10 Feb	60	Reformed Grave Yard	pleurisy
Gesser, Frank Edward	12 Feb	-/3/22		pneumonia
Ways, William Henry	1 Mar	7/2/6		typhoid pneu.
Finny, Miss Julia Lee	6 Mar	19/3/3		consumption
Fout, Mrs. Susan	11 Mar	77/5/-		laryngitis
Dixon, Cora Virginia	12 Mar	1/5/15		brain fever
Kennedy, David	16 May	76/7/16	Reformed Grave Yard	cramp cholic
Moore, Daisie Marie	28 May	1/6/-		meningitis
Tyler, Mrs. Catharine M.	6 Jun	73/-/-	Georgetown, DC	
Scholl, Dennis	20 Jun	71/8/1		paralysis
Schultz, Theodore	27 Jun	56/7/1		consumption
Getzendanner, Mrs. Catharine A.	10 Jul	48/5/21		"
Rice, Mrs. Henrietta	12 Jul	81/7/10	Reformed Grave Yard	paralysis
Dixon, Mrs. Sophia	13 Jul	69/11/11		inflam. of bowels
Delashmutt, Elias E.	17 Jul	-/2/21		cholera infantum
Jones, Edgar	20 Jul	-/-/28	Episcopal Grave Yard	pneumonia
Roelke, Monroe Franklin	22 Jul	-/2/11		cholera infantum
Lipps, Bessie	27 Jul	-/2/7		" "
Brunner, Mrs. Susan	17 Aug	85/6/-		
Kantner, George	2 Sep	88/5/2		
Fout, John H.	5 Sep	81/11/15		paralysis
Staley, George Albert	19 Aug	1/6/5	Doubs	
Chew, Maud May	24 Aug	-/1/10		cholera infantum
Akers, Carrie Estelle	6 Sep	-/1/10	Reformed Grave Yard	
Akers, Mabel Irene	14 Sep	-/1/17	Reformed Grave Yard	
Measell, Clarence C.	15 Sep	12/-/28		
Derr, Mrs. Catharine	11 Oct	70/3/4		dropsy
Derr, Daniel	5 Nov	72/10/23		heart disease
Brengle, Mrs. Rebecca	9 Nov	76/8/15		
Umberger, Roy Eugene	10 Nov	1/11/29	Reformed Grave Yard	

Deaths and Burials of Evangelical Reformed
United Church of Christ
Frederick, Frederick County, Maryland

Name	Date	Age	Cemetery	Cause
Reese, Mrs. Catharine	10 Nov	87/6/10		old age
Walling, Ruth, d/o J. H.	8 Dec	-/7/6		pneumonia
Smith, Mrs. Eleanor	14 Dec	78/1/15	Reformed Grave Yard	paralysis
Scholl, Mrs. Margaret	26 Dec	70		pneumonia
1885				
Wilcoxon, Rufus H.	18 Jan	46/5/8		heart disease
Getzendanner, Christian	5 Feb	68		pneumonia
Rhodes, John	6 Feb	78/1/17		softening of brain
Sponseller, infant child of John	10 Feb	-/-/14		
Holbruner, Thomas M.	17 Feb	61/-/6		apoplexy
Holtz, Mrs. Agnes	25 Feb	73/5/10	Charlesville, Mt. Zion	debility
Nichols, C. Randolph	23 Mar	71		paralysis
Byerly, Mrs. Catharine Elizabeth	4 Apr	72/5/4	Reformed Grave Yard	apoplexy
Hauer, Mrs. Ann Catharine	5 Apr	61		pneumonia
Hallar, Eliza M.	27 Apr	79/3/20		dropsy
Gring, Vida Rebecca	3 Jun	11		diphtheria
Sinn, Mrs. Parmelia F.	7 Jul	68	Reformed Grave Yard	lung congestion
Schroeder, Frederick	20 Jul	69/5/7		consumption
Smith, Mary E. Bruner	22 Jul	-/4/19		cholera infantum
Brust, Virginia	23 Jul	1/4/15		" "
Lamar, Robert G.	26 Jul	37/4/26		Brights disease
Eichelberger, Mrs. Grayson	26 Jul	63/-/11		
Bailley, George Franklin	28 Jul	-/6/11		cholera infantum
Cronice, Isaac	20 Aug	72/5/9		paralysis
Conrod, John Robert	? Aug	in 3rd yr		diphtheria
Brunner, Henry	14 Sep	66/6/27		paralysis
Ely, Ella, d/o James	5 Oct	1/7/-	Reformed Grave Yard	pneumonia
Dixon, Matilda Rebecca	8 Oct	-/7/-		
Zeiler, Clarence	25 Oct	7/3/-	Mt. Olivet	
Stone, Mrs. Orfie E.	22 Oct	28	Reformed Grave Yard	
Albaugh, Bessie Ann	30 Oct	2/8/22		diphtheria
Gurlach, Christian	2 Nov	14/7/9		"
Gurlach, Elizabeth	8 Nov	9/2/18		"
Picking, Thomas	8 Nov	77/6/28		Brights disease
Gurlach, Lewis Clarence	20 Nov	1/6/1		diphtheria
Wolfe, George H.	21 Nov	51/3/-		apoplexy
Feaga, Lillie Hester	21 Nov	10/6/7		pneumonia
1886				
Wolfe, Elizabeth Ryon, d/o Thomas	1 Jan	in 5th yr		diphtheria
Lampe, Emma Augusta	12 Jan	3/5/25		..
Houck, Mrs. Catharine	16 Jan	79/7/10		apoplexy
Rice, Perry	23 Jan	844/2/20		old age
Fauble, David	25 Feb	75/5/-		..
Wolfe, Enoch Pratt	9 Mar	1/4/27		diphtheria
Whalen, John W.	11 Mar	47		heart disease
Gonso, Susan	12 Mar	87/11/6		paralysis
King, Columbus Roe	13 Mar	-/-/13		
Anderson, Oliver P.	9 Apr	47/5/9		consumption
Fox, Harry O.	17 Apr	16/3/9		Brights disease

Deaths and Burials of Evangelical Reformed
United Church of Christ
Frederick, Frederick County, Maryland

Name	Date	Age	Place	Cause
Lamar, Mrs. Kate	3 May	38		consumption
Glessner, William	10 Jun	82/7/9		old age
Ritter, Edward Allen	10 Jun	-/-/5		spasms
Killian, William H.	22 Jun	46		consumption
Heitshue, Susan	18 Aug	80		old age
Ricketts, Daniel Zachariah	20 Aug	10		blood flux
Ramsburg, Clara Maynard	6 Aug	1/1/-		cholera infantum
Marble, Mrs. Julia Ann B.	30 Aug	37/1/13	Rocky Ridge	heart disease
Thomas, Ethel Sarah	25 Sep	-/7/2		cholera infantum
Gonso, William H.	26 Sep	32/5/-		consumption
Gittinger, Miss Anna R.	30 Sep	56/5/14	Reformed Grave Yard	tumor
Gittinger, George	19 Oct	88/5/22	Reformed Grave Yard	old age
Ridgley, John H.	22 Oct	-/-/12	Reformed Grave Yard	spasms
Grove, Clayton Eugene	27 Oct	28/2/14		consumption
Derr, Mrs. Fannie G.	4 Nov	43		diabetes
Allshesky, Susan Agnes	14 Nov	2/2/7	Reformed Grave Yard	paralysis
Brunner, Mrs. Mary E.	7 Nov	70		paralysis
Cover, Thomas Franklin	16 Nov	57	Taneytown	carbuncle
Abrecht, Katie L.	18 Nov	8/9/21		
Waters, Ann Eliza	23 Nov	43/5/8		typhoid malaria
McDonald, Mary Hauer	23 Nov	7/7/6		diphtheria
Butler, Gennette E.	1 Dec	29		paralysis
Smith, Mrs. Mary	5 Dec	78/5/11		old age
Hafner, Mrs. Henrietta	21 Dec	52/7/11		brain trouble
Reese, Charles S.	24 Dec	25/11/7		consumption
Shank, Edward H.	24 Dec	11/1/-		heart disease
Keefer, Frederick	26 Dec	75/4/5		exhaustion
1887				
Hallar, Percy William	7 Jan	-/5/3		spasms
Akers, Addie May	24 Jan	12/-/-	Reformed Grave Yard	diphtheria
Cassin, Nannie A.	2 Feb	17		typhoid fever
Getzendanner, Margaret A.	4 Feb	60/5/16		heart disease
Meister, Anna Christie	4 Feb	78/11/15		found dead
Mantz, Emanuel	5 Feb	63/6/5		paralysis
Haller, Mrs. Eliza M.	8 Feb	66		--
Albright, Mrs. Elizabeth	11 Feb	78/11/0		dropsy
Akers, Ruth Ann	20 Feb	8/8/28	Reformed Grave Yard	croup
Akers, Cora Celestia	23 Feb	7/4/20	Reformed Grave Yard	croup
Black, Mrs. Barbara	24 Feb	80	Rocky Ridge	paralysis
Stull, Mrs. Elizabeth	3 Mar	89/6		old age
Forney, Mrs. Abbe Rebecca	23 Mar	64/7	Haugh's Ch, Carroll Co.	Heart disease
Herring, Mrs. Caroline	28 Mar	82/2/14		old age
Percival, Dr. Charles F.	5 Apr	70	Reformed Grave Yard	heart disease
Staley, Mrs. May Jane	18 Apr	31/9/29		childbed fever
Glaze, Nevin Hamilton	20 Apr	1/1/-		consumption
Hinkle, George	24 Apr	88/6/1	Doubs	old age
Gurlach, Mrs. Ann Catharine	9 May	68/5/24		paralysis
Flemming, Mrs. Matilda	12 May	67		spinal trouble
Michael, Charles L.	13 May	21	Baltimore	consumption

Deaths and Burials of Evangelical Reformed
United Church of Christ
Frederick, Frederick County, Maryland

Name	Date	Age	Burial	Cause
Bruner, Mrs. Ann R.	16 May	73/4/18	Reformed Grave Yard	lung congestion
Trimmer, Harry Clay	25 May	14/6/119		lockjaw
Hallar, Silas L.	4 Jun	34		consumption
Wachter, Mrs. Susan Elizabeth	6 Jul	70/2/25	Utica Reformed Grave Yard	
Picking, Mrs. Barbara	23 Jul	68/1/24		
Bantz, Gideon	25 Jul	74		found dead
Ebert, Octavius A.	26 Jul	57		Brights disease
Zimmerman, Mrs. Mary E.	4 Aug	69/4/5		lung congestion
Markell, Mrs. Mary A. E.	24 Aug	67/6/7		paralysis
Burke, Jacob L.	29 Sep	20		consumption
Ott, Thomas	3 Oct	64/-/24		dysentery
Mantz, William	5 Oct	69		
Brengle, Mrs. Florence C.	8 Oct	35/9/3		sudden death
Hallar, Grant L.	9 Oct	23		consumption
Blumenauer, Mrs. Frederick	15 Oct	68/6/5		paralysis
Bantz, Carrie B.	4 Nov	1/-/5		
Brengle, B. F.	11 Nov	21/2/28	Reformed Grave Yard	consumption
Ebbert, Gustavus Adolph	18 Nov	45		heart disease

1888

Name	Date	Age	Burial	Cause
Pettingall, Miss Eliza	2 Jan	78/3	Middletown	paralysis
Renner, Clara Elizabeth	3 Jan	16/3/5		consumption
Glaze, Maria V.	18 Jan	48/3/7		heart disease
Staley, Altah Irene	22 Jan	1/7/14		inflam of stomach
Brengle, William H.	24 Jan	59/10/-	Reformed Grave Yard	consumption
Dehoff, Mrs. Annie M.	31 Jan	53		"
Houck, Henry	16 Feb	82nd yr	Reformed Grave Yard	old age
Comfort, Rev. H. I.	21 Feb	57/5/29		Brights disease
Ramsburg, Mrs. Catharine	27 Feb	84th yr	Reformed Grave Yard	old age
Shook, Mrs. Susan R.	1 Mar	74/10/21		heart disease
Seaman, Mrs. Margaret A.	7 Mar	74/10/21		consumption
Bell, Mrs. Catharine Elizabeth	14 Mar	50	Reformed Grave Yard	asthma
Brengle, Mrs. Louisa	21 Mar	79/-/10		paralysis
Koester, Christina L.	11 Apr	76/1/25		cancer
Markell, Louis	21 Apr	69/8/12		diabetes
Danner, Cicero	2 May	32		
Thomas, Henry C.	1 Aug	not given		cancer
Strailman, Martha	4 Aug	"		
Oberlander, Louis	26 Jun	"		
Baker, Miss Leah	23 Jul	"		consumption
Steiner, Mrs. Mary	28 Sep	82/7/17		old age
Ramsburg, Mrs. Mary A.	24 Oct	72/3		heart disease
Stull, Mrs. Sarah Sophia	25 Oct	65/10/18		cancer
Shook, Mrs. Susanna	5 Nov	74/10/8	Shook Grave Yard	
Anders, Caleb A.	21 Nov	60		heart disease
Steiner, Miss Mary Ellen	1 Dec	58/3/2		" "
Fauble, Mrs. Mattie E.	3 Dec	50/8/10		cancer
Chew, Mrs. Mary Ann	16 Dec	67/6		heart disease
Miller, Mrs. Fannie	16 Dec	43/8/29		tumor

Deaths and Burials of Evangelical Reformed
United Church of Christ
Frederick, Frederick County, Maryland

1889

Name	Date	Age	Cemetery	Cause
Smith, Dorsey H.	8 Jan	35/-/29		Brights disease
Blumenour, Mrs. Cordelia	15 Jan	39/4/6		cancer
Stoner, Edna Maud	28 Jan	8/7/-		pneumonia
Lerch, Henry	9 Feb	61		pleurisy
Gring, Rev. William Aug.	11 Feb	51/-/16		consumption
Zimmerman, Robert Fleming	28 Feb	-/6/22		dropsy
Bentz, Mrs. Catharine M.	12 Mar	59/1/-		pneumonia
Duvall, Miss Mary R.	30 Mar	74		heart failure
Hallar, Nicholas T.	9 Apr	76		paralysis
Bopst, Edna Ruth	12 Apr	2/1/-		
Meyer, Mrs. Mary J.	5 May	82/11/3	Mt. Olivet	paralysis
Rhodes, Mrs. Susan S.	9 May	47/5/15	Reformed Grave Yard	cancer
Bentz, Henry	12 May	45		jaundice
Hildebrand, Mrs. Lydia A.	6 Jun	83/8/7	Doubs	old age
Best, Mrs. Martha I.	14 Jul	47/4/24		
Shultz, Miss Catharine M.	21 Jul	79	Reformed Grave Yard	old age
Herman, Thomas Jefferson	19 Aug	1/9/1		cholera infantum
Ways, Mrs. Margaret H.	28 Sep	36/9/28		consumption
Quynn, John T.	30 Sep	73		kidney trouble
Stone, Miss Georgia V.	5 Oct	18		shot by a rejected lover
Thomas, William Mantz	7 Oct	7/3/25		diphtheria
Ray, infant child of Samuel	7 Oct	-/-/5	Reformed Grave Yard	
Shawbaker, Mrs. Annie M.	? Oct	not given		
Shindler, Iona J.	29 Oct	50/6/19		liver cancer
Hoskins, Mrs. Mary A.	12 Nov	82		sudden death
Smith, John	12 Nov	82	Reformed Grave Yard	kidney trouble
Thomas, Henry Leven	25 Nov	1/2/-		dentition
Rice, Ada May	8 Dec	17/8/9		spasms
Koontz, Mrs. Frances A. V.	28 Dec	24/3/7		inflam & stones

1890

Name	Date	Age	Cemetery	Cause
Nichols, Edward	18 Jan	69/8/16		
Hafner, Julius F.	21 Jan	63/1-/9		diabetes
Smith, Miss Margaret Louisa	25 Jan	62/3/23	Doubs	pneumonia
Haller, Williiam Bernard	2 Feb	6/6/15		diphtheria
Abbott, George A.	20 Feb	50/5		Brights disease
Miller, Edgar Little	4 Mar	3/1/21	Mt. Olivet	diphtheria
Anderson, infant child of Richard	15 Mar	-	Reformed Grave Yard	stillborn
Kaufman, Mary Catharine	19 Mar	28/4/14		tumor
Ways, William H., Sr.	20 Mar	74/3/5		hernia
Kreh, Louis F.	3 Apr	62/1		heart trouble
Haller, Mrs. Margaret	4 May	66		heart disease
Goodmanson, Mrs. Mary	5 May	70		" "
Lipps, Ethel, d/o Thomas	21 Jun	-/-/9		
Roth, Dr. Amos A.	26 Jun	433/8/4		angina pectoris
Derr, Adelaide, d/o of Mill.	1 Jul	1/10/18	Mt. Olivet	cholera infantum
Byerly, Grace	2 Jul	37/8/14	Reformed Grave Yard	paralysis
Hafner, Sallie Blanch	3 Jul	-/4/8		cholera infantum
Ramsburg, Samuel Maynard	5 Jul	-/5/9	Reformed Grave Yard	" "
Riggs, Mary Hobbs	7 Jul	60/11/29	Glade Ref Grave Yard	paralysis

Deaths and Burials of Evangelical Reformed
United Church of Christ
Frederick, Frederick County, Maryland

Name	Date	Age	Cemetery	Cause
Englar, Alice	14 Jul	-/2/14		cholera infantum
Carson, Alonzo	15 Jul	43		paralysis
Brust, Caroline B.	18 Jul	15/11/10		dysentery
Aubert, Louis H.	21 Jul	28/7/18		typhoid fever
Main, Mary Ann Magdalen	22 Jul	53/2/22		la grippe
Grumbine, Eleanor May	1 Aug	-/-/5		
Cramer, Anna Barbara	2 Aug	93/5		exhaustion
Ramsburg, James Maynard	4 Aug	1/2/29		brain congestion
Lakin, Daniel F.	9 Aug	48/5/29		dysentery
Wolfe, Thomas M.	10 Aug	53/7/1		paralysis
Poole, Mr. Adam	25 Aug	69		catarrh-stomach
Bentz, Louis	25 Aug	81/4/18		paralysis
Mehrling, Rev. J. Maurice	15 Sep	21/11/21		blood poison
Krantz, Frederick	18 Sep	70		typhoid fever
Fleming, Miss Harriet	30 Sep	85/6/7		old age
Baltzell, Miss Elizabeth H.	20 Oct	78/6/25		old age
Ebert, Mrs. Elizabeth	29 Oct	79		heart disease
Dorsey, Elizabeth (colored)	15 Nov	83		
Cramer, Mrs. Mary O.	3 Dec	40/4/8		diphtheria
Cramer, Mary Reynolds	7 Dec	5/9/25		"
Young, Mrs. Mary Ann	9 Dec	73/3		sciatica
Poole, John	18 Dec	65/7/6		paralysis
Zimmerman, Miss Mary D.	20 Dec	30/8/17		rheumatism
1891				
Harley, G. W. Tauman	17 Jan	59/7/10		Brights disease
Ramsburg, Mrs. Margaret J.	4 Feb	79		paralysis
Aubert, James Bruner	10 Feb	23/5		pneumonia
Witter, Joseph Henry	14 Feb	-/1/20		
Fleming, Mrs. Mary A.	15 Feb	61/5/20		paralysis
Myers, Miss Catharine	3 Mar	66	Reformed Grave Yard	lung congestion
Cronise, Miss Clara Adelia	12 Mar	43	Mt. Olivet	Brights disease
Bennett, Miss Julia	5 May	75		la grippe
Nusbaum, Miss Catharine	12 May	86/3	Reformed Grave Yard	heart disease
Lindsay, Mrs. Laura J.	11 Jul	43/11/15		consumption
Bruner, Joshua	11 Jul	75	Reformed Grave Yard	general debility
Heim, Mrs. Anna	28 Jul	68		
Krise, Buchanan K.	13 Aug	18/9/8	Mechanicstown	killed in a mine
Cashour, Mrs. Kate H.	25 Aug	40/10/17		cancer
Quynn, Mrs. Harriet	28 Aug	68		failure
Rice, Mary Louisa, d/o Thomas	3 Nov	-/4/-		spasms
Smith, Caroline Ross	14 Nov	3/3/-		diphtheria/croup
Schley, Mrs. Sophia M.	23 Nov	68		died in Baltimore
Rice, Mrs. Mary Elizabeth	25 Nov	62/11/19		paralysis
Byerly, John	1 Dec	20		
Mateny, George W.	5 Dec	3/9/11	Mt Olivet	chronic croup
Thomas, Christian	10 Dec	81/4/7		paralysis
Chew, William	11 Dec	72		heart disease
Taylor, Mabel Lucy	15 Dec	2/3/3		pneumonia

Deaths and Burials of Evangelical Reformed
United Church of Christ
Frederick, Frederick County, Maryland

Name	Date	Age	Burial	Cause
Schley, Lewis Fairfax	23 Dec	2/5/13		"
Mehrling, Nellie Louisa	23 Dec	8/6/16		heart failure
James, Mrs. Catharine	24 Dec	90/-/23		old age
Pettingall, Robert	28 Dec	73/1		paralysis
1892				
Kina, Edith May	6 Jan	4th yr		diphtheria
Bantz, William S.	6 Jan	73		heart disease
Berger, Miss Ann	9 Jan	84	Reformed Grave Yard	pneumonia
Bürucker, Miss Sophia	9 Jan	73/10/3		paralysis
Berger, Miss Elizabeth	19 Jan	78	Reformed Grave Yard	pneumonia
Fauble, Mrs. Mary Ann	22 Jan	75		heart disease
Zellers, Flora Emma	12 Feb	2/6/-		diphtheria
Bruner, Miss Elizabeth	17 Feb	72/3/11		heart disease
Lerch, Ruth Naomi	22 Feb	-/5/24		pneumonia
Steiner, Dr. Lewis H.	23 Feb	64/9		apoplexy
Babel, J. Christian	29 Feb	53/1/19		paralysis
Miller, Mrs. Ettie	2 Mar	59		bowel trouble
Williams, Mrs. Eleanor	12 Mar	78	Shriver Lot	congestion
Reed, Ethel May	21 Mar	1//5/-	Shriver Lot	pneumonia
Ramsburg, Franklin W.	21 Mar	-/1/-	Reformed Grave Yard	heart disease
Kuhn, Mrs. Elizabeth	26 Mar	91/7/19		old age
Staley, Mrs. Jane Elizabeth	29 Mar	54/6/27		heart disease
Main, Ethel Riene	31 Mar	6/4/3		diphtheria
Talbott, Mrs. Lillian Baker	7 Apr	26/6/21		typhoid fever
Brengle, Franklin Christ	19 Apr	20/4/10		epilepsy
Kramer, Ralph William	20 Apr	-/5/9		bronchitis
Glaze, Mrs. Margaret Ann	6 May	61/5/19		heart disease
Hanschew, Mrs. Catharine S.	7 May	90/4/24		old age
Heck, Mrs. Elizabeth	8 May	77/0/10		paralysis
Koontz, Fannie Myrtle	19 May	2/8/18		meningitis
Thomas, Miss Caroline S.	25 Jun	34/8/23		peritonitis
Forrest, Lucretia A.	8 Jul	1/5/22		inflammation
Bruner, Mrs. Ann Sophia	11 Jul	84/8		paralysis
Burger, Ethel May, twin	12 Jul	-/4/6(?)		malnutrition
Burger, Elsie Marie, twin	16 Jul	-/4/12(?)		malnutrition
Eckstein, Mrs. Elizabeth	19 Jul	69		asthma
Davis, Mrs. Annie E.	9 Aug	75/8/21		debility
Hooper, Mrs. Mary Elizabeth	9 Aug	55		rheumatism
Gittinger, James Cyrus	8 Sep	6/11/24		diphtheria
Keefer, George	15 Sep	52/2/13		cerebral rupture
Bell, William	25 Sep	78	Reformed Grave Yard	found dead
Schley, Rebecca Steiner	? Sep	5/10/28		diphtheria
Baile, Mrs. Annie M.	12 Oct	not given		cancer
Bentz, Mrs. Sophia Ann	21 Oct	61/3/29	Reformed Grave Yard	
Rigney, John H.	23 Oct	57		paralysis
Englebrecht, George J.	26 Oct	60/3/20		heart disease
Gilbert, Mrs. Sarah A.	28 Oct	54/5/28		catarrh-stomach
Rigney, John H.	30 Oct	57		
Hedges, Lycurgus E.	3 Nov	57		fell dead

Deaths and Burials of Evangelical Reformed
United Church of Christ
Frederick, Frederick County, Maryland

Name	Date	Age	Cemetery	Cause
Getzendanner, Mrs. Mary E.	4 Nov	79		pneumonia
Huber, Mrs. Gertrude E.	10 Nov	38		consumption
Blumenouer, Mrs. Catharine	18 Nov	80		old age
Johnson, Mrs. Mary	20 Nov	72		pneumonia
Sweigert, Mrs. Jane	22 Nov	56		liver abscess
Houck, Dr. Henry J.	26 Nov	51		took poison by mistake
Akers, Rowena Houghton	29 Nov	5/5/14	Reformed Grave Yard	dropsy
Bentz, Horatio W.	14 Dec	75/1/9		heart disease
Gittinger, Eugene Irving	16 Dec	2/7/2		diphtheratic croup
1893				
Englebrecht, Mrs. Elizabeth	1 Jan	57/-/1		heart disease
Lidie, Mrs. Fannie M.	5 Jan	29/1/27		consumption
Fox, Charles H. O.	6 Jan	76		brain congestion
Warner, Ruth Elizabeth	19 Jan	2/2/23	Mechanicstown	croup
Cole, Lamartine	10 Feb	42		consumption
Miller, Paul Biser	15 Feb	17/1/2		marasmus (?)
Rhodes, William H.	17 Feb	48		heart disease
Bentz, Jacob M.	12 Mar	71/5/17		" "
McDannel, Mrs. Mary Elizabeth	21 Mar	32		puerperal fever
Bell, Mrs. Margaret	26 Mar	78	Reformed Grave Yard	general decay
Kemp, Eleanor	8 Apr	71/3		
Rhodes, Calvin A.	29 Apr	56	Reformed Grave Yard	heart disease
Custer, Miss Margaret E.	30 Apr	63/-/19		paralysis
Edmonds, Honor Burnice	22 May	17/8/12		spinal meningitis
Suman, Mrs. Mary E.	7 Jun	64		pneumonia
Gittinger, Mrs. Anna M. C.	19 Jun	51/-/5		
Brust, John Albert	13 Jul	-/6/1		cholera infantum
Wachter, Charles E.	19 Jul	41/10/29	Utica	broken back
McMan, Anna Mary	21 Jul	1/10/-		cholera infantum
Akers, Abner	22 Jul	56/11/26	Reformed Grace Yard	catarrh
Edmonds, Loritto Pauline	4 Aug	-/6/26		cholera infantum
Nuss, M. Emory	5 Aug	27		R. R. accident
Kemp, Robert Birely	9 Aug	-/6/4		cholera infantum
Main, John Lewis	31 Aug	32/8/27		fell from elec.pole
Cashour, Mrs. Martha	9 Sep	77/7/23		hernia
Best, Miss Elizabeth	13 Sep	60/9/9		typhoid dysentery
Brengle, Mrs. Maria	2 Oct	78		cholera morbus
Boetler, Miss Lucy	6 Oct	51		consumption
Crum, Mrs. Susan	? Oct	59/1/4		
Rhodes, Mrs. Ann Minerva	15 Oct	84/1/1		paralysis
Dixon, Mrs. Laura Virginia	24 Oct	49/3/28		heart trouble
Thomas, John B.	25 Oct	74		exhaustion
Cramer, George W.	11 Nov	60/-/10		shot himself
Rice, William Henry	16 Nov	56/4/18		Brights disease
Wilcoxon, Andrew Jackson	20 Dec	64/7/7		Pleuro pneumonia
Schultz, George J.	22 Dec	62/2/23	Reformed Grave Yard	apoplexy
1894				
Bentz, Mrs. Ann M.	3 Jan	75/2/17		paralysis

Deaths and Burials of Evangelical Reformed
United Church of Christ
Frederick, Frederick County, Maryland

Name	Date	Age	Place	Cause
Keefer, Miss Ann Elizabeth	13 Feb	53rd yr		apoplexy
Bair, Joseph D.	14 Feb	56		nervous debility
Colliflower, Mrs. Ann E.	28 Feb	83		paralysis
Steiner, Mrs. Mary A.	11 Mar	71		lung congestion
Folsom, Mrs. Ann Elizabeth	16 Mar	77/-/2	Reformed Grave Yard	exhaustion
Main, Mrs. Elizabeth Ellen	18 Mar	63/5/8		heart failure
Hood, James M.	5 Apr	72/11/19		paralysis
Kreh, Florence Bertha	23 Apr	8//6/26	Mt. Oliver	meningitis
Clingan, Mrs. Maria	28 Apr	85th yr		old age
Hildebrand, Frank T.	28 Apr	24/10/26		lock jaw
Thomas, Mrs. Elizabeth	4 Jun	77		paralysis
Reed, George Kenneth	26 Jun	-/8/-		convulsions
Forrest, William McComas	26 Jun	-/7/15	Reformed Grave Yard	cholera infantum
Wertheimer, Mildred Lee	8 Jul	-/10/4		brain trouble
Bantz, Algernon Sidney	10 Jul	69/8/3		
Cronise, Mrs. Margaret R.	12 Jul	73/-/1		heart trouble
Haller, Nellie May	16 Jul	-/5/-		cholera infantum
Whitter, Mrs. Susan E.	2 Sep	82/-/6		hemorrhage
Haller, Charles W.	9 Dec	82		general debility
Fleming, J. Alfred	19 Dec	66		heart failure

1895

Name	Date	Age	Place	Cause
Ziegler, Henry Edward	8 Jan	45/4/11		burned
Titlow, George W.	21 Jan	46		pneumonia
Staley, Jonathan Aug.	17 Feb	68/1/8		paralysis
Keller, Charles Henry	27 Feb	65/1/10		consumption
Miller, Elizabeth Rebekah	1 Mar	2/10/26		meningitis
Fisher, Herman J.	29 Mar	55		general decay
Simmons, Capt. Charles E.	31 Mar	66		cancer of liver
Holtz, John	3 Apr	87/8	Zion Church	
Tyson, Nathan S.	5 Apr	63		pneumonia
Dixon, Thomas O.	9 Apr	54/1/26		"
Hoffmeier, Rev. Henry W.	15 Apr	62/3/18	Middletown	
Hardt, Mrs. Sarah J.	16 Apr	69		heart failure
Brane, Grandison G.	22 Apr	78/10/15		old age
Hedges, Mrs. Mary E.	14 May	76		heart disease
Maynard, Dr. James H.	2 Jun	62	Hagerstown	paralysis
Wise, Mrs. Ellen R.	4 Jun	62		died Brooklyn, NY
Miller, Mary Irene	16 Jun	-/4/15		
Heckathorne, Alice	26 Jun	50		consumption
Lipps, Catharine E.	5 Jul	51st yr		died suddenly
Markey, David J.	15 Jul	48		killed at Harpers Ferry
Zacharias, Mrs. Catharine Z.	27 Jul	80		heart disease
Staley, Mrs. Laura	6 Aug	47/3/6		cancer
Ramsburg, Harry Bernard	6 Oct	-/9/10	Reformed Grave Yard	inanition
Zeigler, Mrs. Rosanna	7 Oct	68/2/18		
Miller, Charles Marion	12 Nov	31/3/27		consumption
Best, Mrs. Margaret Johana	21 Nov	54/10/3		spinal trouble
Glaze, Samuel F.	28 Nov	70/5/22		paralysis

Deaths and Burials of Evangelical Reformed
United Church of Christ
Frederick, Frederick County, Maryland

Name	Date	Age	Cemetery	Cause
Adams, Lewis Bruner	30 Nov	-/10/17	Reformed Grave Yard	croup
Ricketts, Blanche	6 Dec	1/4/22		
Sherer, Daniel	11 Dec	69/-/23		paralysis
Kohlenburg, Mrs. Rachel	23 Dec	75/3/7		old age
Oland, Lucy Belle	23 Dec	2/6/-		scalded
1896				
Conrad, Bernice Ethel	9 Jan	1/10/7		rheumatism
Schley, Mrs. Ann Rebecca	10 Jan	67		paresis
Schindler, Mrs. Cordelia E.	25 Jan	56/10/5		paralysis
Knodle, Mrs. Christiana L.	11 Feb	40		consumption
Krantz, Mrs. Laura V.	15 Feb	54		heart trouble
Cronise, Joseph	21 Feb	72/11/9		heart trouble
Chew, Joseph F.	27 Feb	43rd yr		Brights disease
Buxton, Basil	10 Mar	79/6/15		pneumonia
Forrest, Mrs. Sarah C.	14 Mar	39/10/12		consumption
Bierly, John William	17 Apr	79/4/7		pleurisy
Kolb, William Aug.	19 May	52		
Ott, William H.	10 Jun	67/7/3	Reformed Grave Yard	Brights disease
Ebbert, John	30 Jun	63/2/4		heart failure
Bierly, Mrs. Mary R.	1 Jul	72/11		heart failure
Grove, George W.	11 Jul	56/6/20		consumption
Nicholas, Mrs. Eliza M.	13 Jul	83	Reformed Grave Yard	old age
Stone, Mrs. Ann Maria	21 Jul	88	Pleasant Hill	old age
Bruner, George H.	1 Aug	2/10/13		
Ramsburg, Allen Miller	24 Aug	-/3/04	Reformed Grave Yard	inanition
Sheppard, John K.	24 Aug	58/4/8		Brights disease
Stull, Adam	6 Sep	73/-/15		paralysis
Hauer, Mrs. Lucretia	6 Sep	64		brain abscess
Cramer, Mrs. Henrietta	7 Sep	61/5/20		found dead
Quynn, Mrs. Mary M.	20 Sep	69		complications
Doll, John L.	21 Oct	72		heart disease
Kauffman, George Walter	9 Nov	4/10/13		diphtheria
Shephard, Eleanor	11 Nov	2/9/12		diphtheratic croup
Williams, John H.	14 Nov	82/7/1		paralysis
Apple, Mrs. Mary R.	3 Dec	27/7/13	Clarion, PA	consumption
Dixon, Mrs. Julia A. C.	5 Dec	50/11		heart disease
Duval, William H. E.	17 Dec	35/7/29		consumption
Measell, Catharine Elizabeth	22 Dec	54/6/10		consumption
Houck, William James	27 Dec	25		typhoid fever
1897				
Gilbert, Stewart Meredith	2 Jan	-/10/5		pneumonia
Droneburg, Joseph	9 Jan	-/5/-	Reformed Grave Yard	
Rhoderick, E. Franklin	17 Jan	-/8/1		
Bentz, Mrs. Lydia	27 Jan	70/2/27		pneumonia
Davis, Frank T.	29 Jan	55/3		consumption
Rhodes, Orion Bernard	30 Jan	1/8/17		pneumonia
Blumenauer, Gertrude Catharine	30 Jan	74/7/5		pneumonia
Getzendanner, Edward T.	17 Feb	72/-/23		inflam. of bowels
Castle, Mrs. Georgianna M.	17 Feb	55/5/26		cancer

Deaths and Burials of Evangelical Reformed
United Church of Christ
Frederick, Frederick County, Maryland

Name	Date	Age	Cemetery	Cause
Ramsburg, Alice E.	19 Feb	12/11/8		heart disease
Dudrow, Joseph S.	23 Feb	50/1/14		Columbus, OH
Kemp, Mrs. Ruanah R.	18 Mar	66/11/6		dropsy
Kreh, William Jennings B.	18 Mar	1/7/-		cholera infantum
Roelky, Mrs. Mary Jane	24 Mar	52/11/10		cancer
Rice, Mrs. Barbara J.	24 Mar	59/-/18		brain fever
Beckenbaugh, Miss Sarah	9 Apr	72		general decay
Hedges, Mrs. Amanda S.	19 Apr	62/2/16		angina pectoris
Brust, Mrs. Ann Florence	25 Apr	41/8/5		found dead in bed
Glessner, George W.	2 May	65/9/26		heart disease
Markell, Louis	8 Jun	65/9/26		Brights disease
English, Mrs. Jane R.	1 Jul	76		catarrh-stomach
Coblentz, Edward Franklin	9 Jul	64/11/23	Middletown Ref. Cem	Brights disease
Bennett, Mrs. Fannie L.	24 Jul	33/4		consumption
Brengle, Earle W.	38 Jul	-/4/-		meningitis
Haller, Nannie L.	29 Jul	50/6		consumption
Lipps, Mrs. Catharine	31 Jul	81/11/20		
Shriner, Mary Phoebe	23 Aug	78/5/2		died in Baltimore
Remsberg, George P.	8 Oct	74/4/23		Brights disease
Mehrling, Mrs. Susan	22 Oct	57/3/3		blood poison
Abbott, Mrs. Julia A.	9 Oct	88/6/17		old age
Bender, Katie R. C.	6 Nov	5/-/25	Reformed Grave Yard	malarial fever
Conrod, David Russell	24 Nov	1/3/11		scarletina
Roelky, John	30 Nov	74/1/5		Brights disease
Derr, William H.	4 Dec	75		heart disease

1898

Name	Date	Age	Cemetery	Cause
Measell, Christianna	23 Jan	84/8/8		old age
Jones, Ethel Florence	24 Jan	-/-/7		
Bruner, Lewis	30 Jan	87/3/10	Reformed Grave Yard	old age
Herndon, Annie	12 Feb	28		insane
Babel, Mary Jane	19 Feb	62/-/3		apoplexy
Smith, Mrs. Mary A.	28 Feb	72/-/13		heart failure
Main, Annie Elizabeth	8 Mar	16/4/10		typhoid fever
McDannell, Abraham Sowers	2 Apr	46/8/20		suicide
Schaffer, Jonathan A.	3 Apr	69/6/3		paralysis
Roelky, Mrs. Susannah	12 Apr	72		pneumonia
Bennett, William S.	20 Jun	76/5/17		Brights disease
Hight, Mrs. Caroline	11 Aug	78		dysentery
Wolfe, Thomas Melville Soldier, Tampa, FL.	24 Aug	21/3/3		typhoid fever
Picking, Miss Lottie	25 Aug	51/11/16		erysipelas
Knock, Henry Frederick	31 Aug	67/-/25		paralysis of heart
Jenkins, Mrs. Amanda J.	9 Sep	65		neuralgia of heart
Adams, Thomas Nelson	7 Oct	-/2/5	Reformed Grave Yard	cholera infantum
Bealle, William S.	3 Nov	74/9/5		general debility
Holbruner, Lewis C.	16 Nov	30/7/21		heart failure
Miller, Mrs. Mary E.	19 Nov	38/3/5		cancer
Biser, Thomas Sherwood	22 Nov	5/10/9		diphtheratic croup
Gittinger, Mrs. Catharine	28 Nov	79/-/23		old age

Deaths and Burials of Evangelical Reformed
United Church of Christ
Frederick, Frederick County, Maryland

Name	Date	Age	Location	Cause
Thomas, Mrs. Mary	26 Dec	79th yr		paralysis
Moffatt, Bertie	26 Dec	17	Reformed Grave Yard	grippe
1899				
McDonald, Frank P.	2 Jan	51/4/23		paralysis
Miller, Nina	9 Jan	9/8/27		bronc.pneumonia
Hanshew, George Edward	9 Jan	36/9/25		grippe
Kemp, Mrs. Columbia A.	26 Jan	67/5/6		pneumonia
Mealey, Isaiah	28 Jan	97/6/18		old age
Buxton, Mrs. Mary	6 Feb	79/5/19		old age
Yost, Mrs. Catharine	7 Feb	73/9		pneumonia
Dertzbaugh, John W.	9 Feb	76/-/18		paralysis
Snyder, Mrs. E. Jane	22 Feb	63		heart disease
Wharthen, Mrs. May Jane	10 Mar	66	Jefferson	dropsy
Simmons, Mrs. Martha M.	27 Mar	60		burned
Boetler, Ruth	3 Apr	-/2/1		inanition
Zimmerman, Ruth	9 Apr	7/2/25		diphtheria
Rhoderick, Mrs. Mary A.	15 Apr	87/4/3		paralysis
Hauer, Jennie May	30 Apr	30/2/14		heart disease
Mantz, Mrs. William E.	29 May	30		consumption
Thomas, Mrs. Susan M.	7 Jul	77/9		heart failure
Poole, Hanson	30 Jul	79		paralysis
Barrick, Daniel	30 Jul	74/3/25		softening of brain
Main, Mrs. Eleanor S.	2 Aug	63		cancer
Bantz, Mrs. Julia Ann	12 Aug	85		old age
Shriner, George W. B.	16 Aug	53		Brights disease
Ramsburg, Henry B.	13 Sep	36/5/6		Brights disease
Remsberg, Mrs. Mary G.	17 Oct	79		apoplexy
Rice, Mrs. Margaret	15 Nov	84/1-/13		septicemia
Kessler, Miss Ann E.	3 Dec	87/1		brain concussion
Glessner, Jesse Marie	15 Dec	4/8/13		membr. croup
Fout, Mrs. Elizabeth	23 Dec	77		paralysis
Albaugh, Miss Matilda	31 Dec	79/11/13		old age
1900				
Zimmerman, Merle Henry	22 Jan	4/9/18		diphtheria
Burucker, John S.	23 Jan	84		old age
Kunkel, Philip Baker	29 Jan	79/6/22		heart trouble
Rice, William P.	31 Dec	66		paralysis
Ramsburg, Dennis C.	3 Feb	80/-/22		old age
Reese, Carrie May	5 Feb	28/6/11		consumption
Bell, Mrs. Ann Martha	6 Feb	79/1/4		neuralgia of heart
Bennett, Mrs. Catharine	9 Feb	59/6/23		heart disease
Danner, Thomas A.	20 Feb	67/-/21		heart disease
Markell, George	15 Mar	83		paralysis
Knauff, Mrs. Annie M.	7 Apr	63		apoplexy
Aubert, Mrs. Harriett	18 Apr	71		heart trouble
Miller, William H.	25 Apr	62		heart failure
Derr, George C.	26 Apr	60		husband and wife
Derr, Mrs. Frances V.	26 Apr	58		in same grave
Hauer, Miss Susan	28 May	76		diabetes

Deaths and Burials of Evangelical Reformed
United Church of Christ
Frederick, Frederick County, Maryland

Name	Date	Age	Cemetery	Cause
Shearer, Mrs. Amelia	29 May	67/7/15		congested lungs
Head, Miss Mary	13 Jun	82/9/24	Reformed Grave Yard	dropsy
Cramer, Ezra Lewis	21 Jul	73/1/6		Brights disease
Rohrbach, Martin N.	21 Jul	68		cancer of bowels
Hildebrand, Lewis N.	1 Aug	66/1/17		heart disease
Knock, Mrs. Annie E.	1 Aug	35/4/22		
Father and daughter buried by one service.				
Phebus, Charles Motter	1 Aug	-/3/19		cholera infantum
Obenderfer, A. Augustus	22 Sep	52		heart trouble
Hergesheimer, Sophia	24 Nov	70		general debility
Hauer, Bradley Fritchey	29 Nov	1/5/21		brain fever
Hauer, George Nicholas	19 Dec	16/1/15		typhoid fever
1901				
Rice, Albert Thomas	29 Jan	77/6/14		pneumonia
McDevitt, Christiana Louisa	2 Feb	60		peritonitis
Dull, Henry G.	6 Feb	62		pneumonia
Thomas, John G.	14 Feb	55		apoplexy
Conner, infant	4 Mar			
Gittinger, Daisy Irene	4 Mar	23/7/28		consumption
Hauer, Charles Nicholas	13 Mar	42		Brights disease
Lease, Mrs. Mahala	2 Apr	74/-/25		
Lough, George W.	5 Apr	23/5/9		pneumonia
Main, David M.	21 Apr	69/7/6		heart failures
Dutrow, Mrs. Kate	22 Apr	66		apoplexy
Albaugh, William V.	18 Jun	64/-/2		heart trouble
Blumenouer, Mary Katherine	12 Jul	49/-/28		paralysis
Pearre, William Walter	24 Jul	1/-/11		meningitis
Haller, Robert Edward	29 Jul	-/22/11		consumption
Burkhart, Ezra C. J.	16 Aug	80	Reformed Grave Yard	
Lorentz, Mrs. Catharine J.	9 Sep	59/-/13		cancer
Krantz, Catharine Elizabeth	6 Nov	14/-/13		typhoid fever
McLane, Rufus Almer	27 Nov	58/7/12		consumption
Krantz, Mrs. Mary Catharine	2 Dec	46/1/2		typhoid
Shriner, Edward A.	26 Dec	71/10/28		gen. prostration
1902				
Meyer, Elizabeth Matilda	4 Jan	22/2/25		consumption
Feete, Hattie Ella Elizabeth	14 Jan	22/8/14		consumption
Cramer, Mrs. Susan R.	20 Feb	69/1/9		heart trouble
Stone, Maude Estelle	3 Mar	-/11/1-		kidney trouble
Wolfe, Charles Edward	11 Mar	73		sudden death
Ellis Bertha May	25 Mar	-/-/3	Feagaville	
Kauffman, Mrs. Fannie M.	2 Apr	33/3/18		heart failure
Steiner, John A.	23 Apr	86		old age
Best, John T.	25 Apr	63		apoplexy
Foland, Anna M. E.	30 Apr	-/2/15	Reformed Grave Yard	spasms
Barrick, Mary Catharine	14 May	51/11/27		cancer
Mehrling, Mrs. Barbara	23 May	73		heart failure
Newman, Mrs. Kate	12 Jun	58	Woodsboro	cancer
Main, Mrs. Elizabeth	19 Jun	77/11/2		old age

Deaths and Burials of Evangelical Reformed
United Church of Christ
Frederick, Frederick County, Maryland

Name	Date	Age	Location	Cause
Fitez, William Edward	19 Jun	-/10/0		cholera infantum
Trimmer, Mary Elizabeth Lease	15 Jul	3/1/28		meningitis
Houck, William	6 Aug	-/9/-		cholera infantum
Brooks, Harriet A.	27 Aug	69/7/16		heart failure
Hafer, Ada M.	31 Aug	45/6/15		Brights disease
Roelky, Charles C. A.	7 Sep	47/5/13		killed on R. R.
Roelky, Mrs. Sarah A.	11 Sep	85		old age
Snyder, Miss Elizabeth	16 Sep	80		old age
Houck, Miss Elizabeth G.	16 Nov	68/4/3		typhoid fever
Smith, Mrs. Christiana	22 Nov	68		
Rhodes, George Philip	14 Dec	-/2/6		
Apple, Charlotte Elizabeth	16 Dec	7/3/25		diphtheria
Hildebrand, Mrs. Laura V.	16 Dec	61/7/6		paralysis
Steiner, Mrs. Marietta	18 Dec	60/3		paralysis
Haller, Mary Genivieve (sic)	31 Dec	24/6/28		typhoid fever
1903				
Thomas, Jesse E.	16 Jan	20		Drowned while skating
Brengle, J. Nicholas	27 Jan	82/3/6		old age
Blumenouer, John N.	30 Jan	58		consumption
Schley, Fairfax M. D.	3 Feb	78/3/20		heart failure
McLain, Harry Oscar	13 Feb	35/8/11		consumption
Houck, James	14 Feb	1/6/-		eczema
Glessner, Jennie L.	28 Feb	46/3/15		
Oberlander, Roger J.	12 Mar	7/1/9		diphtheria
Houck, Elizabeth	23 Mar	-/-/13		diphtheria
Keefer, Mrs. Annie M.	6 Apr	63/5/27		Brights disease
Brust, Mrs. Louisa	12 Apr	68/3/21		dropsy
Cramer, Ethan A.	14 Apr	72/11/14		blood poisoning
Rodgers, Mrs. Josephine	22 Apr	78/8/12		paralysis
Cramer, Franklin Edward	28 Apr	5/3/5		paralysis of heart
Morse, Mrs. Barbara	2 may	72		exhaustion
Clarke, Gen. James C.	6 May	79th yr		
Clarke, Mrs. Susan	6 May	55		reinterred with husband, died 1885
Zimmerman, Horace	6 May	77		old age
Keefer, Harry Clay	28 May	56/1/24		cancer
Hedges, Helen Hendrix	1 Jun	-/6/6		meningitis
Knauff, George H.	2 Jun	83/2		heart failure
Blumenouer, Lewis Michael	14 Jun	2/8/14		
Houck, Matilda Simmons	14 Jun	33/6/8		pneumonia
Lyon, Susanna M.	26 Jun	47	Baltimore	
Reel, Catharine M.	15 Aug	86	Reformed Grave Yard	old age
Eyler, Harry Edmond	16 Aug	-/-/25		
Biser, Jonathan	1 Sep	75/3/18	Middletown Ref Cem	bladder trouble
Long, Ralph Alvin	13 Sep	10/10/18		peritonitis
Gittinger, Mrs. Mary M.	26 Sep	73		apoplexy
Thomas, Samuel Donald	13 Oct	8/4/20		diphtheria
Schaeffer, David Luther	18 Oct	71/7/28		apoplexy

Deaths and Burials of Evangelical Reformed
United Church of Christ
Frederick, Frederick County, Maryland

Name	Date			Cause
McLane, Helen Stull	19 Oct	2/-/22		tub. meningitis
Albaugh, Franklin Henry	25 Oct	6/9/20		membr. croup
Rice, Susan Matilda	29 Oct	66/9/21		Brights disease
Cole, Mrs. Julia Ann	5 Nov	83/5/2		old age
Marsh, Nevelyn Kenneth	15 Nov	-/-/14		
Hersperger, Tilghman T.	24 Nov	79		kidney trouble
Main, Lewis H.	2 Dec	71/11/1		heart trouble
Cassin, John	7 Dec	64/5/14		
Garber, Virgie J.	23 Dec	18/-/18		heart trouble
Boetler, Augustus L.	27 Dec	66/9/22		consumption
Glessner, Harry L.	29 Dec	26/1/22		consumption
1904				
Adams, Fannie E. C.	4 Jan	65/0/12		kidney trouble
Mantz, Mrs. Ann U.	19 Jan	84/3/20		liver trouble
Mainhart, Ann Elizabeth	20 Jan	78/11		
Conner, Paul Stauffer, s/o Rev.	20 Jan	1/3/3		
Grove, David	22 Jan	71/3/4		heart trouble
Nichols, J. Lewis B.	1 Feb	57/2		diabetes
Stull, Effie Gertrude	11 Feb	33		consumption
Hedges, Cora Blanche	12 Feb	20/7/8		consumption
Starr, Ira Nelson	13 Feb	=/3/29		hemorrhage
Measell, Charles Thomas	15 Feb	64/11/29		paralysis
Main, Frederick W.	22 Feb	76		
Gittinger, Zach. James	27 Feb	80/4/11		shock
Haller, Thomas Johnson	27 Feb	20/4/16		consumption
Zimmerman, Mrs. Caroline R.	7 Mar	72/-/9	Utica Burying Ground	pneumonia
Starr, Ida R.	22 Mar	37		consumption
DeGrange, Daniel W. F.	28 Jun	63/11/20		paralysis
Roelky, Mrs. Lena	10 Jul	78		cancer
Fox, Mrs. Sarah Catharine	11 Jul	74/1/24		paralysis
Hiteshew, Mrs. Fannie	4 Aug	55		heart failure
Zeiler, Mrs. Ann Sophia	20 Oct	84		old age
Brengle, David M.	24 Oct	59/1/22		consumption
Clabaugh, Bradley	29 Nov	2/2/-		died Washington
Thomas, Zacharias G.	8 Dec	65/7/21		stomach cancer
Whisner, Mrs. Minnie Z.	27 Dec	37/8/5		Brights disease
1905				
Billingslea, Mrs. Elizabeth	16 Jan	80		old age
Glessner, William T.	24 Jan	71/9/25		general debility
Brengle, Francis	8 Feb	60/10/24		general debility
Markell, Mrs. Sophia	28 Feb	88/5/22		fall
Rohrback, Allen - died 1 Mar	12 Apr	32/2/1	remains in vault	consumption
Frazier, Mrs. Matilda E.	17 Apr	77/1/4		pneumonia
Remsberg, Margaret E.	19 Apr	50/4		blood poison
Hargett, Charles N.	20 Apr	55/1/21		
Yost, George	23 Apr	85/8/2		old age
Trimmer, Samuel	25 Apr	59/6/25		heart failure
Houck, Mrs. Laura V.	28 Apr	58/-/26		cancer
Walker, James E.	16 May	56		Brights disease

Deaths and Burials of Evangelical Reformed
United Church of Christ
Frederick, Frederick County, Maryland

Name	Date	Age	Place	Cause
Mergardt, Mrs. Charlotte	16 May	75		cancer
Dutrow, Samuel	19 May	69/10		Brights disease
Rhodes, Cornelia A.	25 Jun	75/9/19		paralysis
Burger, Anna Margaretha	12 Jul	75/3/20		paralysis
Ruland, Mrs. Kate	21 Jul	47		cancer
Oberland, Harry K.	25 Sep	15/5/7		injured on R. R.
Keefer, Alice V.	24 Oct	47		Brights disease
Myer, John	26 Oct	86		old age
Miller, Linol Matthias	3 Nov	5 days		
Albaugh, Frank Eugene	14 Dec	2/3/2		pneumonia
Wachter, Lewis	21 Dec	79th yr		paralysis
1906				
Grove, Mrs. Jemima B.	20 Jan	60th yr		cancer of liver
Nusbaum, Lydia Ann	8 Feb	85/11/10	Reformed Grave Yard	died Montevue
Grumbine, Stewart Daniel	11 Feb	-/5/24		brain trouble
Lambert, John George	15 Feb	76/6		pneumonia
Nusbaum, Mrs. Susan J.	26 Feb	82/10/16	Glade Grave Yard	old age
Zimmerman, Bernard F.	5 Mar	25/11/28		consumption
Mantz, Manzella Malinda	11 Mar	83rd yr		old age
Wilcoxen, Mrs. Annie V.	8 Apr	66th yr		consumption
Gittinger, John Edward	16 Apr	74/3		heart failure
Tyson, Mrs. Margaret	19 May	75/9/27		kidney trouble
McDonald, Mrs. Harriett M.	21 May	58/3/3		result of operation
Wood, Mrs. Grace B.	4 Aug	33/0/3		typhoid fever
Derr, Mary Lugenbeel	30 Aug	72/5/19		dysentery
Haller, Harry T.	5 Sep	55		pneumonia
DeLashmutt, Edward T. H.	11 Sep	57		paralysis
Zacharias, Jane	11 Oct	64/5/12		dropsy
Lambert, Mrs. Mary A. R.	12 Oct	80/10/13		old age
Rhodes, Frances T.	23 Oct	71/3/15		sexton for 46yr
Hanschew, Fritchie	29 Oct	77/7/16		kidney trouble
Hanschew, Mrs. Martha	26 Nov	68		strangulation
Topper, Mrs. Margaret E.	5 Dec	70/9/18		consumption
Anderson, Mrs. Laura V.	9 Dec	62/7/6		kidney trouble
Lampe, Rev. Lewis Theodore	28 Dec	40/5/22		pneumonia
1907				
Haller, Charles Edward	22 Jan	59		heart trouble
Knight, Miss Margaret L.	22 Jan	59		heart trouble
Comfort, Mrs. Lucy L.	4 Feb	42		consumption
Bentz, Alice V.	14 Feb	58/8/24	found dead from natural causes, double
Bentz, Charles Edward	14 Feb	50/8/24		funeral
Hauer, John Henry	28 Feb	52/6/6		heart trouble
Zimmerman, Walton Roelky	26 Mar	6/-/10		tub. meningitis
Glessner, Mrs. Mary Ellen	19 Apr	75/11/19		paralysis
Haller, Harry N.	30 Apr	27		meningitis
Holbruner, Mrs. Florence	30 May	45		complications
Marsh, Alonzo Pierce	1 Jun	54/5	Westminster	Brights disease
Ricketts, Harry Edward	12 Jun	14/7/17		heart failure
Howard, Charles T. F.	15 Jun	69/5/24		paralysis

Deaths and Burials of Evangelical Reformed
United Church of Christ
Frederick, Frederick County, Maryland

Name	Date	Age	Cause
Dertzbaugh, Mrs. Catharine E.	19 Jul	83/-/1	old age
Blair, Mrs. Annie Elizabeth	19 Jul	58/9/8	cancer
Kemp, Charles Edwin	22 Aug	50/6/14	Brights disease
Schell, Grace Elizabeth	25 Aug	-/1/7	
Linton, Mrs. Sarah Elizabeth	28 Aug	34th yr	childbirth
Renner, Ada May	7 Sep	25	consumption
Hafer, Samuel	10 Sep	76	consumption
Brunner, Mrs. Margaret J.	6 Oct	86/5	heart failure
Crum, Raymond Rosen	18 Oct	7/10/14	diphtheria
Mealy, Rosanna Rebekah	4 Nov	61/7/10	pneumonia
Holbruner, Thomas	20 Nov	51	heart trouble
Thomas, Dr. S. Frank	24 Nov	66/1/14	heart trouble
Myers, George W.	30 Nov	80	infirmity
Notnagle, Mrs. Carrie B.	2 Dec	45/7/15	kidney trouble
Shawen, Mrs. Sarah A.	27 Dec	71	heart trouble
McDaniel, Miss Jane E.	30 Dec	abt 78	
1908			
Steiner, Mrs. Louise Irene	1 Jan	55th yr	brain trouble
Ramsburg, Mrs. Drusilla H.	20 Jan	72	heart failure
Getzendanner, F. Marion	8 Feb	72/8/6	
Holbruner, Edward E.	28 Feb	47/5	consumption
Shultz, Mary Margaret	7 Apr	91/3/23	paralysis
Rhodes, Vernon Maynard, Jr.	7 May	-/-/2	
Davis, Mrs. Rose Elizabeth	10 Jul	34/10	consumption
Jones, Miss Martha M.	13 Jul	29/-/27	consumption
Brunner, Mrs. Ann Sophia	21 Sep	89/8/6	old age
Rowe, Mrs. Mary Ellen	28 Sep	38	typhoid fever
Hargett, Douglass H.	29 Sep	62/2/13	pneumonia
Rowe, Nettie Adelia	3 Oct	1/6/14	cirrhosis of liver
Magill, Dr. Lloyd T.	1 Nov	79/3/17	bladder trouble
Kennedy, Daniel Francis	13 Nov	66/-/24	stomach cancer
Clapp, Robert Douglass, s/o Robert	14 Nov	-/4/1	
Holbrunner, Philip Sheridan	7 Dec	44th yr	Brights disease
Stoener(sic), Almedia Susan	9 Dec	65/1/23	diabetes
Cronice, John Calvin	12 Dec	65/1/10	paralysis
1909			
Brust, Conrad	8 Jan	71	
Green, Howard Lee	7 Feb	41/8/26	Brights disease
Worman, Mrs. Mary Elizabeth	29 Mar	81/-/8	old age
Chew, Mary Jane	2 May	60th yr	
Fout, Ann Rebecca	21 May	72/7/8	
Burger, William H.	6 Jun	81/6/6	old age
Burger, Catharine Irene	30 Jun	-/1/2	
Metcalf, Catharine	27 Jul	37/-/16	consumption
Brengle, Miss Laura E.	26 Aug	68/9/21	complications
Lavanture, Mrs. Charlotte	27 Aug	63/1-/8	paralysis
Shook, Mrs. Barbara Ann	10 Sep	69/11/17	heart trouble
Diehl, Frederick W. Edward	19 Sep	50	rheumatism
Stonebraker, Daniel K.	28 Sep	57	

Deaths and Burials of Evangelical Reformed
United Church of Christ
Frederick, Frederick County, Maryland

Name	Date	Age	Place	Cause
Miller, C. Henry	20 Oct	42/6/16		spinal meningitis
Whisner, Mrs. Catharine Elizabeth	4 Dec	19/7/1		
Wilcoxen, Mrs. Anna Mary	21 Dec	77/6/14		pneumonia
1910				
Glaze, Miss Sarah A.	6 Jan	69th yr		
Zacharias, Rev. George Merle	25 Jan	61/3/12		
Doll, Charlotte Wolff	10 Feb	75/10/13	Martinsburg, WV	senility
Koontz, Mrs. Mary E.	14 Feb	53		paralysis
Hiteshew, Capt. Philip L.	15 Feb	69/6/2		paralysis
Poole, Mrs. Anna Mary	14 Mar	77		general debility
Brown, Mrs. Jeannette	29 Mar	not given		liver trouble
Lampe, J. Henry	2 Apr	68/10/15		liver trouble

From this point recordings were made by Rev. Henri L. G. Kieffer. In place of remarks he lists date of death.

Name	Date	Age	Place	Date of Death
Hooper, Elmer B.	28 Jun	42		25 Jun
White, Roscoe Conklin	5 Jul	36/10/18		3 Jul
Howard, Charles Sotheron	25 Aug	49/1/15		23 Aug
Biser, Thaddeus McCauley	21 Sep	55/10/26		18 Sep
Ritter, Alfred	26 Sep	54		22 Sep
Landers, Washington F.	14 Oct	67		12 Oct
Wilcoxen, Urner	29 Oct	32/11/6		26 Oct
Buxton, Ruth Mussetta	10 Nov	80/6/11		8 Nov
Getzendanner, Milton Eugene	16 Dec	65		14 Dec
Derr, Anna H.	24 Dec	not given		21 Dec
1911				
Zumstein, Catherine	7 Jan	84/6/26		4 Jan
Rice, Lillian Catharine	24 Jan	53/9/15		21 Jan
Bantz, Peter S.	16 Feb	80		14 Feb
Murphy, James D.	20 Feb	53/9/15		18 Feb
Myers, Kate Estelle	23 Feb	not given		21 Feb
Thomas, Walter Graham	15 Mar	30/1		13 Mar
Meisner, Naomi	4 Apr	stillborn		3 Apr
Rhoades, Gideon Mantz	27 Apr	53/11/8		24 Apr
Riehl, Charles Jacob	17 May	55/1		15 May
Parsons, Laura J.	23 Jun	64		21 Jun
Lambright, Annie E.	28 Jul	not given		26 Jul
Hooper, James	6 Aug	78		3 Aug
Stull, William H.	8 Aug	67/4/16	Charlesville Ref Cem	6 Aug
Schley, Steiner	18 Aug	62/3/22		16 Aug
Cramer, Katherine Loretta	13 Sep	-/6/5		12 Sep
Gerlach, Mary Dora	16 Sep	not given		12 Sep
Hafer, Catherine	18 Sep	83/6/4		16 Sep
Linton, Joseph	10 Oct	40		8 Oct
Delashmutt, Susan R.	17 Oct	41/5/15		15 Oct
Schaeffer, Paul	8 Nov	not given		6 Nov
Simmons, George A.	25 Nov	17/3/27		22 Nov
Chew, Benjamin Franklin	10 Dec	57/8/23		7 Dec

Deaths and Burials of Evangelical Reformed
United Church of Christ
Frederick, Frederick County, Maryland

1912

Name	Date	Age	Place	Burial
Hauer, Nicholas Daniel	24 Jan	94/6/14		22 Jan
Kemp, Sarah Margaret Miller	16 Feb	90/6/30		14 Feb
Shook, Lewis A.	20 Feb	not given		18 Feb
Blumenauer, George	21 Feb	not given		19 Feb
Blair, Henry	28 Feb	not given		not given
Cronise, Charles L.	27 Mar	63/5		25 Mar
Garber, Solomon	30 Mar	65/4/24		27 Mar
Chew, Christine Roelke	6 May	56/8/10		3 May
Johnson, Alice Camille	9 May	62/2		6 May
Zieler, Charles E.	20 May	59		18 May
Dutrow, Adele Nelson	14 Jun	not given		12 Jun
Gardiner, Henry Tabler	25 Jun	2/3/1		24 Jun
Michael, Mary Custard	25 Jul	72/8/19		23 Jul
Hauer, Mary L.	? Aug	93/7/10		not given
Levy, Charles Perry	26 Aug	not given		24 Aug
Stitely, Florence M.	3 Sep	52/3/11		1 Sep
Lampe, Elizabeth Ross	11 Sep	70/5/17		8 Sep
Reynolds, Mangen Stanhope	21 Sep	-/-/7	Waynesboro	19 Sep
Snyder, Christian Hegler	22 Sep	60/3/11	Hagerstown	19 Sep
Chew, Samuel	17 Oct	64/6/20		15 Oct
Lakin, Francis Thomas	29 Oct	72/2/25		27 Oct
Peck, David B.	31 Dec	not given	Cleveland, OH	27 Dec

1913

Name	Date	Age	Place	Burial
Houck, Emma Bentz	7 Jan	76		4 Jan
Hood, Margaret Elizabeth Scholl	15 Jan	79/6/5		12 Jan
Kennedy, Mary A.	17 Feb	73		15 Feb
Lease, Luther Edward	18 Feb	76/6/17		15 Feb
Thomas, Francis Granville	24 Feb	68/-/5		22 Feb
Kemp, Lewis George	25 Feb	88/7/28		23 Feb
Gittinger, Evelyn Virginia	13 Mar	75		11 Mar
Schaeffer, Charles Edward	14 Mar	68/9/27		12 Mar
Foland, Anne Elizabeth	25 Mar	6/2/19		23 Mar
Main, Lewis C.	31 Mar	24/9/5		29 Mar
Linton, Elizabeth	1 Apr	50		30 Mar
Rhodes, Elizabeth Jane	3 Apr	77/4/1		29 Mar
Anders, Alice Virginia	4 Apr	73/7/12		2 Apr
Schaeffer, Eliza Ann	11 Apr	76/8/14		9 Apr
Whaley, Isabelle Frances	5 May	84/1/2		3 May
Dunott, Catharine Forne	12 May	40/10/9		9 May
Fleming, Nicholas Hughes	25 May	60/11/23		23 May
Ritschy, Drue Hekiner Lipps (?)	1 Jun	68/4/4		29 May
Howard, Mary Louise	8 Jun	72/10/18		6 Jun
Foland, Helen Gertrude	16 Jun	11/4/2		13 Jun
Shelton, Lewis Donovan	15 Jul	/-3/7		14 Jul
Forberger, Katherine Gally	29 Jul	26/4/13		26 Jul
Brown, William Victor	30 Jul	25/11/9		29 Jul
Lough, Katharine Virginia	4 Aug	-/-/6		3 Aug
Kiefer, Ann Sophia	10 Aug	78/1/18		8 Aug

Deaths and Burials of Evangelical Reformed
United Church of Christ
Frederick, Frederick County, Maryland

Name				
Brandenburg, Jeannie May	26 Sep	24/6/26		24 Sep
Doll, Hannah Margaret	11 Oct	78/10/20		9 Oct
Blumenauer, Ann Catharine	1 Nov	not given		30 Oct
Rice, Eliza Jane	26 Nov	50/1/8		24 Nov
Chew, Adam Richard	11 Dec	54/9		9 Dec
Gittinger, Eleanor Hannah	26 Dec	77/11/1		24 Dec
1914				
Foland, Delia Martha	7 Jan	43/7/21		5 Jan
Markey, Richard Simpson	10 Jan	1/5/20		9 Jan
Schroeder, George Adam	13 Jan	64/3/22		11 Jan
Ardecker, Lula Walling	8 Feb	32/4/4		5 Feb
Waters, Richard C.	12 Feb	78		9 Feb
Byerly, John Davis	21 Feb	75/-/1		18 Feb
Grazer, Mary M.	25 Feb	81		not given
Obenderfer, Susan Virginia	26 Mar	58/8/2		23 Mar
Doll, Melville Ezra	9 Apr	77/1/3		7 Apr
Shriner, Alice Eader	30 Apr	67/11/13		25 Apr
Remsburg, Albert Irving	11 Jul	19/8/12	Middletown Ref Cem	9 Jul
Harley, Anna Elizabeth	19 Jul	87/10/20		16 Jul
Link, Addie V.	24 Jul	50/2/15		23 Jul
Boteler, Silas	5 Aug	not given		2 Aug
Simmons, Georgiana	8 Aug	not given		6 Aug
Bentz, Catharine Elizabeth	26 Aug	64/11/26		23 Aug
Ashbaugh, Aquilla	30 Aug	69		27 Aug
Tice, Nannie B.	10 Sep	58	Rose Hill, Hagerstown	6 Sep
Cramer, Lula Ent	12 Sep	-/2/4		11 Sep
Roth, Laura J.	25 Sep	not given		21 Sep
Jacobs, Catharine S.	27 Sep	not given		25 Sep
Brengle, William Avery	4 Oct	65/4/14		2 Oct
Shipley, Mary Ketler	1 Nov	69/4/27		29 Oct
Haller, William	19 Nov	61		17 Nov
Riddlemoser, Lewis W.	28 Nov	77		26 Nov
1915				
Glessner, Thomas K. H.	3 Jan	56/1/20		31 Dec
Renner, Andrew	15 Jan	not given		not given
Baker, Laura Sophia	6 Feb	68		4 Feb
Davis, Lucinda	19 Feb	64/1/4		16 Feb
Misner, Martha Linton	27 Feb	38		25 Feb
Kunkel, Aurelia Frances	26 Feb	79/2/6		24 Feb
Hersperger, Helen Scholl	6 Mar	59/4/6		4 Mar
Thomas, Calvin Augustus	6 Mar	73		5 Mar
Blumenauer, Margaret Ann	15 Mar	not given		13 Mar
Schultz, Caroline Amelia	22 Mar	83/6/2		19 Mar
Hunkel, Ann Catharine	27 Mar	not given		24 Mar
Firestone, Rebecca	31 Mar	89/1/20		28 Mar
Thomas, Ira Newton	5 Apr	28		3 Apr
Knauff, Charles E.	7 Apr	not given		5 Apr
Eschbach, Mary Susan	26 Apr	not given		20 Apr
Rice, Susan Font	30 Apr	not given		28 Apr

Deaths and Burials of Evangelical Reformed
United Church of Christ
Frederick, Frederick County, Maryland

Name	Date	Age	Notes	Burial
Ramsburg, Loraine Kemp	4 May	31/1/11		1 May
Main, Joshua Thomas	20 May	70/6/10		17 May
Murphy, Annie Mary	23 Jun	82/2/10		21 Jun
Miller, Christina	1 Sep	not given		30 Aug
Rowe, William C.	19 Oct	44/4/25		16 Oct
Sheppard, Emma R.	21 Oct	57/7/26		19 Oct
Holtz, Harriet Victoria	22 Oct	75/8/12		20 Oct
Milyard, Robert Biehl	17 Nov	-/1/4		16 Nov
Mateny, Thomas Clinton	28 Nov	57/10/26		26 Nov
1916				
Stull, George L.	28 Jan	75/4/16		26 Jan
Forney, Samuel J.	3 Apr	52		1 Apr
McKenzie, James Fenwick	23 May	1/2/25		22 May
Foland, Edward	24 May	34/11/2		22 May
King, George Joseph	7 Jun 1916	0/1/0		6 Jun
Brish, Margaret S.	12 Jun	76/2/8		10 Jun
Mehrling, John	24 Jul	79/2/27		22 Jul
Biggs, Clara Virginia	10 Aug	62/6/1		8 Aug
Getzendanner, Laura V.	2 Sep	79/3/26		31 Aug
Gittinger, Mary Eleanor	15 Sep	61/7/23		13 Sep
Biser, John Jacob	9 Sep	76/6/6		7 Sep
Yost, Minnie Elizabeth	24 Sep	24		21 Sep
Stauffer, David Murray, Jr.	2 Oct	4/0/0		1 Oct
Gomber, John	18 Oct	76		15 Oct
Hanshew, Emily	20 Oct	90/8/15		17 Oct
Steiner, Georgianna	21 Oct	83/7/26		19 Oct
Mantz, Lucy J.	30 Oct	64/9/11		28 Oct
Chaney, Sarah Elizabeth	15 Nov	85/2/22		13 Nov
Carlin, Ann Cecelia	25 Nov	79/5/26		23 Nov
Hagan, Charles McCauley	17 Dec	63/0/22	15 Dec	
1917				
Bopst, Joshua D.	4 Jan	87		2 Jan
Schell, Mathias B.	12 Feb	67		10 Feb
Rowe, Margaret Lucretia	22 Mar	18/5/19		20 Mar
Dill, Joshua Ada	13 Apr	71/4/16		10 Apr
Saunders, Caroline E.	21 Apr	80/11/18		18 Apr
Kefauver, George Harvey	30 Apr	50/3/11		27 Apr
Colleflower(sic) Sarah C. B.	19 May	76		16 May
Layman, Mary J.	7 Jun	65/3/26	Hill Church, Lewistown	5 Jun
Dill, Lavinia Virginia	3 Sep	70/10/7		1 Sep
Knock, William H.	13 Sep	15/6/16		11 Sep
Glessner, James Schley	8 oct	53/3/8		5 Oct
Stauffer, Daniel Valentine	13 Oct	72		11 Oct
Thomas, Elizabeth C.	10 Dec	66113		7 Dec
1918				
Remsburgh, Courtnay May	2 Jan	32/1/12		31 Dec 1917
Doll, Mary Lucretia	1 Feb	70/0/8		29 Jan
Null, Kenneth Ruthford	8 Feb	2/7/21		6 Feb
Grove, John D.	6 Mar	65/6/9		3 Mar

Deaths and Burials of Evangelical Reformed
United Church of Christ
Frederick, Frederick County, Maryland

Name	Date	Age	Burial Place	Burial Date
Haller, Charles Edgar	24 Mar	31		21 Mar
Routzahn, Charles Emory	6 Apr	59/11/29		4 Apr
Brengle, George W.	17 Apr	73/2/27		15 Apr
Gephart, Louisa Virginia	24 Apr	87/3/20		21 Apr
Gittinger, George Metzger	24 Apr	55/1/19		21 Apr
Johnson, Eugene Augustus	8 May	74/4/11		5 May
Abbot, John H.	14 Jun	81/11/12		11 Jun
Roderick, Samuel Hallar	26 Jun	0/1/23		24 Jun
Kidd, Grace Darlene	27 Jun	28		25 Jun
McDonald, Georgiana Bostick	1 Jul	79		27 Jun
Rice, C. Frank	2 Jul	65/10/26		28 Jun
Feete, Kate A.	2 Jul	78/4/24		29 Jun
Ebert, Mary Elizabeth	2 Jul	88/0/0		30 Jun
Gittinger, George W.	30 Aug	77/10/4		28 Aug
Whisner, S. Guy	6 Sep	29/5/7		4 Sep
Hobbs, John Robert	17 Sep	71/8/22		15 Sep
Wolfe, Alice Virginia	20 Sep	7/2/21		29 Sep
Knipple, Jesse Franklin	11 Oct	18/1/13		9 Oct
Garrett, Harry Norman	13 Oct	26/4/2		8 Oct
Redmond, Lewis Benjamin	23 Oct	0/4/24		22 Oct
Roelke, Arthur Grover	1 Nov	33/0/24		30 Oct
Paisley, Fannie Hiteshew	5 Nov	32/0/21		3 Nov
Buckey, William Augustus	16 Nov	49/4/28		14 Nov
Thomas, Catharine Harriet	23 Nov	78/2/9		21 Nov
Mateny, Nellie May	28 Nov	36		26 Nov
Keefer, Margaret Quynn	29 Nov	69/4/27		26 Nov
Keeney, Minerva Alice	2 Dec	67/5/145		28 Nov
Harry, William H.	2 Dec	78/3/4		30 Nov
Shankle, Philip H.	3 Dec	80/8/11	Zion Luth, Middletown	1 Dec
Kuhn, Nellie Fleming	6 Dec	52/0/13		4 Dec
Wachter, William Noah	19 Dec	33/2/17		16 Dec
Gittinger, Mary Catharine	22 Dec	49		20 Dec
Stup, Jonathan	26 Dec	66/10/0		22 Dec
1919				
Knauff, Alcinda	3 Jan	not given		1 Jan
Tyson, Katharine Aubert	20 Jan	18/10/15		18 Jan
Comfort, Willie Anna	27 Jan	76/2/22		22 Jan
Shelton, John Edward	29 Jan	60		27 Jan
Brish, Louis Edgar	10 Feb	10/5/1		8 Feb
Yinger, Harry Eugene	11 Feb	43/0/17		8 Feb
Miller, Joseph Getzendanner	14 Mar	101/0/19		11 Mar
Neidig, Emma Barbara	21 Apr	61/3/10		18 Apr
Stull, Rose Bavaria	8 Jul	not given		6 Jul
Doll, Samuel Valentine	17 Jul	79/10/11		15 Jul
Winkelman, Paul	25 Jul	41		24 Jul
Hagerman, Henry	2 Aug	79	Rose Hill, Hagerstown	23 Jul
Dixon, Ann Mary	2 Aug	39		31 Jul
Schaeffer, Long Rhoads	14 Aug	59/7/13		12 Aug
Nitzler, Ellen Achey	22 Aug	32/0/6	Mt. Olivet, Hanover, PA	19 Aug

Deaths and Burials of Evangelical Reformed
United Church of Christ
Frederick, Frederick County, Maryland

Name	Death Date	Age	Place	Burial Date
Staley, Clara J.	10 Oct	not given		8 Oct
Clingan, Lewis S.	20 Oct	not given		17 Oct
Feaga, Ida F.	30 Oct	57/0/7		27 Oct
Suter, Laura Virginia	13 Nov	63/7/2	Rose Hill, Hagerstown	10 Nov
Hargett, Anna M.	17 Nov	not given	15 Nov	
Knock, Hannah T.	1 Dec	81/5/24		28 Nov
Odell, Hazel Harrison	9 Dec	24/11/2		8 Dec
Cost, Lloyd Albert	11 Dec	24/8/15	Rose Hill, Hagerstwon	7 Dec
Thomas, Samuel D.	27 Dec	not given	24 Dec	
1920				
Wachter, Helen Krepps	17 Jan	not given		15 Jan
Cost, Cyrus	24 Jan	not given	Fairview, Mercersburg, PA	22 Jan
Riddlemoser, Alice E.	26 Jan	not given		23 Jan
Leilich, Catharine E.	26 Jan	not given		23 Jan
Gannon, Charlotte Ellen	19 Feb	1/11/10		17 Feb
Haller, William Snyder	26 Feb	48/1/10		23 Feb
Smith, Mary Ann Rebecca	29 Feb	71/0/5		27 Feb
Lerch, Frank	17 Mar	60		14 Mar
Mainhart, Caroline	20 Mar	85		18 Mar
Cronise, John F.	23 Mar	68/5/19		20 Mar
Benner, John E.	24 Mar	81/10/20	Rose Hill, Hagerstown	21 Mar
Engelbrecht, Bessie E.	14 Apr	23		11 Apr
Birely, Martha E.	19 Apr	not given		17 Apr
Castle, Thomas F.	26 Apr	84/6/1		23 Apr
Null, Joseph Arthur	13 May	0/4/17		11 May
Hawthorne, Margaret Virginia	26 May	1/6/0	Rose Hill, Hagerstown	24 May
Silance, J. Vernon	29 Jun	63/10/14		27 Jun
Wiles, Ella Louise	23 Jul	0/1/21		21 Jul
Young, Annie K.	24 Jul	59/9/10		22 Jul
DeVine, Earl W.	3 Aug	not given		1 Aug
Thomas, George F.	12 Aug	77/2/26		9 Aug
Clingan, Minerva Elizabeth	16 Aug	81		14 Aug
Beachley, Silas Rex	3 Sep	7/4/11		1 Sep
Engle, Roanna Stull	3 Sep	82/6/14		1 Sep
Thomas, Helen	29 Sep	3		28 Sep
Slick, George F.	2 Oct	37/6/2		30 Sep
Davis, Isabelle	7 Oct	not given		5 Oct
Dunott, Elizabeth	8 Oct	not given		5 Oct
Stull, Mary Ann	9 Oct	87		7 Oct
Mantz, Medora W.	13 Oct	62/4/20		11 Oct
Castle, Harriet D.	1 Nov	not given		29 Oct
Schley, John Reading	2 Nov(reinterred)	not given	died in France	22 Oct 1918
Burkett, Hester	11 Dec	1/11/10		10 Dec
Thomas, Louise	18 Dec	80		16 Dec
Robinson, James William	19 Dec	not given	Woodsboro	16 Dec
Dertzbaugh, William Lee	23 Dec(reinterred)	not given	died in France	not given
1921				
Winkelman, Wilhemina	10 Jan	75		7 Jan

Deaths and Burials of Evangelical Reformed
United Church of Christ
Frederick, Frederick County, Maryland

Name				
Taylor, Florence Barrick	29 Jan	not given		27 Jan
Hildebrand, Isadora V.	30 Jan	48		28 Jan
Schultz, Mary H.	10 Feb	60		8 Feb
Clingan, Frank G.	9 Mar	59		6 Mar
Kolb, David Denmead	6 Jun	not given		4 Jun
Engle, Lewis Henry, Sr.	14 Mar	not given		12 Mar
Stauffer, Willie Anna	4 Apr	not given		2 Apr
Staub, Fannie	16 Apr	not given		14 Apr
Bentz, Mary E.	5 May	not given		2 May
Clarke, Wendell B.	20 May	not given		21 Mar 1920(sic)
Clarke, Charles S.	20 May	not given		12 Nov 1920(sic)
Baker, Clifford Monroe, Jr.	20 May	0/0/2		18 May
McLane, Margaret J.	4 Jun	77		2 Jun
Eyler, Benjamin Franklin	19 Jun(reinterred)	not given	died in France	19 Oct 1918
Hargett, Earlston L.	26 Jun(reinterred)	not given	died in France	not given
Rudy, Annie E.	2 Jul	81		30 Jun
Hildebrand, George	19 Jul	not given		17 Jul
Thomas, Lauretta	23 Jul	not given		21 Jul
Derr, Eugene L.	6 Oct	77		4 Oct
Smith, Donald R.	18 Nov	37/8/26		15 Nov
Feete, William C.	17 Nov	71		14 Nov
Main, Anna C.	21 Nov	not given		17 Nov
Patterson, Caroline H.	26 Nov	76		24 Nov
Fout, Charles	5 Dec	not given		3 Dec
Carnahan, Barbara Ann	9 Dec	not given	Keedysville Cem	6 Dec
Miller, George P.	20 Dec	74		17 Dec
1922				
Brust, Carl Edward	16 Feb	0/0/21		15 Feb
Krantz, Laura Virginia	21 Feb	70		19 Feb
Gardner, Olga Lee	3 Mar	0/1/3		3 Mar
Krantz, Alice Elizabeth	4 Mar	76/5/0		2 Mar
Hermann, Charles M.	13 Mar	79		11 Mar
Chambers, Clara	14 Mar	not given		not given
Null, Joseph M.	17 Apr	not given		15 Apr
Cronise, E. Margaretta	26 May	not given		24 May
Martz, Phoebe C.	26 May	not given	24 May	
Albaugh, Carrie Virginia	2 Jun	not given		30 May
Beal, William H.	8 Jun	60	Liberty Cem.	5 Jun
Chew, Charles Edward	27 Jun	74		25 Jun
Thomas, Sarah E.	24 Aug	74		22 Aug
Schley, Jennie Schley(sic)	19 Sep	71		17 Sep
Kolb, David	23 Sep	83		20 Sep
Remsburg, Fannie R.	7 Oct	not given		4 Oct
Hanshew, Daniel S.	21 Nov	85/7/26		18 Nov
Burger, William A.	29 Nov	65/11/10		27 Nov
Kefauver, H. Edward	13 Dec	81	Ref. Cem, Middletown	11 Dec
1923				
Blumenauer, John W. N.	2 Jan	not given		31 Dec 1922

Deaths and Burials of Evangelical Reformed
United Church of Christ
Frederick, Frederick County, Maryland

Name	Date	Age	Place	Burial
Wilcoxen, George E.	19 Jan	51		17 Jan
Bucheimer, Caroline E.	26 Jan	77		24 Jan
Dertzbaugh, William Henry	7 Feb	not given		5 Feb
Albaugh, Christian Thomas	22 Feb	91/1/4		19 Feb
Rhoderick, Thomas Bernard	24 Feb	0/1/1		23 Feb
Main, Catharine	26 Feb	88/2/8		24 Feb
Little, Sarah Louise	1 Mar	not given		27 Feb
McCardell, Alforetta R.	2 Mar	75		28 Feb
Ragan, Annie	15 Mar	not given	Rose Hill, Hagerstown	12 Mar
Lipps, John A. C.	26 Mar	81/0/4		24 Mar
Harwetel, Emma J.	30 Mar	55		28 Mar
Crum, Henry H.	6 Apr	64/4/21		4 Apr
Gerlach, Christian	10 Apr	82/3/8		8 Apr
Gilbert, Charles	17 May	not given		15 May
Kaufman, Violet	18 May	not given		16 May
Brandenburg, Amanda C.	5 Jun	66/4/4		3 Jun
Nicthman, Jennie I.	9 Jun	58/3/21		7 Jun
Garber, Isabella	14 Jun	76		12 Jun
Gittinger, Henry Mehrl	20 Jun	69		17 Jun
Abbott, Julia Hanshew	3 Jul	83/9/29		30 Jun
Harry, Mary Catharine	27 Jul	81/10/23		25 Jul
Cashour, Fannie Kemp	5 Aug	not given		2 Aug
Wills, Alice V.	25 Sep	73		23 Sep
Glessner, Richard Ross	27 Sep	32		25 Sep
Grumbine, Lester R.	1 Oct	not given		29 Sep
Hooper, Sarah Blanche	8 Nov	not given		6 Nov
Anders, Aaron Repp	1 Dec	44/6/17		28 Nov
1924				
Getzendanner, Annie G. H.	5 Jan	not given		4 Jan
Edmonds, Eyster W.	19 Jan	73		16 Jan
Miller, Oscar Henry, Jr.	18 Jan	6/11/21		16 Jan
Main, Sophia B.	21 Jan	83/0/28		18 Jan
Zimmerman, Laura K.		19 Feb	not given	17 Feb
Notnagle, Helen L.	27 Feb	6/7/18		25 Feb
Knock, James H.	10 Mar	68/5/11		8 Mar
Mantz, Maggie	17 Mar	63/8/1		15 Mar
Tabler, Kate S.	5 Apr	not given		3 Apr
Rice, Marion C.	5 Apr	not given		3 Apr
Starr, Mary K.	20 Apr	not given		17 Apr
Brunner, George H.	28 Apr	83/4/26		26 Apr
Truett, Mabel G.	25 Apr	41		23 Apr
Thomas, Sarah Ellen	17 May	48/6/17		14 May
Windsor, James	19 May	not given		17 May
Bready, E. Tobias	21 May	70/10/11		18 May
Wachter, Phoebe	21 May	61		18 May
Miller, Simon S.	31 May	82		28 May
Ramsburgh, John S.	5 Jun	88		2 Jun
Kaufman, George L.	7 Jul	not given		5 Jul
Cramer, George L.	12 Jul	73/1/15		9 Jul

Deaths and Burials of Evangelical Reformed
United Church of Christ
Frederick, Frederick County, Maryland

Name	Date	Age	Cemetery	Burial Date
Appleman, Philip S.	15 Jul	74/9/12	Rose Hill, Hagerstown	12 Jul
Wolfe, Alice V.	4 Aug	76/3/28		2 Aug
Gittinger, Maggie	5 Sep	not given		not given
Gerlach, Dora E.	10 Sep	75		8 Sep
Meister, Fred	1 Oct	not given		29 Sep
Miller, Fannie Stull	8 Oct	59		6 Oct
Rhoderick, Hannah Beatrice	15 Nov	0/0/2		15 Nov
Krantz, Ruth Helena	11 Dec	7/7/20		9 Dec
Zentz, Newton M.	15 Dec	72/4/16		12 Dec
Houck, Ella V.	30 Dec	not given		27 Dec
1925				
Kefauver, H. Milton	3 Jan	87/8/23		1 Jan
Miller, Mary G.	16 Jan	81/4/8		13 Jan
Young, Manzella	24 Jan	83		21 Jan
Floyd, Addie Winona	10 Feb	23/1/0		6 Feb
Roelkey, John W.	16 Feb	not given		14 Feb
Paisley, Pauline R. V.	5 Mar	16/1/1		2 Mar
Worman, Amanda J.	11 Mar	73		8 Mar
Gittinger, Laura C.	11 Apr	not given		9 Apr
Anders, Lillian R.	11 Apr	not given		8 Apr
Geisbert, Nannie M.	20 Apr	not given		17 Apr
Wills, no first name	22 Apr	not given		20 Apr
Michael, John L.	8 Jun	88		5 Jun
Stup, Sophia Ann	21 Jul	75		19 Jul
Bartgis, William	23 Jul	not given		21 Jul
Hiteshew, Martans E.	25 Jul	not given		23 Jul
MacGill, Charles	no further information			
Wise, Florence M.	11 Sep	not given	Rose Hill, Hagerstown	not given
Butler, Pearl	19 Sep	48/4/17		17 Sep
Marman, Sallie M.	27 Oct	47/0/18		24 Oct
Gittinger, Edward A.	21 Nov	90		19 Nov
Hagan, Rose Catharine	23 Nov	75		21 Nov
Rhoderick, Melvin Dorsey	30 Nov	71/9/14		27 Nov
1926				
Thomas, David Otho	2 Jan	76		1 Jan
Harley, Minnie E.	14 Jan	63/0/15		11 Jan
Mike, Miriam M.	8 Mar	1/4/13		6 Mar
Derr, Alice V.	13 Mar	not given		10 Mar
Krantz, Edward C.	23 Mar	73		21 Mar
Brust, August F.	30 Mar	64/7/22		27 Mar
Kunkel, Mary C.	1 Apr	not given		30 Mar
Fleming, William W.	no further information			
Burger, Nettie Irene	15 Apr	63		13 Apr
Frazier, Clifford A.	26 Apr	64		23 Apr
Abbott, Clementine B.	27 Apr	83		24 Apr
Pettingall, Sarah	28 Apr	not given		26 Apr
Brengle, Charles E.	3 May	51/6/15		1 May
Hallar, Annie C.	not given	not given		2 May
Gittinger, Clara M.	11 May	not given		9 May

Deaths and Burials of Evangelical Reformed
United Church of Christ
Frederick, Frederick County, Maryland

Name	Date	Age	Place	Burial
Zimmerman, Nettie E.	7 Jun	not given		5 Jun
Rice, Susan Addie	24 Jul	not given		22 Jul
Unger, Sophia Elizabeth	19 Aug	75/2/3	Fairview, Mercersburg, PA	16 Aug
Zimmerman, Marion	24 Aug	92/0/23		21 Aug
Crutchley, Milton Clay	30 Aug	81/9/10	Clarksburg	28 Aug
Biser, Catharine	17 Sep	97		15 Sep
Strauff, Della M.	5 Oct	51/2/8		2 Oct
Urban, Carrie Y.	23 Oct	49/9/0		21 Oct
Lough, Margaret A.	29 Oct	80		27 Oct
Boteler, Margaret E.	6 Nov	not given		4 Nov
Derr, Hiram A.	24 Nov	75		22 Nov
Mantz, E. Peter	4 Dec	70		2 Dec
DeLashmutt, Elias	24 Dec	not given		23 Dec
1927				
Zimmerman, Hester C.	1 Jan	70/11/16		30 Dec 1926
Smith, George Edward	27 Jan	76		24 Jan
Newman, Jacob M.	29 Jan	83		27 Jan
Birely, Frances D.	2 Feb	not given		31 Jan
Brengle, Elizabeth	10 Feb	not given		8 Feb
Blumenauer, Nicholas J.	26 Feb	74/3/26		23 Feb
Brunner, Theodore	26 Feb	80		24 Feb
Motter, Gabe M.	3 Mar	75/1/10		1 Mar
Ramsburg, Josiah A.	26 Mar	not given		24 Mar
Stup, Mary Ann	10 Apr	88/6/5		8 Apr
Worman, George M.	23 Apr	not given		20 Apr
Brish, Annie V.	7 May	not given		4 May
Thomas, K. Virginia	18 May	not given		16 May
Ramsburg, Cornelia V.	22 May	not given		19 May
Haller, Anna M.	4 Jul	not given		2 Jul
Obenderfer, Eva Margretta	13 Sep	96		11 Sep
Thomas, Maria Virginia	18 Sep	76		16 Sep
Ramsburg, William H.	28 Sep	not given		26 Sep
Larkin, Ella	3 Nov	61		30 Oct
Getzendanner, Mary Elizabeth	26 Nov	not given		23 Nov
Motter, John C.	26 Nov	not given		24 Nov
Chew, Ida L.	23 Dec	67/4/9		21 Dec
1928				
Krantz, Mary Martha	30 Jan	not given		28 Jan
Wiles, Ida M.	26 Mar	not given		24 Mar
Keefer, Edward P.	27 Mar	86		25 Mar

New record book and format.

Name	Place of residence	Age	Date of death	Date of burial	Place of burial
As above, place of burial is Mt Olivet Cemetery unless otherwise shown.					
1928					
Rice, Anna Othetta	Frederick	40/5/17	17 Apr	20 Apr	
Storm, Alice O.	Lancaster, PA	83	19 Apr	21 Apr	
Herbert, Margaret E.	Frederick	75/10/4	26 Apr	28 Apr	Zion, Middletown

Deaths and Burials of Evangelical Reformed
United Church of Christ
Frederick, Frederick County, Maryland

Name	Place	Age	Died	Buried	Notes
Quynn, Harriet Eleanor	Frederick	67	27 Apr	30 Apr	
Billy, Anna M.	Frederick	84/1/12	8 May	10 May	
Rhoads, Harriet E.	Frederick	58/11/6	17 May	20 May	
Lough, Uriah A.	Frederick	not given	18 May	21 May	
Buckey, Edward	Frederick	not given	26 May	28 May	
Ramsburg, John H. L.	Frederick	80	30 Jun	2 Jul	
Lakin, Mary F.	Frederick	not given	21 Jul	23 Jul	
Kaufman, Jesse D.	Frederick	72	24 Jul	26 Jul	
Culler, John J.	Frederick	not given	28 Jul	30 Jul	Church Hill
Brust, Clara	Morgantown, WV	not given	24 Sep	26 Sep	
Zimmerman, Clara	Walkersville	not given	6 Oct	6 Oct	Utica Mills
Flautt, Lewis C.	Frederick	72	12 Nov	14 Nov	
Birely, Margaret Ellen	Frederick	77	16 Nov	18 Nov	
Ramsburg, Dennis Casper	Lewistown	74/11/5	27 Nov	30 Nov	
Paisley, George A.	Frederick	71/1/4	19 Dec	21 Dec	
Zeigler, Charles C.	Frederick	not given	26 Dec	29 dec	

1929

Name	Place	Age	Died	Buried	Notes
Neighbours, Fleet R.	Frederick	81	12 Jan	15 Jan	
Hanshew, Eleanor	Frederick	not given	15 Jan	18 Jan	
Kemp, Julian E.	nr Frederick	79/9/20	16 Jan	19 Jan	Rocky Springs
Thomas, Cephas M.	Frederick	78	23 Jan	25 Jan	
Hauer, Susan Elizabeth	Frederick	66/8/12	28 Jan	31 Jan	
Rowe, Julia Elaine	Washington, DC	not given	4 Mar	7 Mar	
Miller, Mary G.	Frederick	not given	8 Mar	11 Mar	
Roelke, Ginevera	Frederick	65	8 Mar	10 Mar	
Richards, Wallace W.	Baltimore	not given	? Mar	20 Mar	
Geisinger, Charlotte	Frederick	not given	25 Mar	27 Mar	
Stull, Susan Virginia	Frederick	67/4/10	24 Apr	26 Apr	
Dutrow, Richard S. J.	Frederick	62/8/8	29 Apr	1 May	
Wolfe, Mary A.	Mt. Vernon, AL	not given	6 May	8 May	
Lipps, George Lewis	Frederick	83/2/12	22 May	24 May	
Waters, F. Gordon	Frederick	31/8/27	30 May	1 Jun	
Horine, Malinda	Frederick	not given	15 Jun	17 Jun	
Edmonds, no first name	Frederick	not given	26 Jun	28 Jun	
Hargett, Eva Rebecca	Frederick	39/5/2	5 Jul	7 Jul	
Motter, Janet C. W.	Frederick	45/10/20	19 Sep	27 Sep	
Smith, William S.	nr Frederick	not given	25 Sep	27 Sep	
Chambers, George M.	Frederick	not given	9 Oct	12 oct	
Hopwood, William	Frederick	not given	26 Oct	28 Oct	
Davis, J. Francis	Frederick	not given	1 Nov	4 Nov	
Roelkey, Elroy L.	Frederick	not given	9 Nov	12 Nov	
Duvall, James E.	Frederick	89	30 Nov	2 Dec	
Brunner, Mary	Frederick	not given	20 Dec	22 Dec	

1930

Name	Place	Age	Died	Buried	Notes
Saunders, Sophia E.	Frederick	68/2/28	15 Feb	17 Feb	
Blumenauer, Charles D.	Frederick	39/6/28	3 Mar	5 Mar	
Thomas, John D.	Frederick	75	3 Mar	5 Mar	
Wolfe, Janet Hinks	Washington, DC	not given	10 Mar	11 Mar	
McDannel, Elizabeth P.	Niagra Falls, NY	not given	13 Mar	17 Mar	

Deaths and Burials of Evangelical Reformed
United Church of Christ
Frederick, Frederick County, Maryland

Name	Place	Age	Death	Burial	Notes
Bartgis, Belle R.	Frederick	70/1/17	17 Mar	19 Mar	
Diehl, Laura G.	Frederick	not given	25 Apr	28 Apr	
Shriner, Edward D., Sr.	Frederick	68/3/16	29 Apr	2 May	
Murphy, James G.	Frederick	53	2 May	5 May	
Gring, Emma A.	Frederick	84/0/3	4 May	6 May	
Stauffer, D. Murray	Frederick	43	6 May	8 May	
Birely, P. Henry C.	Frederick	not given	10 May	12 May	
Hall, Harry C.	Frederick	not given	29 May	30 May	
Miller, Emma June	Frederick	70	2 Jun	4 Jun	
Kemp, C. Thomas	Frederick	not given	1 Jul	3 Jul	
Crum, Emory C.	Frederick	46/2/11	10 Aug	12 Aug	
Duvall, Belle E.	Frederick	68	10 Aug	12 Aug	
Glessner, Millard M.	Frederick	not given	11 Sep	13 Sep	
Cramer, Noah E.	Frederick	70/1/0	11 Sep	14 Sep	
Houck, Ezra	Frederick	not given	12 Sep	15 Sep	
Geisbert, William H.	Frederick	66/11/9	25 Sep	28 Sep	
Cashour, Charles W. F.	Frederick	77/1/20	27 Sep	30 Sep	
Dertzbaugh, Emma I.	Frederick	not given	12 Oct	14 Oct	
Shipley, J. Franklin	Frederick	21	7 Nov	10 Nov	
Brengle, Jennie	Frederick	not given	5 Dec	8 Dec	
Johnson, Manzilla	Frederick	not given	25 Dec	27 Dec	
1931					
Krantz, William H.	Shookstown	86/7/2	11 Feb	13 Feb	
Thomas, Louisa P.	Frederick	72	16 Feb	18 Feb	Tiffin, OH
Harding, Clara R.	Frederick	78	18 Mar	20 Mar	
Zimmerman, Alberta F.	Frederick	75	29 Mar	31 Mar	
Hallar, Eliza A.	Frederick	77	2 Apr	4 Apr	
Hargett, Emma M.	Frederick	78/8/28	30 Apr	2 May	
Flautt, Jennie Catherine	Frederick	78/3/20	11 May	14 May	
Abbott, Henry H.	Frederick	not given	28 May	30 May	
Lovejoy, Sara C.	Frederick	not given	? Jul	25 Jul	
Fisher, Moses	Frederick	not given	17 Jul	19 Jul	
Dutrow, Samuel P.	Frederick	not given	19 Jul	21 Jul	
Schroeder, Mary A.	Frederick	not given	19 Aug	21 Aug	
Knock, Charles F.	Frederick	not given	20 Aug	23 Aug	
Motter, Serene K.	Frederick	not given	5 Oct	7 Oct	
Quynn, Casper	Frederick	not given	3 Nov	5 Nov	
1932					
Eichelberger, Lily C.	Frederick	not given	14 Feb	16 Feb	
Lampe, Nettie Lee	Frederick	not given	12 Feb	14 Feb	
Obenderfer, Elizabeth	Frederick	not given	28 Feb	1 Mar	
McCardell, Adrian C.	Frederick	86/3/1	30 Mar	2 Apr	
Poole, Jane	Frederick	81	1 Apr	2 Apr	
Winebrener, Annie L.	Frederick	84/7/8	24 May	26 May	
Zimmerman, Harry Franklin	Pottsville, PA	not given	28 May	30 May	Charlesville Ref.
Garrett, Ella J.	Frederick	not given	10 Jun	12 Jun	
Remsberg, Emory C.	Frederick	63	10 Jun	12 Jun	Middletown Ref.
Shaw, Breckinridge	Frederick	71	23 Jul	26 Jul	Manchester, MD
Zimmerman, Spencer G.H., Sr.	Frederick	not given	6 Aug	8 Aug	

Deaths and Burials of Evangelical Reformed
United Church of Christ
Frederick, Frederick County, Maryland

Name	Place	Age	Death	Burial	Notes
Zeigler, Mrs. Caroline C.	Frederick	72/3/8	10 Sep	12 Sep	
Lipps, Annie P.	Frederick	75/5/23	29 Sep	1 Oct	
Routzahn, Albert B.	Frederick	68/11/26	23 Oct	25 Oct	
Harner, Mrs. Lola R.	Baltimore	37/7/18	20 Dec	22 Dec	
Richards, Mrs. Minnie D.	Baltimore	not given	23 Dec	26 Dec	
Markell, Mrs. Mary Kate	Frederick	not given	25 Dec	28 Dec	
1933					
Schmidt, Mazie C.	Frederick	44	4 Jan	6 Jan	
Lipps, Mrs. Eleanor M.	Frederick	84	8 Jan	10 Jan	
Duvall, Rosa V.	Frederick	45/9/28	30 Jan	1 Feb	
Buchheimer, Miss Catherine	Frederick	89/2/10	9 Feb	13 Feb	
Gittinger, Samuel J.	Frederick	74	6 Mar	8 Mar	
Motter, Samuel Lewis, Jr.	Elizabeth NJ	25	15 Mar	22 Mar	
Bentz, Mrs. Lillie May	Frederick	not given	20 Mar	23 Mar	
Eichelberger, Francis Marion	Frederick	73/10/19	2 Apr	5 Apr	
Keith, Mrs. Ellen B.	Frederick	48	6 Apr	8 Apr	Memorial Park
Ramsburgh, Mary Catharine	Frederick	not given	30 May	1 Jun	
Main, Mrs. Clara Z.	Frederick	77	13 Jun	14 Jun	Charlesville
Cramer, Mrs. Lulu Ent	Frederick	61/2/18	7 Jul	10 Jul	
Blumenauer, Mrs. Julia Ann	Detroit, MI	65	13 Jul	16 Jul	
Heagey, Jesse F. R.	Frederick	59	13 Jul	16 Jul	Gettysburg, PA
Anders, Orra Washington	Middletown	73/7/27	24 Jul	28 Jul	Middletown Ref.
Albaugh, Eugene H.	Friendship Hgts.	not given	5 Aug	7 Aug	
Frazier, Stanley F.	Washington, DC	68	2 Sep	5 Sep	
Krantz, Mrs. Nannie E.	Frederick	67	7 Sep	9 Sep	
Rice, Thomas P.	Frederick	76	23 Sep	26 Sep	
Bartgis, Mary W.	Frederick	73/3/3	12 Oct	14 Oct	
Schell, George E.	Frederick	35/0/1	18 Oct	21 Oct	
Measell, Susan R.	Meadows	83	3 Dec	6 Dec	
Quynn, Emily C.	Frederick	84	7 Dec	9 Dec	
Harrison, James Victor	Frederick	2/6/0	25 Dec	27 Dec	
Kaufman, Mrs. Ann R. C.	Frederick	68	29 Dec	31 Dec	
1934					
Mull, Florence G. M.	Frederick	61	23 Jan	31 Jan	
Cole, Mrs. Ida M.	Frederick	70/10/8	1 Feb	3 Feb	
Conrad, Mrs. Catherine A.	Frederick	78	11 Feb	14 Feb	
Phleeger, Mrs. S. Laura	Frederick	76/11/17	14 Feb	17 Feb	
Thomas, Mrs. Emily V.	Frederick	84	16 Feb	19 Feb	Manor Graveyard
Main, Clinton E.	Frederick	not given	7 Mar	9 Mar	
Heffner, Mrs. Maggie E.	Frederick	55	9 Apr	12 Apr	
Gittinger, J. Albert	Frederick	77/5/14	3 May	6 May	
Marsh, Mrs. Martha W.	Frederick	50	15 May	18 May	
Hankey, Mrs. Myrtle B.	Erie, PA	not given	9 Jun	12 Jun	Waynesboro, PA
Chew, Thomas	Frederick	77	29 Jun	1 Jul	
Thomas, Miss Edith M.	Frederick	not given	11 Jul	14 Jul	
Bennett, Miss Jane	Frederick	not given	13 Jul	15 Jul	
Hildebrand, Miss Hattie May	Frederick	not given	29 Aug	31 Aug	
Walker, Mrs. Annie M.	Frederick	80	6 Sep	9 Sep	
Krantz, Miss Margaret Ann	Frederick	not given	10 Sep	13 Sep	

Deaths and Burials of Evangelical Reformed
United Church of Christ
Frederick, Frederick County, Maryland

Name	Place	Age	Death	Burial	Notes
Mateny, Elmer E.	Petersville	73	2 Oct	4 Oct	Middletown Ref.
Blumenauer, Miss Georgia	Frederick	85	4 Oct	6 Oct	
Lampe, Allen R.	Frederick	54	25 Oct	27 Oct	
Ramsburg, Elias B.	Frederick	72	18 Nov	20 Nov	
Cramer, Miss Susan P.	Frederick	71	22 Nov	24 Nov	
Clingan, Miss Marie L.	Frederick	68	2 Dec	5 Dec	
Doll, Charles D.	Frederick	80/6/-	29 Dec	1 Jan '35	
1935					
Stockman, Franklin E.	Frederick	1 day	7 Jan	9 Jan	
Stockman, Marion L.	Frederick	1 day	7 Jan	9 Jan	
Biser, Ira E.	Frederick	not given	31 Jan	3 Feb	Middletown Ref.
Crum, Irving H.	Frederick	69/3/19	8 Feb	11 Feb	Union Chapel
Simmons, Louis	Frederick	76	21 Mar	23 May	
McCardell, Mrs. Helen L.	Frederick	not given	3 Apr	5 Apr	
Tyson, Mrs. Katharine A.	Frederick	77/6/7	29 May	1 Jun	
Chipley, Mrs. Katherine	Pittsburgh, PA	not given	11 Jun	13 Jun	
Hauer, Fritchie H.	Baltimore	71	11 Jun	14 Jun	
Kemp, C. Edwin	Frederick	45	21 Jun	23 Jun	
Miller, Mrs. Roberta	Frederick	not given	26 Jun	28 Jun	
Dutrow, Miss Ada R.	Frederick	not given	29 Jun	2 Jul	
Lawson, Charles A.	Bartonsville	not given	1 Jul	4 Jul	
Mantz, Miss Mary Ann	Frederick	not given	13 Jul	15 Jul	
Jones, Mrs. Jane Rice	Frederick	44/0/25	23 Jul	25 Jul	
Derr, Dr. Ezra Z.	Frederick	not given	24 Aug	26 Aug	
Glessner, Harry F.	Frederick	38/4/14	10 Sep	12 Sep	
Rhoads, Mrs. Grace A.	Frederick	not given	29 Sep	1 oct	
Staley, Mrs. Bertha C.	Frederick	not given	9 Oct	11 oct	
VanDevanter, Lillian M.	Baltimore	72/7/21	12 Oct	14 Oct	Rose Hill, Hagerstown
Troxell, Charles P.	Frederick	not given	28 Oct	31 Oct	
Lampe, Christian L. C.	Frederick	87	22 Nov	25 Nov	
Santee, Charles A.	Ft Washington, PA	not given	12 Dec	16 Dec	Sharpsburg
1936					
Hahn, Charles S.	Frederick	not given	11 Jan	14 Jan	
Culler, Mrs. Annie E.	Frederick	77	15 Jan	18 Jan	Church Hill
Birely, Mrs. Laura V.	Frederick	82	22 Jan	25 Jan	
Dertzbaugh, Charles J.	Frederick	79/2/20	25 Jan	27 Jan	
Martin, William C.	Frederick	71	14 Feb	17 Feb	
Martz, John H.	Frederick	61	16 Feb	18 Feb	
Engle, Calvin L.	Frederick	63	16 Feb	19 Feb	
Rhoderick, Miss Rebecca	Frederick	92	19 Feb	22 Feb	
Lampe, Henry R.	Frederick	71/8/12	16 Mar	18 Mar	
Sinn, Miss Eva B.	Frederick	not given	18 Apr	20 Apr	
Kefauver, Mrs. Laura V.	Middletown	89	26 Apr	28 Apr	Middletown Ref.
Feaga, Mrs. Emma M.	Frederick	67/0/27	20 Jul	23 Jul	
Biser, Mrs. Jennie Thomas	Shookstown	69/3/7	29 Jul	31 Jul	
Glaze, Worthington O.	Frederick	77	1 Aug	4 Aug	
Haller, Ruth Evaline Lewis	Frederick	20/2/22	3 Aug	5 Aug	
Hiltner, Christian	Frederick	not given	3 Aug	6 Aug	
Staley, Fleet B.	Frederick	86	19 Sep	22 Sep	

Deaths and Burials of Evangelical Reformed
United Church of Christ
Frederick, Frederick County, Maryland

Name	Place	Age	Died	Buried	Notes
Brengle, Samuel Thomas	Baltimore	abt 76	29 Sep	3 Oct	
Swope, Florence May	Frederick	69	10 Oct	12 Oct	
Bentz, Edward	Frederick	80	16 Oct	19 Oct	
Birely, William C.	Frederick	86/3/14	23 Oct	26 Oct	
Derr, Mrs. Julia L.	Frederick	91/2/25	26 Nov	28 Nov	
Engle, Gladys W.	Frederick	3 days	22 Dec	23 Dec	
Ramsburgh, Mrs. S. Laura	Frederick	72/1/9	22 Dec	24 Dec	
Feaga, John J.	Frederick	not given	31 Dec	2 Jan '37	

1937

Name	Place	Age	Died	Buried	Notes
Rhodes, Mrs. Margaret E.	Frederick	85/2/20	10 Jan	12 Jan	
Sulcer, Emma K.	Frederick	74/3/14	18 Jan	21 Jan	
Worman, Charles W. D.	Frederick	not given	20 Jan	23 Jan	
Neighbours, Mrs. Anna L.	Frederick	69	20 Feb	23 Feb	
Zimmerman, R. Clinton	Frederick	79	23 Feb	25 Feb	
Gittinger, A. Kate	Frederick	71/1/18	25 Feb	27 Feb	
White, Mrs. Alice A.	Frederick	82	17 Mar	20 Mar	Middletown Ref.
Howard, Charles Sothoron	New York, NY	40/4/12	1 Apr	3 Apr	
Eschbach, Mary Susan	Frederick	not given	2 Apr	3 Apr	
Sinn, C. Edward	Frederick	75	14 Apr	16 Apr	
Mantz, Annie Rebecca	Frederick	80/9/11	17 Apr	19 Apr	
Kolb, Mrs. Caroline V.	Frederick	83/9/14	20 Apr	22 Apr	
Hauer, Mrs. Anna Belle	Baltimore	78	27 Apr	29 Apr	
Lipps, Fannie L. C.	Frederick	68	11 May	13 May	
Yost, Mary	Frederick	not given	3 Jun	5 Jun	
Yost, Amelia	Frederick	not given	9 Jun	11 Jun	
Schmidt, Mrs. Laura R.	Frederick	79/3/25	25 Jul	27 Jul	
Riggs, Mrs. Susan A.	Frederick	77	17 Sep	19 Sep	
Keefer, Francis M.	Elkton	31	21 Sep	24 Sep	Elkton Cem
Gittinger, Edward A., Jr.	Frederick	72	10 Oct	12 Oct	
Holtz, Clarence C.	Frederick	77	5 Nov	8 Nov	
Kemp, Robert A., II	Westfield, NJ	15/6/0	12 Dec	15 Dec	

1938

Name	Place	Age	Died	Buried	Notes
DeLashmutt, Arthur	Frederick	53/7/3	5 Mar	7 Mar	
Obenderfer, Frederick W.	Frederick	not given	6 Mar	9 Mar	
Mantz, Henry	Frederick	88	14 Mar	16 Mar	
DeLashmutt, Mrs. Alvida T.	Frederick	80/10/17	8 Apr	11 Apr	
Chipley, Edward B.	Avalon, PA	66	8 Apr	11 Apr	
Zimmerman, Maria A.	Frederic	74/11/10	21 Apr	23 Apr	
Runkles, Frances P.	Mt. Airy	15/9/0	22 Apr	25 Apr	Church Hill
Zimmerman, Harvey S.	Frederick	74/8/22	11 May	13 May	
Brunner, Milton O.	Frederick	not given	1 Jul	3 Jul	
Grove, Vallie R.	Frederick	not given	4 Aug	6 Aug	
Derr, Mrs. Florence M.	Frederick	not given	6 Aug	8 Aug	
Remsburg, Charles J.	Lewistown	77/5/12	6 Oct	9 Oct	Utica
Falconer, Dale	Frederick	0/1/18	12 Oct	13 Oct	
Dertzbaugh, Cornelia	Frederick	45	15 Oct	17 Oct	
Droneburg, Ethel H.	Frederick	not given	17 Oct	19 Oct	
Zimmerman, Mrs. Laura M.	Frederick	85	18 Oct	20 Oct	
Staley, William T.	Lewistown, PA	not given	15 Nov	17 Nov	

Deaths and Burials of Evangelical Reformed
United Church of Christ
Frederick, Frederick County, Maryland

Name	Place	Age	Death	Burial	Cemetery
Delaplaine, Eleanor Frances	Frederick	15/11/22	23 Nov	28 Nov	Memorial Park
Horine, Luther M.	Frederick	63	26 Nov	29 Nov	Zion Middletown
Derr, Frances	Baltimore	not given	26 Nov	28 Nov	
Keefer, A. Kemp	Frederick	71/8/16	29 Nov	1 Dec	
Null, Mrs. Maggie S.	Frederick	84	9 Dec	11 Dec	
Krantz, Charles E.	Frederick	65	30 Dec	1 Jan '39	

1939

Name	Place	Age	Death	Burial	Cemetery
Kemp, Mrs. Florence V.	Frederick	74/10/0	12 Jan	15 Jan	
Harding, Everest C.	Frederick	84	19 Jan	21 Jan	
Staples, Katherine	Washington, DC	not given	28 Jan	31 Jan	
Duvall, Margaret A.	Frederick	92/0/22	2 Feb	4 Feb	
Schmidt, Jacob H.	Frederick	61/6/27	8 Feb	10 Feb	
Rhoads, Vernon M.	Frederick	not given	not given	not given	
Hersperger, W. Scholl	Frederick	not given	not given	not given	
Hafer, Ella V.	Frederick	not given	16 Apr	18 Apr	
Keefer, Katharine S.	Frederick	not given	not given	not given	
Quynn, D. Hauer	Frederick	78/0/20	4 Nov	6 Nov	
Murphy, A. Kate	Frederick	72/9/27	7 Nov	9 Nov	
Fisher, Mary E.	Frederick	76	19 Nov	22 Nov	
Doll, Florence I.	Frederick	81/10/15	21 Nov	24 Nov	
Myers, Thomas F.	Mt. Airy	78/10/10	21 Nov	24 Nov	
Carty, Mrs. Minnie D.	Frederick	73	10 Dec	12 Dec	
Harrington, Harvey A., Sr.	Frederick	56/10/21	23 Dec	26 Dec	
Smith, Mrs. Emma	Frederick	79/0/21	31 Dec	2 Jan '40	

1940

Name	Place	Age	Death	Burial	Cemetery
Rodrick, Margaret G.	Frederick	59	11 Jan	13 Jan	Jefferson Ref.
Rebert, Naomi S.	Frederick	49/6/21	14 Feb	16 Feb	Littlestown, PA
Shearer, Walter E.	Frederick	68/10/6	1 Mar	4 Mar	
Condon, Albert W.	Frederick	66	16 May	19 May	
Brust, John N.	Morgantown, WV	73	19 May	22 May	
Keith, Charles T.	Frederick	68/5/24	9 Jun	11 Jun	Memorial Park
Stockman, William E.	Frederick	82	22 Jun	25 Jun	Jefferson Ref.
Garrett, Willard N.	Frederick	77	11 Sep	13 Sep	
Eckstein, C. Thomas	York, PA	62	11 Sep	13 Sep	
Burger, Charles E.	Frederick	79	18 Sep	20 Sep	
Kemp, Mary Matilda	Frederick	79/1/12	28 Sep	30 Sep	
Thomas, Clinton C.	Frederick	84	25 Oct	27 Oct	
Zentz, Mrs. Jennie M. C.	Frederick	79/1/7	4 Nov	6 Nov	
Gonzo, Ariana	Frederick	not given	not given	not given	
Obenderfer, Nellie M.	Frederick	59	6 Dec	8 Dec	
Zimmerman, Charles E.	Frederick	not given	28 Dec	31 Dec	

1941

Name	Place	Age	Death	Burial	Cemetery
Glaze, Anne M.	Frederick	77/11/20	12 Jan	14 Jan	
Ramsburg, Walter J.	New York, NY	not given	13 Jan	16 Jan	
Rice, Lewis R.	Frederick	79/3/6	23 Jan	25 Jan	
Kohlenberg, Edythe A.	Frederick	not given	29 Jan	1 Feb	
Lampe, Mary E.	Frederick	92	20 Feb	23 Feb	
Wachter, Steiner R.	Frederick	not given	4 Mar	6 Mar	
Zimmerman, Florence M.	Frederick	68/10/21	23 Mar	26 Mar	

Deaths and Burials of Evangelical Reformed
United Church of Christ
Frederick, Frederick County, Maryland

Name	Place	Age	Died	Buried	Notes
Duvall, William T.	Washington, DC	58/0/28	4 Apr	7 Apr	
Lambert, Jacob J.	Frederick	84	6 Apr	8 Apr	
Stoner, Harry A.	Frederick	59/3/6	7 Apr	9 Apr	
Murphy, Richard W.	Gaithersburg	81/3/7	10 Apr	12 Apr	
Hermann, Elizabeth	Frederick	95/3/26	17 Apr	20 Apr	
Kolb, Betty R.	Frederick	81/6/4	18 Apr	21 Apr	
Herwig, Theodore	Baltimore	78/7/3	7 Jun	16 Aug (sic)	
Winebrenner, Arie	Frederick	not given	8 Oct	11 Oct	
Falconer, Carol	Frederick	2/3/7	30 Oct	1 Nov	
Smith, Raymond	Frederick	5	13 Nov	16 Nov	Thurmont UB
VanFossen, Carrie B.	Frederick	75/7/10	15 Nov	17 Nov	Middletown Ref.
Null, Lillian Regina	Frederick	26	26 Nov	29 Nov	
Ramsburgh, Lucie T.	Frederick	83/8/16	13 Dec	15 Dec	
Worman, Emma J.	Frederick	86	23 Dec	26 Dec	
Moberly, Mrs. Sallie S.	Frederick	not given	24 Dec	26 Dec	
1942					
McLane, Robert C.	Washington, DC	81	4 Jan	6 Jan	
Lambert, Georgette	Frederick	86/1/19	18 Jan	20 Jan	
Stroup, Elizabeth	Frederick	not given	20 Jan	22 Jan	
Rhoads, Austin E.	Frederick	43	4 Feb	7 Feb	
Rohrbach, Ida R.	Frederick	74/2/26	8 Feb	10 Feb	
Kemp, Robert A.	Frederick	77/0/24	4 Mar	6 mar	
Brunner, Franklin E.	Los Angeles, CA	63/7/13	7 Apr	14 Apr	
Bowers, Mrs. Harriet M.	Frederick	76/3/3	21 Apr	23 Apr	
Kemp, Alvin Edward	nr Frederick	55/3/20	12 May	15 May	Rocky Springs
Hiteshew, Floy	Frederick	56/0/5	26 May	28 May	
Paisley, Mrs. Wililetta	Frederick	82/6/7	27 May	29 May	
Milyard, John W.	Frederick	not given	13 Jul	16 Jul	
Krantz, Frederick B.	Frederick	not given	21 Jul	23 Jul	
Routzahn, Mrs. Ida L.	Frederick	80/8/23	6 Aug	8 Aug	
Kneck, Frederick B.	Frederick	40/0/20	8 Aug	11 Aug	
Myers, Garrison E.	Washington, DC	not given	20 Aug	24 Aug	Jefferson Ref.
Dixon, Clarence B.	Frederick	61	22 Sep	26 Sep	
Brish, Harry H.	Frederick	78/10/20	3 Oct	5 Oct	
Wolfe, Guy F.	Frederick	73	14 Oct	16 Oct	
Mateny, May Ida Rebecca	Frederick	82/11/13	22 Oct	25 Oct	
Pearre, Mrs. Nannie R.	Frederick	71/9/16	12 Nov	15 Nov	
Shearer, Mrs. Florence M.	Frederick	71/0/20	4 Dec	6 Dec	
Neidig, William C.	Frederick	88/7/17	9 Dec	12 Dec	
Quynn, Kitty S.	Frederick	not given	28 Dec	30 Dec	
1943					
Smith, Granville M.	Frederick	82	3 Jan	5 Jan	
Oberlauder, Emma C.	Frederick	83/2/15	11 Jan	14 Jan	
Hermann, Mrs. Emma B.	St. Louis, MO	61/5/14	17 Jan	21 Jan	
Miller, Mrs. Cecelia K.	Frederick	77	2 Feb	5 Feb	
Martz, Mrs. Emma E.	Frederick	80	15 Feb	18 Feb	
Staley, Charles A.	Frederick	not given	23 Feb	25 Feb	
Delashmutt, William R.	Chevy Chase	61/11/14	22 Mar	25 Mar	
Cramer, Harry M.	Frederick	72/1/1	24 Mar	27 Mar	

Deaths and Burials of Evangelical Reformed
United Church of Christ
Frederick, Frederick County, Maryland

Name	Place	Age	Death	Burial	Notes
Smith, F. Lester	Frederick	62	5 Apr	7 Apr	
Kinsey, Robert P.	Frederick	19/0/6	13 Apr	16 Apr	Mt. Airy
Howard, Francis D.	Frederick	44	25 Apr	28 Apr	
Ramsburg, Guy R.	Frederick	not given	27 Apr	29 Apr	
Delaplaine, William T., III	Frederick	23/11/25	27 Apr	4 May	Memorial Park
	Lt. in US Navy, died in airplane accident near Oakland, CA				
Blair, Charles F. F.	Frederick	56/10/19	5 May	9 May	
Sinn, Mary E.	Frederick	72	24 May	27 May	
Sparrow, Helen M.	Baltimore	27	3 Jun	5 Jun	
Quynn, Charles W.	Frederick	85/6/12	24 Jul	27 Jul	
Brish, J. Murray	Frederick	75/7 13	24 Aug	26 Aug	
Montgomery, Irma Lucille	Frederick	19/0/11	4 Oct	6 Oct	
Hanshew, H. Lee	Frederick	69/9/6	31 Oct	2 Nov	
Bruchey, Richard A.	Frederick	55	30 Nov	2 Dec	
Feaga, Lydia A.	Frederick	92	2 Dec	6 Dec	
Miller, Ira L.	Frederick	70	4 Dec	7 Dec	
Epps, infant twins	Frederick	1 day	20 Dec	20 Dec	
			1944		
Zimmerman, infant	Frederick	stillborn	3 Jan	4 Jan	
	Child of Harry and Octavia Zimmerman				
Gomber, Margaret F.	Frederick	73/6/25	11 Jan	14 Jan	
Parkinson, Lillie M.	Hagerstown	81	13 Feb	16 Feb	
Gittinger, George M.	Frederick	84/10/9	11 Mar	13 Mar	
Bruchey, Richard T., Jr.	Frederick	9/8/26	15 Mar	18 Mar	
Null, Carroll F.	Frederick	not given	23 Mar	26 Mar	
Zimmerman, Elsie R.	Frederick	68	21 Apr	24 Mar (sic)	
Wachter, Ralph F.	Frederick	56/5/20	8 May	10 May	
Cramer, Ella K.	Frederick	not given	22 May	25 May	
Peck, Margaret C.	Frederick	79/11/4	11 Jun	13 Jun	
Brown, James W.	Cumberland	not given	23 Jun	27 Jun	
McDevitt, Guy H.	Braddock Hgts.	58/4/18	10 Jul	13 Jul	
Grumbine, Cora M.	Hagerstown	78	12 Jul	14 Jul	
Pearre, Albert L.	Frederick	78/4/1	15 Jul	18 Jul	
DeLashmutt, Mildred L.	Frederick	48/5/20	2 Sep	5 Sep	
Snook, Hallie F.	Frederick	69	11 Sep	14 Sep	Utica
Downing, Robert L.	Middletown	86	1 Oct	4 Oct	
Shaw, Joseph M.	Frederick	not given	7 Aug	not given	killed in action, Europe
Shafer, Earlston F.	Frederick	not given	21 Aug	nit given	killed in action, Europe
Cramer, Henrietta	Frederick	70/0/17	10 Oct	12 Oct	
Werking, Dove E.	Frederick	68/0/6	13 Oct	16 Oct	Woodsboro
Dutrow, Katie L.	Frederick	76	20 Oct	22 Oct	
Dill, Mary Ellen	Frederick	83	29 Nov	1 Dec	
Motter, Lewis E.	Emmitsburg	90/3/4	5 Dec	8 Dec	
Ramsburg, Ethel V.	Harmony Grove	52	6 Dec	9 Dec	
Haller, Lucretia W.	Frederick	71/1/27	28 Dec	31 Dec	
			1945		
Main, Ella S.	Frederick	not given	7 Feb	10 Feb	
Gannon, Lewis B.	Frederick	58/4/14	22 Mar	24 Mar	
Hoover, Lillian R.	Frederick	50	8 Apr	10 Apr	

Deaths and Burials of Evangelical Reformed
United Church of Christ
Frederick, Frederick County, Maryland

Name	Place	Age	Date of Death	Date of Burial	Notes
Wilcoxen, Rebecca	Frederick	73/9/21	25 Apr	27 Apr	
Comfort, Willian H.	Frederick	78/1/13	5 May	8 May	
Santee, Rebecca R.	Ft. Washington, PA	88	2 Jul	6 Jul	Sharpsburg
Rohrbach, Jacob	Frederick	81/10/23	16 Jul	18 Jul	
Lansdale, Annis Elizabeth	Frederick	not given	17 Aug	cremated	
Zimmerman, Georgia W.	Frederick	82/8/1	19 Sep	22 Sep	
Graser, Florence Elizabeth	Frederick	25	17 Oct	20 Oct	
Gilman, Anna	Frederick	62	2 Nov	4 Nov	
Hammond, Fannie O.	Frederick	75/11/21	12 Nov	15 Nov	
Simmons, Martha Elizabeth	Frederick	86/0/23	19 Nov	21 Nov	
Johnson, Albert L.	Frederick	61	30 Nov	2 Dec	Wernersville, PA
McCardell, A. LeRoy	Frederick	72/10/5	9 Dec	11 Dec	
Winebrenner, Laura A.	Frederick	85/10/5	25 Dec	27 Dec	
			1946		
Zimmerman, Jessie M.	Washington, DC	not given	27 Jan	30 Jan	

Deaths and burials recorded by Rev. Paul L. Althouse

Name	Place	Age	Date of Death	Date of Burial
Quynn, Katherine S.	Frederick	88	16 Feb	18 Feb
Perry, Katherine Mehrling	Lewistown	83	17 Feb	20 Feb
Roelkey, Celeste M.	Frederick	83	27 Feb	2 Mar
Cramer, Bertram S.	Sykesville	60	13 Apr	16 Apr
Gephart, Charles William	Frederick	91	13 Apr	17 Apr

Book changed again to following format. As before, if burial place is not listed, it is Mt. Olivet Cemetery.

Name	Age	Date of Birth	Date of Death	Place of burial	Date of burial
			1946		
Hallar, Jessie	86/7/9	7 Aug 1859	16 May		18 May
Larkin, Rose	74	1872	30 May	Jefferson Luth	1 Jun
Bowman, John H.	50	17 Dec 1896	4 May	Memorial Park	7 Jun
Swadener, Mrs. Anna Bertha	77	1869	7 Jun		10 Jun
Eppley, Francis, Jr.	68/4/11	22 Feb 1887	3 Jul		5 Jul
Berry, Edith Bantz	80	1866	15 Aug		17 Aug
Hooper, Mrs. Mary Simmons	62	1884	22 Sep		25 Sep
Ramsburgh, Henry B.	59/9/3	3 Dec 1886	26 Sep		28 Sep
Rowe, Mrs. Mary L.	75	14 Jul 1871	27 Sep		30 Sep
Shapro, Frank M.	54	21 Feb 1892	6 Oct		9 Oct
Raver, Mrs. Rose A.	59/9/6	2 Mar 1889	8 Dec		12 Dec
Bentz, William H.	75	1871	29 Dec		2 Jan '47
			1947		
Wolfe, Mrs. Rose May	76/4/3	1871	5 Jan		8 Jan
Gilbert, William L.	80	1867	27 Jan		29 Jan
Shull, Grayson F.	47/11/20	13 Feb 1899	2 Feb		4 Feb
Schmidt, Cora May	69/10/15	3 Apr 1877	18 Feb		21 Feb
Thomas, Susan L.	93/5/6	4 Oct 1853	10 Mar		12 Mar
Poole, George W.	74	1873	5 Apr		8 Apr
Gittinger, Mrs. Emelia A.	87/3/10	1860	14 Apr		17 Apr
Grahe, John A.	70	not given	7 May		10 May

Deaths and Burials of Evangelical Reformed
United Church of Christ
Frederick, Frederick County, Maryland

Name	Age	Birth	Death	Burial Location	Burial Date
Thomas, C. Newton	94/0/18	7 May 1853	25 May		27 May
Gosnell, Herbert E.	64	not given	30 May		1 Jun
Schley, Agnes	89/10/3	not given	1 Jun		3 Jun
Yingling, Mrs. Nora Kefauver	64/1/27	31 Jul 1883	28 Sep	Middletown	30 Sep
Grindle, Mrs. Josie (Thomas)	not given	not given	not given		4 Nov
Holtz, Mrs. Carrie C. (Staley)	82/6/26	13 Apr 1865	9 Nov		12 Nov
Abrecht, Mrs. Mattie C.	58/4/21	2 Jul 1889	23 Nov		26 Nov
Kuhn, Mrs. Della M.	76/0/1	7 Dec 1871	8 Dec		11 Dec
Martz, Ruth E.	48/0/13	30 Nov 1899	13 Dec		15 Dec
Mowry, Virgie M.	82/9/5	8 Mar 1865	13 Dec	Bedford, PA	15 Dec
Lull, Mary Esther	45	1902	14 Dec		16 Dec
Rhoads, Mrs. Grace L.	74/2/9	22 Oct 1873	31 Dec		3 Jan '48
1948					
Glessner, Alice Adora	82/4/6	4 Sep 1865	10 Jan		12 Jan
Shipley, Charles F.	77/6/25	20 Jun 1870	15 Jan		18 Jan
Apple, Joseph H.	82	not given	17 Jan		20 Jan
Little, Marion C.	not given	not given	22 mar		26 Mar
Fisher, James	91	not given	19 Apr		21 Apr
Derr, R. Earl	57/0/18	not given	1 May		4 May
Wiles, Pfc. James Edward	19	not given	2 Jul 1944	reinterred fm France	23 May
Crum, Mrs. Pheobe A.	68	7 Jun 1879	22 May		26 May
Shafer, Pfc. Earlston F.	28	not given	21 Sep 1944	reinterred fm France	27 May
Buckey, Mrs. Mary R.	67/5/15	28 Dec 1880	23 Jun		26 Jun
Grumbine, Marshall S.	84/8/28	6 Oct 1863	4 Jul		6 Jul
Worman, Scott	86/8/12	not given	20 Jul		22 Jul
Plunkett, Thomas Martin	82/10/11	30 Sep 1865	11 Aug	cremated	13 Aug
Bentz, Lawrence E.	49/0/12	3 Sep 1899	15 Sep		18 Sep
Cronise, Adele	not given	not given	8 Oct		11 Oct
Martz, Mrs. Mary	74/4/23	not given	10 Oct		12 Oct
McCardell, Edgar S.	not given	5 Feb 1875	14 Oct		16 Oct
Houck, Mrs. William H.	53	12 Feb 1895	9 Nov		11 Nov
Coblentz, Oscar B.	69/11/29	not given	22 Nov	Middletown	26 Nov
Allison, Comfrey M.	69/2/9	8 Oct 1879	17 Dec	Church Hill	20 Dec
Mealey, Florence H. E.	90/3/16	13 Sep 1858	29 Dec	31 Dec	
1949					
Obenderfer, J. William	63	not given	3 Jan		6 Jan
O'Donnell, Mrs. Mary S.	78/10/21	18 Feb 1870	9 Jan		11 Jan
Sier, Jesse Benson	68/8/2	8 Jun 1880	10 Feb		13 Feb
Shipley, M. Mae	70/1/17	29 Dec 1878	16 Feb		18 Feb
Schaefer, Mrs. Anna	84	19 Apr 1864	6 Mar	Loudoun Park, VA	8 Mar
Flautt, Gilmore R.	63/2/8	18 Jan 1886	26 Mar		28 Mar
Stull, Charles	not given	not given	not given		2 Apr
Baker, William McK., Jr.	24/10/19	12 May 1924	31 Mar		4 Apr
Heiner, Dr. Peter E.	84/6/26	15 Oct 1864	11 may	Memorial Park	14 May
Shaw, Pfc. Joseph M.	Not given	28 Aug 1921	7 Aug	reinterred fm France	21 May
Levy, Mrs. Roberta	not given	not given	12 Jun		14 Jun
Oberlauder, Frederick A.	65/6/11	20 Dec 1883	1 Jul		3 Jul
Brish, William W.	78/0/12	21 Jun 1871	3 Jul		6 Jul
Rimer, William Oscar	74	3 Nov 1874	16 Jul		18 Jul

Deaths and Burials of Evangelical Reformed
United Church of Christ
Frederick, Frederick County, Maryland

Name	Age	Birth	Death	Notes	Burial
Chatman, Harry	81/8/13	12 Nov 1868	25 Jul	cremated	28 Jul
Burger, Anna M.	85	7 Dec 1864	2 Aug		5 Aug
Bowers, James A.	26/1/13	15 Apr 1919	28 May 1945	reinterred fm Japan	4 Sep
Wolfe, Elsie May	65	2 Dec 1883	8 Sep	Marvin Chapel	11 Sep
Dixon, Louis Franklin	70	not given	8 Oct		12 Oct
Houck, Nan Johnson	75	not given	11 Oct		14 Oct
Fahrney, J. Welty	75/6/1	12 Apr 1874	13 Oct		16 Oct
Esworthy, Robert H.	38/1/6	5 Nov 1911	11 Dec		14 Dec
1950					
Grove, Mrs. Cora	78	not given	15 Jan		18 Jan
Michael, William C., III	1 day	31 Jan 1950	31 Jan		1 Feb
Snyder, May K.	abt 75	not given	3 Feb		6 Feb
Smith, Barbara Ann	86/5/2	27 Sep 1863	1 Mar		4 Mar
Garber, Lillian Jane	55/11/20	15 Apr 1894	5 Apr		8 Apr
Remsberg, Viola Thomas	76/11/7	5 Jun 1873	12 May	Middletown	14 May
Stroup, Harry Milton	58/8/13	31 Aug 1891	14 May		17 May
Baer, Raymond	29	not given	18 May	Utica	20 May
Hueting, Eric Scott	3/10/24	29 Aug 1946	23 May		26 May
Wallis, Albert R.	77/6/22	13 May 1878	1 Jul		3 Jul
Null, Roy Calvin	72/1/22	10 Dec 1872	5 Jul		8 Jul
Apple, Miriam Rankin	55/7/22	12 Dec 1894	14 Jul		17 Jul
Lampe, William E.	not given	not given	? Aug		19 Aug
Cutsail, Inda Trapnell	77/3/8	7 Jul 1873	12 Oct		15 Oct
Zimmerman, Mazeppa A.	82	14 Nov 1867	13 Nov		16 Nov
Graser, John William	79/8/28	21 Mar 1871	9 Dec	Rocky Hill	12 Dec
Heffner, William	over 70	not given	24 Dec		27 Dec
1951					
Best, Charles E. T.	84/7/6	10 Jun 1866	16 Jan		19 Jan
Brish, Minnie H.	79/10/3	5 Apr 1871	8 Feb		11 Feb
Butcher, Baby Girl		28 Feb 1951	28 Feb		1 Mar
Buckingham, Hattye B.	69/0/3	3 Mar 1882	6 Mar	Williamsport	8 Mar
Kemp, Mary Ellen	88/2/9	20 Dec 1872	8 Mar	Rocky Springs	10 Mar
Buckey, William A.	74	2 Apr 1877	16 Mar		19 Mar
Derr, Aida Grace	71/5/24	22 Sep 1879	18 Mar		20 Mar
Hahn, Rose Agnes	66/4/1	29 Nov 1884	30 Mar		2 Apr
Virts, Charlotte Inez	41/1/24	15 Mar 1910	9 May		11 May
Nusz, Mary V.	83/0/1	15 Jun 1868	16 Jun		18 Jun
Oberlauder, Lucille S.	84/3/11	10 Mar 1867	21 Jun		23 Jun
Ramsburg, Lester F.	58/1/10	28 May 1893	8 Jul		12 Jul
James, Lewis Franklin, Sr.	60	not given	21 Jul		24 Jul
Garrett, William D.	60/7/22	1 Dec 1890	23 Jul		26 Jul
Foland, John Michael	48/3/11	17 May 1903	28 Aug		30 Aug
Gilmer, James Kerr(?)	45/9/28	31 Oct 1905	29 Aug		1 Sep
Thomas, Hiram G.	80/6/3	11 Mar 1871	14 Sep		17 Sep
Routzahn, Laura G.	86/8/13	4 Feb 1865	17 Oct		19 Oct
Boone, Patrick Ray	stillborn	28 Oct 1951	28 Oct		29 Oct
Culler, Thomas P.	66/6/3	11 May 1885	14 Nov		17 Nov
Culler, Bertha Roderick	66/1/29	15 Sep 1885	14 Nov		17 Nov
Hankey, John Henry, Sr.	72/3/22	11 Aug 1879	3 Dec	Waynesboro, PA	6 Dec

Deaths and Burials of Evangelical Reformed
United Church of Christ
Frederick, Frederick County, Maryland

Name	Age	Date of Death	Date of Burial	Place	
Zimmerman, Lola Bell	72/1/25	12 Oct 1879	7 Dec	Virginia	10 Dec
Mantz, Anna Lee	82	not given	15 Dec		18 Dec
Willard, Mary E. S.	75/4/27	31 Jul 1876	28 Dec		31 Dec
			1952		
Summers, baby		7 Jan 1952	7 Jan		7 Jan
Shaffer, Nellie R.	87/4/14	11 Aug 1864	25 Jan		28 Jan
Foreman, Maurice Eugene	54/7/28	8 Jul 1897	6 Feb	Taneytown	11 Feb
Kieffer, Margaret R.	70/10/26	25 Mar 1881	20 Feb	Rose Hill, Hagerstown	23 Feb
Fetteroff, Nannie G. Shriner	84/8/24	28 May 1867	21 Feb		24 Feb
Sellard, Lillian G.	74	1878	9 Mar	cremated, ashes int.	22 Mar
Swadener, Henry Clinton	not given	18 Sep 1866	3 Apr		6 Apr
Wallis, Fannie Elizabeth	79/3/22	4 Jan 1873	26 Apr		28 Apr
Wiles, George Daniel, Jr.	57/2/2	28 Feb 1895	30 Apr		2 May
Dertzbaugh, Carol Ann	10 days	14 May 1952	23 May		24 May
Mantz, Frank	90	not given	9 Jun		12 Jun
Dittmar, Mrs. Maud W.	78	6 Jun 1874	10 Jun	Jefferson	12 Jun
Kemp, Annie Nixdorff	93/9/9	11 Sep 1858	20 Jun		22 Jun
Biser, Cora Banks	89/7/25	16 Nov 1862	6 Jul	Middletown	9 Jul
Gaither, Millard David	49/9/7	24 Oct 1902	1 Aug		5 Aug
Wills, Cpl. Victor L.	not given	28 Jan 1932	3 Jun	killed in Korea	6 Aug
Albaugh, Mary M.	Not given	4 Jun 1866	13 Aug		16 Aug
Mercer, Mary Ellen	88/0/30	22 Jul 1864	21 Aug		23 Aug
Kline, Harry	86/3/9	13 May 1866	22 Aug		25 Aug
Houck, Margaret Elizabeth	83/1/14	17 Jul 1869	31 Aug		2 Sep
Fauble, Laurence	92	16 Feb 1860	11 Oct		14 Oct
Clary, Adelaide M.	83	25 Oct 1869	31 Oct		3 Nov
Rupp, Ida J.	98	10 Mar 1854	31 Oct	Baltimore	3 Nov
Newman, Mary H.	64/7/26	88/3/14	10 Nov		12 Nov
Kefauver, Harry Joshua	69/4/27	4 Jul 1883	1 Dec		4 Dec
Martin, Hallie	85/1/9	26 Oct 1867	5 Dec		8 Dec
Geisbert, Samuel Stephen Compher	87/3/4	6 Sep 1865	10 Dec		13 Dec
Herwig, Clara E.	78	24 Dec 1873	18 Dec		20 Dec
Ziegler, Susan Chandler	86/10/22	29 Jan 1866	21 Dec		24 Dec
			1953		
Etzler, Walter Paul	54/2/16	10 Nov 1898	26 Feb		1 Mar
Staley, Addie Elizabeth	80/1/16	18 Jan 1873	4 Mar		7 Mar
Stull, Mamie Estelle	68/2/4	7 Jan 1885	13 Mar		17 Mar
Daniels, Mary Elizabeth	80/10/8	25 May 1872	3 Apr		6 Apr
Staley, Ira Biser	73/6/6	29 Sep 1879	5 Apr		8 Apr
Noell, J. Guyon	59/10/23	3 Jun 1893	26 Apr	Hanover, PA	30 Apr
Phillips, Mary I.	64/9/22	22 Jul 1888	14 May		17 May
Burkett, Doris Virginia	0/6/16	8 Nov 1952	24 May		27 May
Heck, Hiram Webster	77/4/29	17 Jan 1876	16 Jun		18 Jun
England, Nathan J.	87	not given	13 Jul		15 Jul
Apple, Gertrude H.	84/7/20	20 Dec 1868	9 Aug		12 Aug
Sanders, Thomas Lee	733/4/2	30 Apr 1880	1 Sep		3 Sep
Lewis, Mrs. Alida A.	79/8/14	21 Dec 1873	4 Sep		7 Sep
Ramsburg, Mrs. Jessie T.	71/3/30	5 May 1882	4 Sep		8 Sep

Deaths and Burials of Evangelical Reformed
United Church of Christ
Frederick, Frederick County, Maryland

Name	Age	Born	Died	Burial	Date
Wilson, Henry Leo, Sr.	56/9/0	28 Jan 1897	28 Oct	Memorial Park	2 Nov
Williams, Mrs. Alma V.	55	26 Mar 1898	27 Nov		30 Nov
Lininger, Fannie Elizabeth	58/9/23	24 Feb 1895	17 Dec		21 Dec
			1954		
Burger, Charles Henry, Sr.	67/3/29	4 Sep 1886	2 Jan		4 Jan
Zimmerman, William Marion	90/6/22	16 Jun 1863	8 Jan		11 Jan
Rice, Ruger Rollins	55	30 Jun 1898	28 Jan		1 Feb
Cutsail, Horace Edgar	73/3/7	26 Nov 1880	3 Mar		6 Mar
Burger, Lewis Bennett	64/4/27	23 Oct 1889	20 Mar		23 Mar
Wachter, Christina Sophia	81	20 Jul 1872	4 Apr		6 Apr
Walter, Mary Kathryn	49/7/28	22 Aug 1904	28 Apr		30 Apr
Stull, Mary Margaret	95/8/9	21 Aug 1858	28 Apr		1 May
Kaufman, Willian Conrad	94/6/5	12 Dec 1859	17 Jun		19 Jun
Miller, Marion Stull	58/2/14	11 mar 1896	24 Jun		26 Jun
Schroeder, Lucy Medora	76/10/19	9 Oct 1877	28 Aug		31 Aug
Worman, Emma K.	84	not given	14 Sep		16 Sep
Gannon, Charles Franklin	26	13 Nov 1926	18 Sep		21 Sep
Cramer, Leslie	not given	not given	9 Oct	died in Seattle, WA	2 Nov
Smith, Dorothy E.	47	not given	26 Nov		29 Nov
Greenwald, Isaac W.	83	not given	5 Dec		9 Dec
Rogers, Katherine Kieffer	45/2/8	17 Oct 1909	25 Dec	Rose Hill, Hagerstown	31 Dec
Bushong, Drusilla H.	83	1 Nov 1871	31 Dec		2 Jan '55
			1955		
Wenger, Msgt John H.	43/10/28	2 Dec 1911	9 Jan		12 Jan
Brish, Devillo Colgate	89/2/15	27 Oct 1865	12 Jan		14 Jan
Culler, Kathryn Rebecca	64/11/24	1 Feb 1891	25 Jan		27 Jan
Saunders, Vina Grace	76/4/27	22 Nov 1878	19 Feb		21 Feb
Measell, Edward B.	85	not given	23 Feb		25 Feb
Diehl, Roland Lee	1/6/21	6 Jan 1953	25 Feb		28 Feb
Shankle, Lola Alberta	48/9/16	3 Jun 1906	19 Mar	Zion, Hagerstown	22 Mar
Sier, Edith Gertrude	63/3/7	23 Dec 1891	30 Mar		2 Apr
Rohrback, Alice M.	78/7/28	6 Oct 1876	3 Jun		6 Jun
Clapp, Bessie M.	72	not given	2 Jul		6 Jul
Miller, Franklin D.	75/1/24	10 May 1880	4 Jul		6 Jul
Shafer, Lester Ezra	65/6/9	25 Dec 1889	4 Jul		7 Jul
MacGregor, Margaret E.	40/11/25	20 Jul 1914	15 Jul		20 Jul
Motter, Samuel Lewis	75/11/1	21 Aug 1879	22 Jul		25 Jul
Horine, Effie Mahoney	65/6/2	29 Jan 1890	31 Jul	Zion, Middletown	3 Aug
Mantz, Nettie K. V.	83/8/27	not given	22 Aug		25 Aug
Zimmerman, Mary Margaret Jeannette	96/9/16	12 Dec 1858	28 Sep	Zion, Hagerstown	1 Oct
Eppley, Virgie Grace	76/11/17	17 Nov 1878	4 Nov		7 Nov
Abbott, Eleanor D.	85/7/2	7 Apr 1870	9 Nov		12 Nov
McLane, Georgianna	88/2/15	4 Sep 1867	19 Nov		21 Nov
			1956		
Stockman, Marshall Henry, Sr.	65/10/5	5 Feb 1890	10 Jan		13 Jan
Lease, Minnie Elsa	86/5/2	9 Aug 1869	11 Jan	Glade Cem	13 Jan
Feaga, Charles	83	not given	25 Jan		28 Jan
Rhoads, George Oscar	78/10/22	19 mar 1877	11 Feb		14 Feb

Deaths and Burials of Evangelical Reformed
United Church of Christ
Frederick, Frederick County, Maryland

Name	Age	Date Buried		Where buried			Death Date
Forney, Ada Estelle	87/7/23	26 Jun 1868	19 Feb				22 Feb
Riehl, Addie Louisa	87	not given	19 Mar				22 Mar
Buesing, Mattie	not given	not given	25 Mar				28 Mar
Martz, Joseph D.	84/5/21	23 Oct 1871	14 Apr				17 Apr
Hahn, Walter Staley	34/9/29	21 Jun 1921	20 Apr	Memorial Park			23 Apr
Snyder, Lucy Wolfe	66/11/9	89/6/3	12 May	Plane No. 4			15 May
Myer, George Ernest	79/6/13	1 Nov 1876	14 May				16 May
Coblentz, John Harman Ezra	78/2/12	18 Mar 1878	10 Jun	Middletown Ref.			12 Jun
Dutrow, Virgie May	71/1/8	4 May 1885	12 Jun				15 Jun
Minor, Lillian Belle	76/11/26	20 Jun 1879	16 Jun				19 Jun
Stockman, May Catherine Virgie	63/4/0	16 Feb 1893	16 Jun				21 Jun
Zimmerman, Clayton Maynard	89/0/22	27 Jun 1867	19 Jul				22 Jul
Culler, Albert Franklin	68/7/23	7 Nov 1887	30 Jul				2 Aug
Thomas, Susan Elizabeth	77/8/20	24 Nov 1878	14 Aug				17 Aug
Niner, Daisy Victoria	77/2/18	30 May 1879	18 Aug				21 Aug
Dyer, Katye R.	85/2/5	4 Jul 1871	9 Sep				13 Sep
Stine, Ethel M.	65/11/15	20 Oct 1890	5 Oct				8 Oct
Harp, Maud Elizabeth	80/8/28	11 Jan 1876	9 Oct	Rest Haven, Hgrstn			12 Oct
Duvall, T. Guy	80	25 Sep 1876	19 Oct				25 Oct
Ramsburg, Russell Upton	59/1/13	11 Oct 1897	24 Nov				28 Nov
Worman, Mary Willetta	88	not given	19 Dec				21 Dec
Shipley, George William	81/3/11	9 Sep 1875	20 Dec				24 Dec
Wolff, Amelia Catherine	89/2/11	10 Oct 1867	21 Dec				24 Dec
Dunn, Charles McFarland	premature	24 Dec 1956	24 Dec				26 Dec
Thomas, Anna May	92	not given	26 Dec				28 Dec
Herwig, Henry August	86/1/27	1 Nov 1870	28 Dec				31 Dec
Holter, Charles R.	86/-/20	8 Dec 1870	28 Dec	Middletown Ref.			31 Dec

Another new book and new format.

Name	Age	Date Buried	Where buried	Birth Date	Death Date
		1957			1957
Miller, Nellie May	71/7/11	15 Jan		30 May 1885	11 Jan
Newman, Francis Jacob	77/0/12	24 Jan		9 Jan 1880	21 Jan
Cramer, James Houck	60/4/8	18 Feb		7 Oct 1896	15 Feb
Brandenburg, Virginia Smith	not given	19 Feb		19 Aug 1902	17 Feb
Cramer, George T.	51	13 Mar		3 Apr 1905	11 Mar
Kenyon, Firm Clark	61/9/5	13 May		4 Aug 1895	9 May
Kefauver, Manville E.	43/0/12	23 May		7 May 1914	19 May
Boileau, Mary Elizabeth	67/4/10	27 May	Christ Ref, Middletown	14 Jan 1890	24 May
Ordeman, Dr. G. Frederick	64/6/20	3 Jun		9 Nov 1892	29 May
LeVan, Dr. Charles Wilburforce	99	19 Jun	Krider's Cem	24 May 1858	17 Jun
Zimmerman, Myra Beatty	87/5/11	26 Jun		12 Jan 1870	23 Jun
Fahrney, Mary Ella	74/8/10	28 Jun		14 Oct 1882	24 Jun
Saunders, Walter Warren	81/8/3	2 Aug		27 Nov 1875	30 Jul
Mahoney, Mary Elizabeth	64	10 Sep		not given	6 Sep
Waltz, Margaret	53	9 Sep		not given	6 Sep
Zimmerman, S. Joseph	79/2/28	11 Oct		10 Jul 1878	8 Oct

Deaths and Burials of Evangelical Reformed
United Church of Christ
Frederick, Frederick County, Maryland

Name	Age	Death	Cemetery	Birth	Burial
Dertzbaugh, Katherine K.	67/7/11	22 Oct		9 Mar 1890	20 Oct
Hooper, George William	8/9/21	2 Nov		9 Jan 1874	30 Oct
Lampe, Ada Elizabeth	78/9/9	21 Nov		9 Feb 1879	18 Nov
Thomas, William H., Sr.	88	21 Nov		19 Jan 1869	19 Nov
Greeman, Cora Diller	71	4 Dec		18 Feb 1886	2 Dec
		1958			**1958**
Roelkey, Margaret	91	22 Jan		17 Dec 1866	12 Jan
Best, Eleanor H.	88	29 Jan		25 Nov 1869	26 Jan
Young, Austin U.	57	11 Feb		1900	7 Feb
Milyard, Mary Ann	74	19 Feb		27 May 1883	15 Feb
Baker, William McK.	68	6 Mar		16 Oct 1889	3 Mar
Burger, Marcia M.	4	11 Mar		13 Oct 1953	8 Mar
Harris, Claire M.	52	24 Mar		24 May 1905	22 Mar
Stull, George David	67	9 May		5 Jul 1890	5 May
Fletcher, James Wood	61	11 May		29 Sep 1896	8 May
Stine, William Sylvester	75	23 May		22 Oct 1882	21 May
Cain, Flossie Elliott	59	21 Jun		29 Dec 1898	19 Jun
Dertzbaugh, Harry B.	82	26 Jun		23 May 1876	23 Jun
Fogle, Lillian F.	25	11 Aug	Union Chapel Cem	4 Jun 1933	8 Aug
Eppley, Samuel	75	25 Aug		1 Apr 1883	21 Aug
Staley, Lurene A.	70	15 Sep	(grave side service)	11 Feb 1888	30 Aug
Dutrow, Dr. Howard V.	not given	3 Oct	" "	not given	not given
Dutrow, Mrs. Howard	not given	3 Oct	" "	not given	not given
Johnson, Ida M.	88	4 Oct		4 Jun 1870	2 Oct
Linton, Mary C.	94	16 Oct		29 Sep 1864	13 Oct
Stoner, Lemmiezine	83/10/28	14 Oct		16 Nov 1874	11 Oct
Derr, Dr. John S.	77	27 Oct		6 Jan 1881	23 Oct
Mathers, William T.	74	26 Nov		14 Sep 1884	23 Nov
Keedy, Edwin R.	78	29 Nov	Mt. View, Sharpsburg	19 Jan 1880	29 Nov (sic)
Miller, John Q.	42	21 Dec		29 Nov 1916	19 Dec
Sinn, Walter E.	62	31 Dec		24 Jan 1894	28 Dec
		1959			**1959**
Young, Joseph	64	3 Jan		4 Mar 1894	29 Dec '58
Miller, Ann G.	56	30 Jan		14 Feb 1902	31 Dec(sic)
Geisey, Franklin K.	89	24 Feb	Utica Cem	14 Dec 1869	21 Feb
Hildebrand. L. Cecilia	87	27 May		28 Feb 1872	25 May
Stine, Mary Alice	82	28 May	Middletown UCC	2 Sep 1876	25 May
Hyssong, Michael A.	2 days	3 Jun	Middletown, Zion	30 May 1954	2 Jun
Routzahn, Charles O.	70	10 Jun		26 Jan 1889	5 Jun
Measell, Annie Belle	77	3 Jul		not given	1 Jul
Mull, Alice Virginia	abt 86	11 Aug		10 Nov 1875	8 Aug
Walter, R. W.	57	17 Aug		not given	14 Aug
Young, Alvey Doub. Jr.	25	20 Aug		15 Sep 1933	15 Aug
Thomas, Dr. Edward P., Sr.	67	28 Aug		26 Feb 1892	25 Aug
Stickel, R. Dean	61	21 Sep		not given	19 Sep
Hargett, Harry	58	22 Oct		12 Feb 1901	19 Oct
Graser, Annie E.	79	10 Oct	Rocky Springs	15 Dec 1879	15 Oct
Schaefer, Edna M.	71	26 Oct	Loudon Park, Baltimore	22 Sep 1888	24 Oct
Thomas, Mary Edith	78/6/20	26 Dec		3 Jun 1881	23 Dec

Deaths and Burials of Evangelical Reformed
United Church of Christ
Frederick, Frederick County, Maryland

			1960			**1960**
Eppley, Anna Mary	79		11 Jan		7 Nov 1880	8 Jan
Haller, Ruth Elizabeth	74		14 Jan		30 Jul 1886	11 Jan
Trundle, Bessie B.	75		21 Jan	St. Luke's, Feagaville	30 Apr 1884	18 Jan
Reese, Franklin B.	58		30 Jan		8 May 1901	27 Jan
Nusz, Emory G.	65		30 Jan		19 Apr 1894	27 Jan
Hollis, Milton Ross	73		3 Feb		6 Sep 1886	31 Jan
Zeigler, George Z.	93		13 Feb		23 Feb 1866	11 Feb
Krepps, Mary Agnes	91		16 Feb		29 Apr 1868	12 Feb
Phebus, Larry Francis	21		16 Feb		4 Nov 1938	6 Feb
Delashmutt, Charlotte T.	70		4 Mar		30 Nov 1889	2 Mar
Marcks, Miriam Lark	54/10/29		19 Apr		17 May 1905	16 Apr
Motter, Guy Kunkel, Sr.	74/4/9		21 Apr		9 Dec 1880	18 Apr
Dertzbaugh, Mabel P.	75/4/0		30 Apr		28 Dec 1884	29 Apr
Shafer, Abbie Maria	70/0/25		4 May		6 Apr 1890	1 May
Staley, Glenna May	72/5/1		18 May		14 Dec 1887	15 May
Vann, Dan MacIntyre	not given		7 Jun		not given	3 Jun
Young, Charles Brown	93/1/18		19 Jun		27 Apr 1867	15 Jun
Dieterich, Anna Mary	74/8/9		2 Jul		21 Oct 1885	30 Jun
Zimmerman, Charles Herbert	76/2/5		5 Jul		26 Apr 1884	1 Jul
Rohrback, Gustavus M.	60		9 Aug		11 Nov 1900	6 Aug
Carty, Joseph W. L.	93		23 Aug		1867	21 Aug
Angleberger, Melvin Edgar	44/10/19		29 Aug		7 Oct 1915	26 Aug
Willard, J. Lee (Jess)	71/4/17		15 Oct		26 May 1889	13 Oct
Murphy, Cora Margaret	93/5/19		22 Oct		30 Apr 1867	19 Oct
Keller, Nellie Irene	85/4/10		11 Nov	Jefferson Ref.	28 Jun 1875	18 Nov
Minor, Miss A. Maude	82/8/13		19 Nov		4 Mar 1878	17 Nov
Eyster, Rev. Dr. Frederick Daniel	58/5/28		19 Nov	Union Cem, York, PA	19 May 1902	17 Nov
			1961			**1961**
Zimmerman, Alfred Glaze	69/2/2		4 Jan		30 Oct 1891	2 Jan
Ramsburg, Donald Fitez	43/1/25		8 Feb		10 Dec 1917	5 Feb
Van, Grace DeLashmutt	65		13 Feb		7 Jan 1914	5 Feb
Kieffer, J. Spangler	47/0/24		13 Feb	Rose Hill, Hagerstown	7 Jan 1914	1 Feb
Nicodemus, Robert Fulton, Sr.	60/10/5		28 Feb		20 Apr 1900	25 Feb
Wiles, Steven Ray	8/10/15		31 Mar	Zion, Middletown	13 May 1952	28 Mar
Harriss, Ruth Noami Hagan	71		1 Apr		31 Oct 1889	30 Mar
Corbet, Charles Frank	70/4/19		19 Apr		27 Dec 1890	16 Apr
Ramsburg, Mehrl H., Sr.	64		29 Apr		17 Nov 1896	26 Apr
Jones, Clara M. C.	87/9/6		7 Jul		25 Sep 1873	3 Jul
Milyard, Minnie L.	86/9/18		26 Jul		5 Nov 1874	25 Jul
Fisher, James Roger	66/10/17		1 Aug		12 Aug 1894	29 Jul
Kolb, Robert L.	78/1/1		21 Aug		18 Jul 1883	19 Aug
Lampe, Mary Christine	89/1/19		23 Aug		1 Jul 1872	20 Aug
Brandenburg, Lewis H.	82		1 Sep	Middletown UCC	17 Nov 1878	29 Aug
Lebherz, Grace Marie Worman	64/4/19		9 Sep		18 Apr 1893	7 Sep
Miller, Birdie May	86/4/19		19 Sep		26 Apr 1893	15 Sep
Burger, Anna Rosetta	90/5/24		31 Oct		5 May 1871	29 Oct
			1962			**1962**
Kefauver, Mrs. Anna Lee	81		5 Feb		19 Jul 1880	2 Feb

Deaths and Burials of Evangelical Reformed
United Church of Christ
Frederick, Frederick County, Maryland

Name	Age	Death	Place	Birth	Burial
Marendt, Robert Paul	64/4/26	7 Feb	Memorial Park	8 Sep 1899	4 Feb
McCardell, Albert N.	85/5/27	1 Mar		29 Aug 1876	26 Feb
McMurry, Luther Vincent	40/0/29	11 Mar		8 Feb 1922	7 Mar
Staley, Catherine Philabena	87/1/18	6 Apr		16 Feb 1875	4 Apr
Staley, Emma Grace	69/7/12	25 Apr		10 Sep 1892	22 Apr
Hobbs, Paul Philip	35/10/5	14 Jun		5 Aug 1926	10 Jun
Rosenberger, Frank Authur	57/6/5	6 Jul	Glade Cm, Walkersville	29 Dec 1904	4 Jul
Wachter, George N.	92	6 Aug		1 Sep 1869	3 Aug
Kline, Lewis L.	68/3/1	9 Aug		5 May 1894	6 Aug
Norris, Hallie V.	69	23 Aug		15 Oct 1892	20 Aug
Michael, Elizabeth M.	69/10/26	4 Sep		5 Oct 1892	1 Sep
Dutrow, Mary Irene	68	16 Sep	Mt. Hope, Woodsboro	19 Nov 1894	13 Sep
Price, Edwin Reynolds	73/8/17	30 Sep		10 Jan 1889	27 Sep
Schley, Lilian Kunkle	74/8/10	19 Aug	interment only	24 Jan 1888	4 Oct
Ramsburg, Clara Sophia	77/7/9	10 Oct		7 Feb 1885	6 Oct
Boyer, Emma Jane	78	16 Oct		22 Oct 1883	12 Oct
Brish, Colegate Hanschew	66/1/21	14 Nov		20 Sep 1896	11 Nov
Boileau, David Russell	80/0/29	26 Nov	Zion, Middletown	23 Oct 1880	22 Nov
Zeigler, Amy Rebecca	75/10/10	4 Dec		21 Jan 1887	1 Dec
Garrett, Franklin Edward	68/11/7	10 Dec		31 Dec 1893	7 Dec
Shipley, Ernest H.	not given	26 Dec	New London Central	not given	22 Dec
Nicodemus, Anna Elizabeth	60/15/17	3 Jan '63		14 Jul 1902	31 Dec
		1963			**1963**
Birely, Mary Rosanna	82/5/8	8 Feb		28 Aug 1880	6 Feb
Dutrow, Grayson David	81	13 Feb		22 Nov 1882	10 Feb
Hamilton, Raymond	77	20 Feb		21 Nov 1886	17 Feb
Crum, Jennie Phoebe	92/0/1	27 Apr		23 Apr 1871	24 Apr
Davis, Walter J.	64	2 May		22 Jul 1898	29 Apr
Harp, Bessie Dell Zentz	82	7 May		24 Sep 1880	5 May
Droneburg, Gloria Jean	1 day	13 May	Rest Haven-Lewistown	12 May 1963	13 May
Tull, Eleanor M.	91	1 Jun		1872	30 May
Abrecht, Ernest	73	24 Jun		20 Jan 1890	22 Jun
Fravel, Rev. Noah H.	76	13 Jul	Manor Ref Cem	20 Jun 1887	11 Jul
Corun, Myra Corine	88	14 Jul		5 Jun 1875	11 Jul
Lough, Eleanor Fisher	89	22 Jul		17 Jun 1874	20 Jul
Derr, Jeannette Rose Humphreys	78	3 Aug		1885	18 Jul
Shipley, Carrie D.	80	21 Oct		9 Apr 1883	18 Oct
Howard, Donald Fleming	81	28 Oct		1881	21 Oct
Gosnell, Orie L.	79	17 Nov		16 Aug 1884	14 Nov
Lakin, Charlotte E.	Not given		died in NY-buried there		17 Sep
Bruchey, Anna Mary	77/8/21	7 Dec		12 Mar 1886	4 Dec
		1964			**1964**
Hess, Mrs. Elizabeth A.	76	5 Jan	Lancaster, PA	not given	not given
Dutrow, Reba Mary	65	8 Jan		8 Nov 1898	8 Jan (sic)
Thomas, Effie S. Hargett	91	1 Feb		27 Dec 1872	29 Jan
Anders, Sarah E. Danby	83	14 Feb		12 Jan 1881	11 Feb
James, Mrs. Sadie F.	79	24 Feb		1884	21 Feb
Himes, Charles Hamilton	67/1/16	6 Mar		17 Jan 1897	3 Mar
Slagle, George C., Sr.	75/5/3	16 Mar		10 Oct 1888	13 Mar

Deaths and Burials of Evangelical Reformed
United Church of Christ
Frederick, Frederick County, Maryland

Name	Age	Death Date	Cemetery	Birth Date	Burial Date
Abb, Dorothy Marker	59	11 Apr		18 Aug 1904	9 Apr
Delaplaine, William T.	73	21 Apr	Frederick Mem Park	22 Jan 1891	18 Apr
Crum, Kathryn Powles	63	8 May		14 Apr 1901	6 May
Davenport, Sadie Pauline	88	9 May		15 Jan 1876	6 May
Smith, William Henry	69/1/5	1 Jun		24 Apr 1895	29 May
Noell, Edna May Wolff	72/8/15	6 Jun	Hanover, PA	18 Sep 1891	3 Jun
Mehrling, Elizabeth	49/10/6	13 Jun	Pleasant View Cem	5 Aug 1914	11 Jun
Newman, Mrs. Grace Viola	80	27 Jun		9 Jan 1884	25 Jun
Kieffer, Henri L. G., D.D.	85	6 Jul	Rose Hill, Hagerstown	24 Jul 1878	4 Jul
Crampton, Luther Boyer, Sr.	63	13 Jul		26 Jan 1901	10 Jul
Wachter, Mrs. Lois Kathryn	39/4/15	22 Jul		5 May 1925	20 Jul
Cagle, Mrs. Mary Ellen	86	24 Jul		10 Apr 1878	21 Jul
Harriss, Charles G. Knill	75	6 Aug		7 Jan 1889	4 Aug
Droneburg, Guy Herbert	83/0/29	20 Aug		18 Jul 1881	17 Aug
Engle, Mary Elizabeth	92	1 Sep		4 Mar 1872	29 Aug
Hobbs, James Fuller	59	15 Sep	Oak Grove Cem	20 Aug 1905	12 Sep
Brust, August Trago	74	27 Oct		27 Dec 1889	25 Oct
Anders, Jesse Brengle	85	8 Dec		17 Sep 1879	5 Dec
		1965			**1965**
Morton, Roberta Dixon	63	2 Jan		2 Jan 1901	30 Dec '64
Schroeder, George T., Sr.	87	10 Feb		15 Sep 1877	7 Feb
Lampe, Anna Thomas	92	13 Feb		15 Dec 1872	11 Feb
Miss, Edward W.	75/8/27	8 Mar	Rocky Springs Cem	8 Jun 1889	3 Mar
Boone, Amy Sophia	74/5/21	21 Jun	Christ Ref, Middletown	26 Dec 1890	17 Jun
Staley, Grayson H.	84	21 Jun		17 Mar 1881	18 Jun
Ramsburg, Roy Hench	81	26 Jul		11 Oct 1883	23 Jul
Cramer, Ruth B. Thomas	60/5/22	7 Sep		12 Mar 1905	3 Sep
McCardell, Pauline R.	79/1/5	22 Sep		15 Aug 1886	20 Sep
Lough, Charles W.	90/10/6	24 Sep		16 Nov 1874	22 Sep
Null, Lillie Regina	77/8/5	2 Oct		25 Dec 1887	30 Sep
Houck, Eleanor W.	84/0/12	21 Oct		7 Oct 1881	19 Oct
Englar, Myrtle Marie	82/2/1	10 Nov		7 Sep 1883	8 Nov
Jaeger, Robert Edward	18/4/0	19 Nov	Arlington Nat'l Cem	15 Jul 1947	15 Nov
Abbott, Jane Elizabeth	88/9/23	26 Nov		30 Jan 1877	28 Nov
Staley, Margaret Burger	63/4/3	3 Dec		27 Jul 1902	30 Nov
Brown, Elizabeth Rebecca	68/10/25	7 Dec		18 Jan 1897	4 Dec
Forney, Walter Samuel	74/3/12	28 Dec		13 Sep 1891	25 Dec
		1966			**1966**
Stauffer, Betty Lee	81/7/2	3 Jan		30 May 1884	1 Jan
Michael, Charles Irving	66/8/14	5 Mar		15 Jun 1899	1 Mar
Cain, Rose Main	89/5/28	31 Mar		1 Oct 1876	29 Mar
Eppley, Samuel Herbert	55/2/29	7 Apr		5 Jan 1911	4 Apr
Griny, Naomi Catherine	87	13 May		26 May 1878	11 May
Hahn, Charles Earl	60	17 May	Union Chapel Cem	15 Apr 1906	14 May
Young, Alvey Doub	71/7/12	19 Jun		4 Nov 1894	16 Jun
Lochner, Mary Stone	89/7/25	20 Jun		23 Oct 1876	18 Jun
Marks, James Daniel, Sr.	63	8 Jul		10 Feb 1903	4 Jul
Frushour, Harold U.	61	14 Jul		9 Dec 1904	12 Jul
Rinehart, Rev. Bernard O.	27	20 Jul	cremated	11 Mar 1939	15 Jul

Deaths and Burials of Evangelical Reformed
United Church of Christ
Frederick, Frederick County, Maryland

Name	Age	Death	Burial Place	Birth	Burial
Notnagle, James Leonard	74	29 Jul		15 Jan 1892	25 Jul
Martz, John W., Sr.	61	31 Jul		3 Jul 1905	26 Jul
Stull, David P.	48	20 Aug	Haugh's, Ladiesburg	28 Sep 1918	16 Aug
Cramer, Charles Edward	74	23 Sep		9 Mar 1892	20 Sep
Miller, Edith	76/3/13	29 Sep		13 Jun 1890	26 Sep
Thomas, Mary Cordelia Boyer	90/1/10	7 Oct		25 Aug 1876	5 Oct
Bowers, Reine Grove	74/4/6	13 Oct		4 Jun 1892	10 Oct
Brust, Millard M.	71	22 Nov		10 Mar 1895	19 Nov
Culler, Ralph Edward	69	8 Dec	Zion Luth, Middletown	17 Nov 1897	6 Dec
		1967			**1967**
England, Emma Newman	89	3 Jan		30 Jan 1877	31 Dec '66
Jacobs, Mrs. Mary Virginia	69	4 Mar	Christ Ref, Middletown	22 May 1897	1 Mar
Kemp, Caroline Ethel Troxell	77/5/22	8 Mar		13 Sep 1889	5 Mar
Brownlow, Edna Estelle	82/11/1	10 Mar		6 Apr 1884	7 Mar
Staley, Mollie May	88	14 Mar		4 Apr 1878	11 Mar
Garrett, Helen D.	77/7/19	14 Mar		21 Jul 1889	10 Mar
Duvall, Walter Harry	80/10	31 Mar		28 May 1886	28 Mar
Shipley, Franklin Nathan	79/10/24	6 May	9 May 1887	9 May 1887	3 May
Shriner, Virginia Musser	77	27 May		3 Aug 1889	25 May
Wachter, Helen Rhoads	57	13 Jul		27 Dec 1909	11 Jul
Hildebrand, Blanche Estelle	88	19 Jul		12 Feb 1879	10 Jul
Haugh, Margaret E.	86	8 Aug		19 Dec 1880	5 Aug
Clapp, Robert Earle, Sr.	88	14 Sep		10 Jul 1879	11 Sep
Blumenauer, Dorothy M. Good	35/2/0	29 Sep	Resthaven Mem Gar	26 Jul 1932	26 Sep
Zimmerman, Irving Franklin	59	26 Oct		15 Mar 1908	23 Oct
Boyer, Marion Davis	60	1 Dec		25 Jun 1907	28 Nov
		1968			**1968**
Carty, Hellie Walker	92	27 Jan		21 Sep 1875	24 Jan
Delashmutt, Sarah Elizabeth	80	1 Feb		13 Nov 1887	29 Jan
Winters, Caroline Fleming	61	2 Feb		4 Mar 1906	29 Jan
Burger, Mary Smith	79	9 Feb		25 Aug 1888	6 Feb
Swope, Mary Elizabeth	71	4 Mar		13 Oct 1896	1 Mar
Thomas, Ralph J.	84	4 Mar		23 Nov 1883	29 Feb
Staley, Mae Estelle	80	9 Mar		25 Mar 1887	6 Mar
Cannon, Charles Burton	73	17 Apr		13 Apr 1895	14 Apr
Kinsey, Virgie Mae Crum	80	17 Apr	Pine Grove, Mt. Airy	7 Jun 1887	15 Apr
Hoffmeier, Edgar F.	88/9/11	20 Apr	Glade, Walkersville	6 Jul 1879	17 Apr
Murray, Lee	71	9 May		6 Aug 1896	7 May
Bell, Mrs. Inna Lorine	82	15 May		23 Feb 1886	13 May
Lipps, Mary Elenora	84	12 Jul		6 Jul 1884	10 Jul
Fry, Austin Thomas	58/10/13	13 Jul		27 Aug 1909	10 Jul
Ramsburg, J. Richard	61/0/15	17 Jul		29 Jun 1907	14 Jul
Ramsburg, Lillian V.	89/4/21	20 Sep		26 Feb 1879	17 Jul
Wachter, Cheryl Anne	21	29 Jul		12 Mar 1947	25 Jul
McCardell, Eleanor Clingan	88/6/14	29 Aug		13 Feb 1880	27 Aug
Blumenauer, John N.	not given	4 Sep	Rocky Hill, Woodsboro	not given	31 Aug
Cramer, Dani Elizabeth	4 ½ hrs	28 Sep		28 Sep 1968	28 Sep
Newman, Helen Elizabeth	95	24 Oct		7 Jul 1873	22 Oct
Davis, Emily Ruth Myers	46	7 Dec		27 Apr 1922	5 Dec

Deaths and Burials of Evangelical Reformed
United Church of Christ
Frederick, Frederick County, Maryland

1969

Name	Age	Death	Cemetery	Birth	Burial
Phebus, Daisy M.	81	1 Jan		1 Mar 1887	29 Dec '68
Garrett, Sadie May	77/11/24	7 Jan		10 Jan 1891	4 Jan
Gannon, Cora Irene	80/3/12	9 Jan		24 Sep 1888	6 Jan
Thomas, Ruth Dixon	75	25 Jan		17 Oct 1893	22 Jan
Burger, William Leslie	75	19 Feb		7 Oct 1893	16 Feb
Murray, Roscoe Covert	77/6/21	21 Feb		27 Jul 1891	18 Feb
Krantz, Bessie C.	80/8/12	28 Feb		14 Jun 1888	26 Feb
Maisel, Ruth Thomas	83	26 Apr		not given	23 Apr
Herbert, Henry H.	84	28 Jun	Zion Luth, Middletown	24 Feb 1885	25 Jun
Hughes, Elinor Markey	85	12 Jul		5 Feb 1994	9 Jul
Martz, Amy Elmira	85/3/20	21 Jul		28 Mar 1884	18 Jul
Crampton, Claude Leroy	69	23 Jul	Resthaven Mem Gar	3 May 1900	20 Jul
Kefauver, Ruth Willard	80	9 Sep	Christ Ref, Middletown	14 Jul 1889	7 Sep
Zimmerman, Elizabeth H.	65/8/15	10 Sep		21 Dec 1903	6 Sep
Grove, Philip Mathias	72/7/10	15 Nov		21 Mar 1897	11 Nov
Hoke, Mildred R.	68/6/26	12 Dec		13 May 1897	9 Dec
Harrington, Harvey A.	61	19 Dec		28 Aug 1906	15 Dec

1970

Name	Age	Death	Cemetery	Birth	Burial
Gosnell, Roy R., Sr.	74	14 Jan	Union Chapel Cem	29 Jun 1895	11 Jan
Fry, Harold Edward	53/2/25	2 Feb		4 Nov 1916	29 Jan
Sanders, Lucy Estelle Derr	81	23 Feb		3 Aug 1888	19 Feb
Elkin, Walter LeRoy	69	10 Mar		not given	6 Mar
Ordeman, Charlotte Sinn	76/6/8	19 Mar		6 Sep 1893	14 Mar
Heffner, Vernon Eugene, Jr.	60/11/8	7 Apr		22 Apr 1909	4 Apr
Myers, George Worthington	78/6/1	9 May		5 Nov 1891	6 May
Stewart, Bernard Roy	62	18 May		3 Dec 1907	13 May
Biehl, Gerald Monroe	57/3/21	9 Jun		15 Feb 1913	6 Jun
Tinney, Lillian R.	76/5/15	24 Jun		16 Jan 1894	21 Jun
Dutrow, Rena Grace	80/2/28	25 Jun		10 Mar 1890	22 Jun
Graham, Roy Webster	81	30 Jul		7 Apr 1889	27 Jul
Rice, Pauline G.	75	4 Aug		25 Mar 1895	2 Aug
Houck, William Harry		10 Aug		1 Jan 1894	7 Aug
Derr, Will May	94	27 Aug		30 Jul 1876	24 Aug
Radcliff, James Ralph	87	2 Sep		23 Feb	30 Aug
Notnagle, Mary Dittmar	74	27 Nov		28 Jan 1896	24 Nov
Maples, Sam Wynne, Sr.	82	1 Dec		12 Nov 1888	28 Nov
Lorentz, George Egbert	59	19 Dec		21 Dec 1910	16 Dec
Radcliff, Myrtle M. Zentz	86	22 Dec		9 Sec 1884	20 Dec
Delashmutt, Alvida Browning	85/9/22	22 Dec		28 Feb 1885	20 Dec
Price, Lillian Elizabeth Motter	82	24 Dec		15 Mar 1898	22 Dec

1971

Name	Age	Death	Cemetery	Birth	Burial
Mori, Eric Hans, Sr.	74/5/4	5 Jan		28 Jul 1896	2 Jan
Swain, Laura Virginia	69	16 Jan	Frederick Mem Park	31 Jan 1901	13 Jan
Derr, Betty Irene Klein	46	20 Feb		15 Jul 1924	15 Feb
Crampton, Dora Crone	67/1/8	15 Apr	Resthaven Mem Gar	3 Mar 1904	11 Apr
Quynn, Allen George	77/0/1	21 Jun		16 Jun 1894	17 Jun
Clark, Dorothy O'Neal	68	23 Jun	Zion Luth, Middletown	14 Mar 1903	21 Jun
Martz, Grace Susan	84	30 Jun		3 Aug 1886	27 Jun

Deaths and Burials of Evangelical Reformed
United Church of Christ
Frederick, Frederick County, Maryland

Name	Age	Born	Died	Cemetery/Place	Born	Died
Ramsburg, Lulu Teresa	89		13 Jul		6 Oct 1882	9 Jul
Hocker, Robert P.	79/10/7		7 Aug		2 Sep 1891	4 Aug
Graham, Vallie Q.	80		12 Aug		22 Nov 1890	9 Aug
Hodges, Katherine	69/10/6		13 Aug		4 Oct 1901	10 Aug
Gaither, Helen Engle	67		31 Aug		19 Oct 1903	27 Aug
Gaver, Pierce Horatio	66		28 Sep		29 Dec 1904	24 Sep
Jaeger, Robert Frederick	56		4 Oct	Arlington Nat'l Cem	3 Jun 1915	28 Sep
Slagle, Margaret Gertrude B.	83/2/18		8 Oct		17 Jul 1888	5 Aug (sic)
Hermann, Edward A. G.	93/2/1		30 Oct		26 Aug 1878	27 Oct
Hossler, Frances L. Sutton	54/9/7		24 Nov	Union Chapel Cem	14 Feb 1917	21 Nov
Doll, Arthur Holtz	75		29 Nov		20 Aug 1896	17 Dec
Harbaugh, Helen Frances	79		21 Dec		6 Sep 1892	17 Dec
			1972			**1972**
Althouse, Mary Elizabeth	90/2/9		3 Jan	Reading, PA	20 Oct 1881	29 Dec '71
Phebus, Harry Edgar	65		31 Jan		14 Jul 1906	27 Jan
Hargett, Richard Schaeffer	90/11/20		14 Feb		21 Feb 1881	10 Feb
Cox, Mary Rebekah Z.	69		10 Mar	cremated	23 Sep 1902	6 Mar
Ramsburg, Alice May	84/11/16		15 Mar		25 Mar 1887	22 Mar
Johnson, Catharine N.	76		14 Apr	Warnersville, PA	9 Feb 1896	22 Apr
Mills, James Benjamin	91		2 May	Glen Haven, Baltimore	24 Oct 1880	29 Apr
Coons, Harold Niver	79/11/2		23 May	Louisville, KY	18 Jun 1892	20 May
Brandenburg, Josiah Henry	78/1/11		3 Jul		19 May 1894	30 Jun
Lang, John Frederick	60/6/7		17 Jul		16 Jan 1912	13 Jul
Zimmerman, Margaret M.	75/8/23		18 Jul		23 Oct 1896	15 Jul
Albaugh, Effie A.	not given		26 Jul	Christ Ref, Middletown	not given	23 Jul
Ramsburg, Mary Florence	71/9/12		19 Sep		28 Nov 1900	16 Sep
Hoffmaster, Meredith R.	52		4 Oct	Zion Luth, Middletown	22 Jul 1920	30 Sep
Stauffer, Bessie M. Kaufman	83/11/17		24 Oct		5 Nov 1888	22 Oct
Martz, George David	91/3/27		4 Dec		4 Aug 1881	1 Dec
Flautt, Walter				Baltimore		
Kuhn, Sarah Rebecca	71/5/4		20 Dec		13 Jul 1901	17 Dec
			1973			**1973**
Hargett, Maud Riggs	86/11/7		8 Jan		28 Jan 1886	4 Jan
Burger, Bertha Mae Wilhide	84		16 Feb		13 Jan 1889	13 Feb
Burkett, Harry Vernon, Jr.	53/4/6		10 Mar		31 Oct 1919	7 Mar
Angleberger, Preston David	49		23 Mar		19 Mar 1924	19 Mar
Null, Joseph Arthur	84/10/16		23 Mar		4 May 1888	20 Mar
Martz, Eleanor Catharine	75/2/2		9 Apr		4 Feb 1898	6 Apr
Boyer, William Edward, Jr.	59/8/3		13 Apr		7 Aug 1913	10 Apr
Hollis, Nellie Beatrice Thomas	84/9/14		7 Jul		11 Sep 1888	5 Jul
Eyler, Miss Mary Ella	81/9/14		14 Jul		27 Sep 1891	12 Jul
Ray, Maurice Butler	48/6/30		8 Aug	Frederick Mem Park	6 Jan 1925	5 Aug
Albaugh, Caroline B.	58		5 Sep		9 Jan 1915	1 Sep
White, Dorothy Sier	62		30 Oct		19 May 1911	26 Oct
Slagle, Mary Pearl "Patsy"	49/4/18		23 Nov		2 Jul 1924	20 Nov
Albaugh, Howard Moore	80		5 Dec		25 Jan 1893	2 Dec
Hane, Barbara Jane	75/2/17		13 Dec		24 Sep 1898	11 Dec
Zimmerman, Isabele E.	83		26 Dec		17 Oct 1890	23 Dec

Deaths and Burials of Evangelical Reformed
United Church of Christ
Frederick, Frederick County, Maryland

Name	Age	1974			1974
Humphreys, Jesse B.	65	15 Jan		25 Apr 1908	11 Jan
Baker, Katie Amelia Zeigler	83/7/14	18 Jan		2 Jun 1890	16 Jan
Rhoderick, Lillian A.	79/10/24	29 Mar		2 May 1894	26 Mar
Haffner, Mrs. Jane	87	16 Apr		13 Jul 1886	12 Apr
Alexander, Martha Mabel	84/11/0	10 May		7 Jun 1889	7 May
Burkett, Harry Vernon, Sr.	80	13 May		28 Jan 1894	10 May
Staley, Irving Edgar	881/10/13	15 Aug		30 Sep 1885	13 Aug
Wiles, Alvie C.	89	16 Oct	Faith Ch, Charlesville	4 Apr 1885	13 Oct
Knock, Pauline Zentz	81/10/29	23 Dec		21 Jan 1892	20 Dec
		1975			**1975**
Cramer, Ethan Alan	71	2 Feb		7 May 1903	31 Jan
Harrington, Mary Lila	89	5 Feb		10 Sep 1885	5 Feb
Derr, John A.	64	18 Mar		2 Aug 1910	14 Mar
Mantz, Leda Catherine	85/0/12	27 Mar		13 Mar 1894	25 Mar
Buell, Carlotta Pratt	78/0/27	11 Apr	Utica Cem	11 Mar 1897	8 Apr
Gannon, Lewis B. "Goose"	51/0/16	6 May		16 Apr 1924	2 May
Fesperman, Rev. Frank L.	80/4/19	15 May	Union, Lovettsville, VA	29 Dec 1894	10 May
Dertzbaugh, Frank M., Sr.	84	19 May		3 Aug 1890	16 May
Dertzbaugh, Lewis R.	92	26 Jul		16 Nov 1882	24 Jul
Schell, Serena Motter	84	28 Jul		21 Nov 1890	25 Jul
Henderson, Mildred K.	64/9/9	2 Sep		20 Nov 1910	29 Aug
MacKenzie, Kathryne Elizabeth	74/4/19	3 Nov		11 Jun 1901	30 Oct
		1976			**1976**
Wachter, Grayson Phillip	70	14 Jan		4 Dec 1905	11 Jan
Brust, Robert Marion	55	28 Jan		7 Aug 1920	26 Jan
Culler, Ella Elizabeth	85	30 Jan	Manor, Adamstown	7 May 1890	28 Jan
Dorsey, George Alfred	61	6 Feb		30 Sep 1914	2 Feb
Shapro, Evelyn Grose	82/2/6	21 Feb		12 Dec 1893	18 Feb
Oberlander, William C.	90/11/0	9 Mar		5 Apr 1885	5 Mar
Falconer, Lucille W.	59	29 Mar		25 Aug 1916	26 Mar
Eicholtz, Mildred Catherine S.	78	9 Apr		29 May 1897	9 Apr
Schell, John Edward, Jr.	82	24 May		9 Dec 1893	20 May
Dutrow, Ruth Patterson	76	15 Jun		18 Sep 1899	14 Jun
Thomas, Clarence C. C.	82	22 Jul		16 Dec 1893	20 Jul
Shawbaker, Jessie June	93	28 Aug		29 Jun 1883	25 Aug
Sheppard, Charles Guy, Sr.	46	13 Sep		30 Oct 1929	10 Sep
Shawbaker, Jacob Garfield	88	4 Oct		1 Jan 1888	30 Sep
Falconer, Howard H.	62	29 Oct		3 Mar 1914	25 Oct
Derr, John S., Jr.	53	15 Dec		27 May 1923	11 Dec

New format

Date of Death	Name	Age	When buried	Where buried
1977			**1977**	
14 Feb	Mathers, Hellen	65/1/8	17 Feb	
9 Feb	Blumenauer, Julia Ann	80	11 Feb	Rocky Hill Cem
21 Feb	Winpigler, Robert Earl	24	24 Feb	Frederick Mem Park

Deaths and Burials of Evangelical Reformed
United Church of Christ
Frederick, Frederick County, Maryland

24 Feb	Cramer, Lucy C.	100	28 Feb	
24 Mar	MacKenzie, C. E. Bernard	75	28 Mar	
22 Apr	Martz, Hattie Irene	75	25 Apr	
5 May	Keller, Clinton E.	74	9 May	Ref Cem, Jefferson

Deaths and burials recorded by Rev. Frederick A. Wenner

1977			1977	
23 May	Thomas, Jessie Lee Diller	81	25 May	
4 Jun	Phebus, Ethel M.	76	7 Jun	
12 Jun	Myers, Julia Roelkey	81	15 Jun	
27 Jun	Holter, Lawrence Fahrney	69	30 Jun	
8 Jul	Hydorn, Walter Rutherford	68	12 Jul	Resthaven Mem Gardens
15 Sep	Kolb, Helen T.	68	19 Sep	
22 Sep	Burkett, Margaret M.	78	24 Sep	
22 Sep	Sofrit, Helen M.	82	26 Sep	
8 Oct	Fisher, Mary Starr	84	10 Oct	
17 Oct	Hocker, Lena Dodd	87/2/2	20 Oct	
18 Oct	Starr, June Estelle	50	22 Oct	
15 Nov	Thomas, Grace A.	94	16 Nov	
26 Dec	Herbert, Sylvia R.	88	28 Dec	
28 Dec	Carter, Franklynn Louise	76/0/23	30 Dec	
1978			**1978**	
14 Jan	Thomas, Catherine Alice	74/2/22	17 Jan	
17 Feb	Kuhn, Charles Bertram	80/8/6	21 Feb	
10 May	Etzler, Norma Wachter	84	13 May	
13 Jul	Delaplaine, Janie Quynn		21 Jul	
10 Sep	Pease, Sarah Dorothy	83/8/15	14 Sep	Lakeview Mem Park
13 Nov	Hahn, Elmira Staley	84/8/3	15 Nov	Union Chapel Cem
17 Nov	Remsberg, Dorothy Maude Derr	76/4/9	20 Nov	
8 Dec	Shaw, Mary Ruthella W.	89	12 Dec	
1979			**1979**	
17 Jan	Dutrow, Richard C.	71		memorial service
25 Jan	Abrecht, Ernest A. "Buck"	69/10/13	27 Jan	
4 Feb	Horine, Willard "Bill"	54/6/25	7 Feb	Zion Luth, Middletown
7 Feb	Hoffmeier, Hester LeVan	92/7/3	12 Feb	Glade, Walkersville
6 Mar	Perry, Louise Ent	83/2/7	9 Mar	
1 May	Shoemaker, Henry R., Sr.	84	3 May	
27 May	Shipley, G. Raymond	79	29 May	
7 Aug	Dutrow, Elizabeth Lee			memorial service
22 Aug	Shriner, Edward Derr, Jr.	84	24 Aug	
3 Sep	Harris, S. Fenton	96	6 Sep	
11 Sep	Roth, Dorothy Abrecht	66	11 Sep	grave side service
31 Oct	Crum, Ethel Myers	93	31 Oct	grave side service
5 Nov	Bartgis, Anna Young	73/9/26	8 Nov	
27 Nov	Zimmerman, Madeline M.	85/8/21	29 Nov	
5 Dec	Myers, Edward Irvin, Sr.	83/6/24	8 Dec	
14 Dec	Gallagher, Thelma Elizabeth	70/11/25	17 Dec	
20 Dec	Blumenauer, Sallie Virginia	74/7/23	24 Dec	

Deaths and Burials of Evangelical Reformed
United Church of Christ
Frederick, Frederick County, Maryland

1980

Date	Name	Age
12 Feb	Gannon, Carol Lynn	29/5/20
16 Mar	Neidig, Grace	96/1/18
20 Mar	Storm, Sperry L.	73
7 Apr	Dutrow, Katharine E.	79/7/23
23 May	Kinsey, Gwynn X.	54/7/26
29 May	Forney, Arthur J.	75
18 Jun	Heffner, Heidi Lynn	stillborn
26 Jun	Hahn, Walter J.	82
30 Jul	Garrett, Willard N.	67
10 Aug	Mateny, Helen	85
20 Aug	Morgan, John W.	77
30 Nov	Brown, Lillian Olive	97

1981

Date	Name	Age
5 Jan	Montgomery, Julia A.	82
7 Feb	Maisel, Edward F.	94
11 Mar	Zimmerman, Helen G.	89/10/7
5 Apr	Harrington, Robert C.	68
15 Apr	Myers, Drew Allen	22
4 May	Dorsey, Russell L.	29/1/23
30 May	Thomas, Louise G.	79
1 Jun	Berry, Robert P.	26/11/13
1 Jul	Stine, Pierce Charles, Sr.	54/11/01
17 Sep	Zimmerman, Thomas H.	76
26 Sep	Filby, Mollie I.	100/4/8
28 Oct	Shatto, Paul Frederick	60/9/21
1 Dec	Willard, Roger H.	74

1982

Date	Name	Age
20 Jan	Umstead, Bernice S.	85
20 Feb	Maples, Annie Kemp	88
27 Feb	Herbert, Nora Ethel	88/1/23
23 Mar	Morgan, Lenora Rudy	73/0/15
8 Apr	Geisbert, Calvin M., Jr.	65
30 Apr	Crummitt, Edna Mae	84/5/5
17 May	Myers, Sally Pearl Delphey	83
19 May	Kefauver, Mrs. Lillie S.	96/10/8
27 May	May, Carl C.	82
28 May	Lumpkin, Mrs. Dorothy E.	66/4/19
1 Jun	Long, Mrs Roberta Carty	84/5/11
13 Aug	Cramer, Kirk Donald, Sr.	77/9/28
14 Nov	Shue, Viola Gwendolyn	76/3/28
22 Nov	Huffer, Charles Jacob	66/12/14
6 Dec	Oden, Mrs. Bertha May	64/6/11
12 Dec	Ramsburg, Elias B., Jr.	79/9/12
31 Dec	Romero, Mrs. Dorothy Ruth	84/11/2

1983

Date	Name	Age
5 Jan	Zimmerman, Raymond R.	91/11/17
12 Feb	VanSwearingen, Charles	83/2/20
6 Mar	Molesworth, Winifred M.	64/10/27

1980 (Burials)

Date	Notes
15 Feb	
21 Mar	grave side service
24 Mar	
21 Apr	
26 May	Pine Grove, Mt. Airy
31 May	
26 Jun	
29 Jun	Chapel Cem, Libertytown
2 Aug	
13 Aug	
23 Aug	
2 Dec	Summit Station, PA

1981 (Burials)

Date	Notes
7 Jan	
10 Feb	
13 Mar	
8 Apr	
18 Apr	Resthaven Mem Gardens
8 May	
2 Jun	
4 Jun	
4 Jul	
22 Sep	
29 Sep	
30 Oct	private service
4 Dec	

1982 (Burials)

Date	Notes
22 Jan	Union, Lovettsville, VA
27 Feb	
2 Mar	Zion Luth, Middletown
26 Mar	
10 Apr	
6 May	
20 May	
21 May	
29 May	Rocky Springs Cem
1 Jun	
2 Jun	
16 Aug	
17 Nov	Christ Ref, Middletown
24 Nov	
9 Dec	
15 Dec	
1 Jan ' 83	

1983 (Burials)

Date	Notes
8 Jan	
15 Feb	
9 Mar	

Deaths and Burials of Evangelical Reformed
United Church of Christ
Frederick, Frederick County, Maryland

11 Mar	Bussard, Walter Luther	69/10/20	14 Mar	
13 Mar	Bell, Jesse Elmer, Sr.	96/5/10	15 Mar	
26 Mar	Wachter, William Noah, Jr.	74/9/13	28 Mar	
26 Mar	Ramsburg, Mildred A.	77/9/13	31 Mar	
24 apr	Brust, Margaret N.	85/7/17	27 Apr	
25 Apr	Marks, Gladys Clerene	77/6/05	28 Apr	
20 May	Gunneau, Betty Ruth	53/10/29	23 May	
28 May	Ramsburgh, Mabel E.	96/3/2	31 May	
13 Jun	Remsberg, Gerald Grosh	81/8/9	16 Jun	
5 Jul	Gainer, Giles Oliver	73/7/4	8 Jul	Mt. View, Ringgold
10 Aug	Smith, Mildred Biser	83/1	12 Aug	
28 Aug	Hoffmaster, Emma Margaret	88/1	1 Sep	Zion Luth, Middletown
30 Sep	Rice, Dr. Louis A.	87/7	4 Oct	
10 Oct	Quynn, Rachel Motter	87/3	14 Oct	
6 Oct	Hersperger, Ella Kea	80/5/3	14 Oct	
12 Nov	Young, Leah Hamilton Lark	80/1/3	15 Nov	
11 Dec	Elton, Ellen Reid	80/4/03	13 Dec	Monocacy Cem, Beallsville
20 Dec	Carlson, Dr. C. Edwin, Sr.	77/6/6	29 Dec	
29 Dec	Gardner, Samuel F., Jr.	77/5/6	3 Jan '84	
1984			**1984**	
14 Jan	Marendt, Ella Mae	81/11/2	17 Jan	Frederick Mem Park
7 May	Troxell, Robert Allen	68/7/15	10 May	
9 May	Shafer, James Elliott, Sr.	71/10/12	12 May	
19 Jul	Paisley, Ray A.	98/9	21 Jul	
11 Oct	Bartgis, Frances Evans	73/1/11	13 Oct	
19 Oct	Mathers, Helen Ramsburgh	94/7/90	22 Oct	
28 Nov	Gardner, Ethel V.	78/12/5	30 Nov	
13 Dec	Motter, Margaret R.	91/2/93	15 Dec	
20 Dec	Routzahn, Erma Lavada		22 Dec	
23 Dec	Paisley, Florence E.	88/5	26 Dec	
30 Dec	Sinn, Myra Elizabeth	86/2	3 Jan '85	
1985			**1985**	
9 Jan	Biser, Thaddeus McCauley, Jr.	82/1/2	12 Jan	
3 Feb	Rohrback, Alice	84/1/1	6 Feb	
7 Feb	Hane, Ruth Ellen		12 Feb	
4 May	Bowers, Alma Staley	62/5/22	7 Mar	
11 Apr	Stup, Charles E.	62/7/22	15 Apr	
20 Apr	Shipley, Ruth Johanna	86/7	29 Apr	
29 Apr	deLillo, Virginia Carty	91/12	2 May	
27 May	Culler, Harold Albert	68/0/21	30 May	Resthaven Mem Gardens
13 May	Mateny, Guy Clinton	90	15 May	
26 Jun	May, Ernest William, Sr.	76	29 Jun	
25 Aug	Baker, Clifford Monroe	93/7/92	28 Aug	
1 Oct	Rinehart, Russell J.	75/10/9	4 Oct	
3 Nov	Higinbotham, Frank Weadon	72/8/12	6 Nov	New Oxford, PA
5 Nov	Hammond, Charles Leonard	49/2	16 Nov	
30 Nov	Harbaugh, Roland W.	90/10/5	2 Dec	
1986			**1986**	
9 Jan	Thomas, Clarence S., Jr.	78	15 Jan	

Deaths and Burials of Evangelical Reformed
United Church of Christ
Frederick, Frederick County, Maryland

24 Jan	Hodges, Elmer Ernest	83/7/2	28 Jan	
8 Feb	Huffer, Alice E.	70/9/11	11 Feb	
18 Mar	Stewart, Harriet Loretta Z.	71/9/14	21 Mar	
6 Jun	Staley, John H., Sr.	99/4	5 Jun (sic)	
29 Jun	Eshleman, Elmer I.	86/3	1 Jul	
21 Jul	Poole, Meleko	infant	24 Jul	
6 Aug	Myers, F. Ross	92	9 Aug	
24 Oct	Remsberg, Emory Earl	87/9/99	27 Oct	
29 Oct	Shafer, Emma		1 Nov	
14 Nov	Crummitt, William E., Jr.	53/2/33	18 Nov	
26 Nov	Steele, Mary Louise Tritapoe	77/1/0	28 Nov	Union, Burkittsville
30 Dec	Rhoads, Mary Evelyn	83/5/3	3 Jan '87	
1987			**1987**	
23 Feb	Hooper, William R.	63/12/23	26 Feb	
23 Feb	King, Grace G.	88/10/99	26 Feb	
3 Mar	Mossburg, F. Doris L.	52/8/34	6 Mar	
21 Mar	Dinterman, Lester Clarence	75/11/11	25 Mar	Resthaven Mem Gardens
10 Apr	Reeder, Carmey Emmonds	76/3/11	25 Mar	
19 May	Neighbours, Mary F.	84/6/2	22 May	
21 Jun	Crum, LeRoy Irvin "Pete", Jr.	69/11/17	24 Jun	
8 Jul	Tobery, Edna Irene	55/11/31	11 Jul	Resthaven Mem Gardens
15 Aug	Dyer, Madaline A.	83/8/3	22 Aug	
6 Oct	Blumenauer, Edward K., Sr.	80/5/7	8 Oct	
8 Oct	Creed, Marion	77/1/10	11 Oct	cremated-memorial service
28 Dec	Sleber, Anthony Jay, Jr.	10 days	31 Dec	Resthaven Mem Gardens
29 Dec	Willard, Jane Russell Meade	73/5/14	2 Jan '88	
1988			**1988**	
24 Jan	Myers, Arthur V.		27 Jan	St. John's Roman Catholic
20 Jan	Johnson, Michael G., Sr.	40/7	23 Jan	Resthaven Mem Gardens
6 Feb	Baumgardner, John A.	65/8/22	9 Feb	
23 Feb	Jones, Grace Virginia	84/3/3	26 Feb	
1 Apr	Burger, William Leslie, Jr.	62	11 Apr	
7 Apr	Hansen, Helen Virginia	79/1/23	11 Apr	
22 Apr	Cramer, Dorothy R.	76/4 12	26 Apr	
24 Apr	Staley, Paul Eugene	72/7/15	26 Apr	
25 Apr	Thomas, Mrs. Rilla V.	79/5/8	28 Apr	
23 May	Hedges, Mary Elizabeth	85/12/2	26 May	
19 Jun	Bugos, Robert Joseph, Sr.	64/11/4	21 Jun	
30 Jun	Morton, William Dare	91/8/8	2 Jul	
29 Jul	Rinehart, F. Evelyn	77/9/27	1 Aug	
1 Aug	Dorsey, Barbara L.	66/10/1	4 Aug	
24 Aug	Beatty, Dorothy Souder	79/12/14	27 Aug	Union, Lovettsville, VA
28 Aug	Bentley, Betty Jane	66/11/16	31 Aug	
7 Sep	Wiles, Charles "Hambone", Sr.	63/4/14	10 Sep	Mt. Zion U. M.
6 Sep	Molesworth, John William, III	73/5/16	14 Sep	
29 Sep	Rice, Elizabeth M.	90/1/21	3 Oct	
5 Oct	Slayman, Charles Henry, Jr.	72/5/19	8 Oct	
17 Oct	Angleberger, Emma	93/1/9	21 Oct	
1 Nov	Schley, Mary Margaret	84/2/12	4 Nov	

Deaths and Burials of Evangelical Reformed
United Church of Christ
Frederick, Frederick County, Maryland

6 Nov	Ranck, James B., Sr.	90/3/18	9 Nov	cremated-Lancaster, PA
25 Nov	Blumenauer, George Daniel	83/2/9	29 Nov	
27 Nov	Brown, Grace Virginia	85	30 Nov	Camp Hill, PA
27 Dec	Elkin, Bertha V. Jones Smith	88/12/17	31 Dec	
1989			**1989**	
3 Feb	Staley, Orvis Marion	78/2/7	6 Feb	cremated
26 Feb	Zimmerman, William Henry, Sr.	87/4/5	28 Feb	
24 Mar	Martz, Lewis Joseph	81/5/22	27 Mar	
2 Aug	Troxell, Helen Staley	75/10/28	4 Aug	
27 Aug	Dutrow, Richard	58	?	
30 Aug	Wilkinson, Jean Collmus	68/12/13	2 Sep	
20 Dec	Hollinger, Harold Clyde	62/6/29	22 Dec	

New format. As previously mentioned, if place of burial is not named, it is Mt. Olivet Cemetery, Frederick, MD.

Name	Birthdate	Deathdate	Burial date	Place of burial
		1990		
Wilkinson, T. D.	16 Jan 1923	8 Jan	12 Jan	
Hodgson, Mary Condon	4 Jul 1903	25 Jan	29 Jan	
Cockrell, Edward W., Sr.	1 Nov 1920	31 Jan	3 Feb	
Abrecht, Eva Elizabeth	19 Jul 1909	14 Feb	17 Feb	
Eschleman, Orpha Susan Showe	29 Jan 1892	23 Mar	26 Mar	
Zimmerman, William Henry, Jr.	31 Mar 1931	9 Apr	11 Apr	
Hahn, Catherine Virginia	31 Mar 1908	30 Apr	3 May	Christ Ref, Middletown
Rice, Lewis A.	24 Jul 1925	26 Jun	29 Jun	
Coblentz, Mary Helen	15 Jul 1896	4 Aug	8 Aug	Christ Ref, Middletown
Staley, I. Mary	28 Jul 1912	2 Sep	7 Sep	
Boone, Russell Loraine	14 Nov 1916	17 Sep	19 Sep	Union Chapel Cem
Staley, Arlene Estelle Grove	3 Sep 1925	19 Oct	22 Oct	
Crum, Evelyn Virginia Gaver	15 Sep 1918	16 Nov	19 Nov	Christ Ref, Middletown
Thomas, Curtis William	23 Mar 1918	14 Dec	19 Dec	cremated
Poole, MacKenzie Autumn	26 Feb 1989	28 Dec	31 Dec	
		1991		
Kintz, Harry	27 Jan 1922	30 Mar	2 Apr	cremated
Carey, Ruth Shipley	22 Jan 1900	9 Apr	12 Apr	
Geisbert, Ruth Perry	31 Aug 1917	19 May	23 May	
Crampton, Dorothy Marie	29 Aug 1903	28 May	31 May	
Delauder, Helen Eppley	9 May 1905	3 Jun	6 Jun	
Harrington, Ruth Dixon	16 Mar 1913	6 Jun	10 Jun	
Werntz, Rev. W. Garner	11 Mar 1937	7 Jun	11 Jun	cremated
Martz, Helen Whitmore	20 Feb 1902	28 Jul	31 Jul	
Nusz, Margaret Young	16 Sep 1895	18 Aug	21 Aug	
Fogle, Rhoda Mary	24 Nov 1899	19 Aug	22 aug	
Griffith, Raymond W.	24 Jun 1906	13 Sep	13 Sep (sic)	
Frushour, Katherine	1 Nov 1905	23 Sep	27 Sep	
Lodge, Frederic George	3 Oct 1912	21 Oct	4 Oct	Resthaven
Boyer, Rhoda Pauline	19 Feb 1911	2 Oct	5 Oct	
Staley, Shirley Brandes	4 Nov 1926	8 Oct	11 Oct	
Kolb, Mary Alice	5 Dec 1925	17 Oct	21 Oct	Frederick Mem Park

Deaths and Burials of Evangelical Reformed
United Church of Christ
Frederick, Frederick County, Maryland

Name	Born	Died	Buried	Notes
Maples, Margaret Quynn	20 Oct 1928	21 Oct	24 Oct	
Hane, Meredith	19 Oct 1906	12 Oct	15 Oct	
Delauder, Bruce	16 Apr 1913	15 Oct	20 Oct	interment of ashes
Bussard, Clarence Lease	9 Feb 1911	1 Dec	5 Dec	
Humphreys, Anna Mary	8 Aug 1904	6 Dec	13 Dec	

1992

Name	Born	Died	Buried	Notes
Shearer, George David	19 Dec 1905	19 Jan	21 Jan	
Gosnell, Helen Rebecca Crum	17 Sep 1898	21 Jan	24 Jan	Union Chapel Cem
Githerman, Helen M.	9 May 1921	20 Apr	22 Apr	
Haugh, Charles Thomas	10 Jan 1918	7 Jul	9 Jul	
Stull, Elizabeth Bussard	12 Feb 1912	20 Jul	23 Jul	
McCormick, Rosebelle Biser	11 Oct 1896	5 Oct	13 Oct	
Hammell, Frederick Paul	1 Aug 1912	11 Oct	15 Oct	
Davis, Mary Louise	19 Aug 1911	9 Nov	11 Nov	
Hydorn, Beryl Bidwell	22 Aug 1910	7 Dec	10 Dec	Resthaven Mem Gardens

1993

Name	Born	Died	Buried	Notes
Storm, Betty Culler	4 Feb 1910	5 Feb	9 Feb	
Schmid, Elsie W.	28 Jun 1903	18 Feb	21 Feb	Philadelphia, PA
Weigle, Anne Elizabeth Korn	28 Oct 1961	24 Feb	27 Feb	
Blumenauer, Albert Leroy	29 Jul 1909	26 Feb	2 Mar	
Shafer, Grace Virginia	26 Feb 1917	23 Mar	27 Mar	
Roderuck, Roscoe E.	18 Jun 1910	26 Mar	30 Mar	Mt. Hebron Cem
Rhoads, Mildred Thomas	30 Jun 1900	3 Apr	6 Apr	
Thomas, William H., Jr.	29 Jun 1918	18 Apr	20 Apr	
Engle, Lewis Henry	10 Aug 1903	28 May	1 Jun	
Fout, Margaret Elizabeth	24 Apr 1921	30 May	2 Jun	
Bruestle, Mildred B.	17 Oct 1906	21 Aug	?	
Bittinger, Anne	25 Jul 1944	26 Sep	1 Oct	Emanuel, Hanover, PA
Rhoderick, Wayne A.	18 Aug 1941	3 Dec	7 Dec	
Pease, Helen R.	24 Oct 1918	10 Dec	13 Dec	

1994

Name	Born	Died	Buried	Notes
Albaugh, Edwin	2 Oct 1913	15 Jan	18 Jan	
Droneburg, John Thomas, Sr.	3 Dec 1947	24 Jan	29 Jan	Resthaven Mem Gardens
Culler, Edna Margaret	27 Jan 1914	12 Feb	15 Feb	St. Paul's, Jefferson
Rhoderick, Helen Elizabeth	4 Aug 1917	18 Apr	21 Apr	
Rhoderick, Earl James	27 Jan 1913	7 Jun	9 Jun	
Werntz, Florine	not given	6 Aug	10 Aug	
Bruchey, David Lee	29 Jan 1950	18 Aug	23 Aug	
Bartgis, William Henry	2 Dec 1909	27 Aug	30 Aug	
Cook, William	3 Jun 1915	1 Sep	3 Sep	
Hueting, Eutha Wachter	15 Oct 1921	22 Sep	27 Sep	
Slagle, Robert Sincell "Brue"	9 Jun 1926	19 Nov	22 Nov	
Albaugh, Ethel Thomas	19 Sep 1903	29 Nov	1 Dec	
Fahrney, Roenna	13 Apr 1911	7 Dec	12 Dec	St. Mary's Episcopal Cem

1995

Name	Born	Died	Buried	Notes
Richmond, Terry	13 Nov 1959	7 Feb	10 Feb	Evergreen, Gettysburg, PA
Eyler, Ella Roberta	15 Sep 1903	30 May	2 Jun	
Zimmerman, Harry "Bud"	10 Aug 1915	18 Jun	21 Jun	Libertytown
Zimmerman, Dorothy Jean	19 Feb 1948	13 Jul	16 Jul	Emmitsburg

Deaths and Burials of Evangelical Reformed
United Church of Christ
Frederick, Frederick County, Maryland

Name	Born	Died	Buried	Notes
Stull, G. Bernard	2 Dec 1908	25 Jul	28 Jul	
Lough, Margaret Eleanor	9 Apr 1906	18 Aug	21 Aug	
Bell, Luther Ellsworth	23 Jun 1897	11 Sep	14 Sep	
Esterly, Fannie Virginia	13 Nov 1915	2 Dec	6 Dec	
Bruchey, Richard Thomas	12 Feb 1911	1 Dec	6 Dec	
Tanner, Lydia Isabel	not given	11 Dec	?	Atchison, KS
Eppley, Jennie Mae	7 Dec 1916	18 Dec	29 Dec	
1996				
Darner, Alice	8 May 1908	28 Apr	2 May	Jefferson Ref Cem
Corby, Ursula Hutton	aged 88		7 Jul	memorial service
Starr, Earl J.	aged 76	15 Jun	20 Jul	memorial service
Thomas, Mildred Lee Wenner	9 May 1905	18 Aug	22 Aug	grave side service
McKeever, Sally Y.	aged 103	30 Aug	1 Sep	Gate of Heaven Cem
Graham, Richard Webster	22 Feb 1917	7 Sep	11 Sep	
Wachter, Helen G.	8 Mar 1898	20 Sep	23 Sep	
May, Lillian M.	15 Aug 1911	19 Nov	22 Nov	
Abbott, Julia E.	18 Nov 1904	8 Nov	5 Dec	
1997				
Wachter, Elmer E.	8 Aug 1923	14 Jan	17 Jan	
Martz, Harriet G.	9 Dec 1913	29 Jan	3 Feb	
Pilgram, Margaret Keiffer	24 Jan 1919	23 Feb	25 Feb	interment of cremains
Hueting, Darwin Albert	24 Feb 1917	28 Mar	31 Mar	
Dertzbaugh, Frank Marion	23 Feb 1918	23 Apr	26 Apr	
Welsch, Jean	15 Dec 1948	1 Jun	5 Jun	Scranton, PA
Cline, Marlowe Melvin	3 Apr 1917	1 Jul	7 Jul	Resthaven Mem Gardens
Barklow, Duane Dale	aged 35	9 Jul	14 Jul	cremains - memorial
Thomas, Hiram Irving	28 Jun 1909	18 Aug	22 Aug	
Boone, Alma Willetta	16 Dec 1911	6 Sep	9 Sep	
Best, Richard Houck	2 Sep 1917	16 Nov	19 Nov	
Clapp, Robert Earle, Jr.	28 Apr 1910	24 Nov	26 Nov	
Pease, Edward Leroy	25 Jun 1917	23 Dec	27 Dec	
1998				
Boyer, Betty R.	16 Nov 1922	6 Jan	8 Jan	
Lease, Ignatius E.	7 Jul 1904	8 Jan	12 Jan	
Ridgley, Alvie Lewis	13 Mar 1922	8 Jan	13 Jan	
Cutsail, J. Alfred	8 Jul 1916	1 Feb	5 Feb	
Lorentz, Gloria Mori	1 Sep 1923	1 Apr	4 Apr	
Abb, Irving A.	22 Jan 1904	3 May	6 May	
Graham, Velma Grace	26 Aug 1924	11 May	14 May	
Parker, Ronald Dixon	1946	7 Jun	11 Jun	
Biser, Reginald A.	1 Mar 1910	28 Jun	1 Jul	
Remsberg, Edith A.	24 Nov 1927	1 Jul	3 Jul	Resthaven Mem Gardens
Best, Denise Elaine	22 Feb 1948	1 Jul	6 Jul	
Mossburg, Paul Michael	7 Jun 1957	20 Aug	22 Aug	
Biser, Alma	27 Apr 1909	29 Aug	1 Sep	
Boyer, Mildred V.	18 Dec 1920	3 Sep	8 Sep	
Ranck, Dorothy	17 Sep 1900	4 Oct	6 Nov(sic)	Greenwood, Lancaster, PA
Culler, Roy C.	18 Sep 1927	9 Oct	16 Oct	
Schroeder, George Thomas	7 Mar 1911	11 Oct	17 Oct	

Deaths and Burials of Evangelical Reformed
United Church of Christ
Frederick, Frederick County, Maryland

Orndorff, Katherine	29 Jul 1905	16 Oct	19 Oct	
Remsberg, Paul D.	9 Oct 1928	2 Nov	5 Nov	Glade Cem, Walkersville
Stahler, Margaret	15 Mar 1913	26 Dec	30 Dec	Greenwood, Allentown, PA

1999

Collmus, Dwight	not given	26 Jan		body donated to science
Gardiner, Jesse	10 Jul 1980	23 Feb	27 Feb	cremated
Mills, Esker	4 Nov 1912	1 Mar	4 Mar	Monocacy Cem, Beallsville
Young, Julia Latham Derr	not given	11 Mar	9 Apr	
Shoemaker, Edna Freeman	2 Jul 1899	23 Apr	26 Apr	
Slayman, Margaretta Fromke	19 Feb 1904	24 Apr	27 Apr	
Keller, Lemuel David	2 Sep 1907	23 Apr	27 Apr	
Reutz, Jan Bowers	7 Nov 1945	27 Apr	3 May	
Gillis, Cecelia Mary	26 Mar 1916	12 Jun	16 Jun	Pine Grove, Mt. Airy
Oland, Agnes Lee	12 Aug 1917	13 Jul	15 Jul	

Deaths and Burials of Evangelical Reformed
United Church of Christ
Frederick, Frederick County, Maryland

INDEX

Abb
  Dorothy Marker, 60
  Irving A., 71
  John H., 37
Abbot
  Clementine B., 41
Abbott
  Eleanor D., 55
  George A., 20
  Henry H., 44
  Jane Elizabeth, 60
  Julia A., 26
  Julia E., 71
  Julia Hanshew, 40
Abrecht
  Ernest, 59
  Ernest A. "Buck", 65
  Eva Elizabeth, 69
  Katie L., 18
  Mattie C., 52
Ackerman
  Elizabeth, 13
Adam
  Valentine, 2
Adams
  Abraham, 9
  Abraham T., 15
  Fannie E. C., 30
  Lewis Bruner, 25
  Thomas Nelson, 26
Akers
  Abner, 23
  Addie May, 18
  Carrie Estelle, 16
  Charles Marion, 15
  Cora Celestia, 18
  infant, 11
  Mabel Irene, 16
  Rowena Houghton, 23
  Ruth Ann, 18
Albaugh
  Bessie Ann, 17
  Caroline B., 63
  Carrie Virginia, 39
  Charles Edward, 16
  Charles Richardson, 9
  Christian Thomas, 40
  Edwin, 70
  Effie A., 63
  Ethel Thomas, 70
  Eugene H., 45
  Frank Bertram, 14
  Frank Eugene, 31
  Franklin Henry, 30
  Harry Lancaster, 14
  Howard Moore, 63
  Justus Roy, 14
  Mary M., 54
  Matilda, 27
  Maurice, 10
  William V., 28
Albright
  Elizabeth, 18
Alexander
  Martha Mabel, 64
Allbach
  William, 4
Allison
  Comfrey M., 52
Allshesky
  Susan Agnes, 18
Althouse
  Mary Elizabeth, 63
Ami
  Charles, 5
Anders
  Aaron Repp, 40
  Alice Virginia, 34
  Caleb A., 19
  Jesse Brengle, 60
  Lillian R., 41
  Orra Washington, 45
  Sarah E. Danby, 59
Anderson
  infant, 20
  Laura V., 31
  Oliver P., 17
Angivine
  Hattie Sophia, 15
Angleberger
  Emma, 68
  Melvin Edgar, 58
  Preston David, 63
Apple
  Charlotte Elizabeth, 29
  Gertrude H., 54
  Joseph H., 52
  Mary R., 25
  Miriam Rankin, 53
Appleman
  Philip S., 41
Ardecker
  Lula Walling, 35
Ashbaugh
  Aquilla, 35
Aubert
  Harriett, 27
  James Bruner, 21
  Louis H., 21
Aurand
  Catharine, 1
  Elizabeth, 1
Babel
  J. Christian, 22
  Mary Jane, 26
Baer
  Raymond, 53
Baile
  Annie M., 22
Bailley
  George Franklin, 17
Bair
  Joseph D., 24
Baker
  Clifford Monroe, 67
  Clifford Monroe, Jr., 39
  Katie Amelia Zeigler, 64
  Laura Sophia, 35
  Leah, 19
  William McK., 57
  William McK., Jr., 52
Baltzel
  William, 1
Baltzell
  Anna Mary, 5
  Elizabeth H., 21
Balzel
  Jacob, 2
  John, 3
Bantz
  Algernon Sidney, 24
  Carrie B., 19
  Elizabeth, 5
  Gideon, 19

Deaths and Burials of Evangelical Reformed
United Church of Christ
Frederick, Frederick County, Maryland

Julia Ann, 27
Peter S., 33
William S., 22
Barklow
  Duane Dale, 71
Barrick
  Allen E., 12
  Daniel, 27
  Mary Catharine, 28
Bartgis
  Anna Young, 65
  Belle R., 44
  Frances Evans, 67
  James, 16
  Mary W., 45
  William, 41
  William Henry, 70
Bastian
  Mary Albertina, 8
Baugher
  Ann E., 10
Baumgardner
  John A., 68
Bayer
  Hubertus, 8
  Susan, 8
Beachley
  Silas Rex, 38
Beal
  William H., 39
Bealle
  William S., 26
Beatty
  Dorothy Souder, 68
Beck
  Elizabeth, 7
Beckebach
  Caspar, 2
  George Michael, 3
  John, 9
Beckenbaugh
  Sarah, 26
Becker
  Frantz, 8
  Magdalen, 5
  Philip, 7
Beisser
  Catharine, 1
Bell
  Ann Martha, 27
  Catharine Elizabeth, 19

Inna Lorine, 61
Jesse Elmer, Sr., 67
Luther Ellsworth, 71
Margaret, 23
William, 22
Beltz
  Rebecca, 1
Bender
  Eliza, 16
  Emma Amelia, 14
  Katie R. C., 26
Benedict
  Sus. Holtz, 7
Benner
  John E., 38
Bennett
  Catharine, 27
  Fannie L., 26
  Jane, 45
  Julia, 21
  William S., 26
Bentley
  Betty Jane, 68
Benton
  Ellen Elizabeth, 16
Bentz
  Alice V., 31
  Ann M., 23
  Catharine A., 13
  Catharine Elizabeth, 35
  Catharine M., 20
  Charles Edward, 31
  Edward, 47
  Henry, 20
  Horatio W., 23
  Jacob M., 23
  John, 3
  Lawrence E., 52
  Lillie May, 45
  Louis, 21
  Lydia, 25
  Mary E., 39
  Rebecca, 11
  Sophia Ann, 22
  William H., 51
Berg
  Anna Catharine, 1
  Catharine, 8
  Julianna, 4
  Willable, 7

Berger
  Ann, 22
  Elizabeth, 22
Bergesser
  Anna Barbara, 6
Beringer
  John Weiss, 7
Bernesius
  -------, 3
Berry
  Edith Bantz, 51
  Robert P., 66
Best
  Charles E. T., 53
  David, 13
  Denise Elaine, 71
  Eleanor H., 57
  Elizabeth, 23
  Frank Lawrence, 14
  John T., 28
  Margaret Johana, 24
  Martha L., 20
  Richard Houck, 71
Betzan
  John, 15
  Susan, 13
Bevan
  Sarah, 15
Biehl
  Gerald Monroe, 62
Bierly
  John William, 25
  Mary R., 25
Biggs
  Clara Virginia, 36
Billingslea
  Elizabeth, 30
Billy
  Anna M., 43
Birely
  Frances D., 42
  Laura V., 46
  Margaret Ellen, 43
  Martha E., 38
  Mary Rosanna, 59
  P. Henry C., 44
  William C., 47
Biser
  Alma, 71
  Catharine, 42
  Cora Banks, 54

Deaths and Burials of Evangelical Reformed
United Church of Christ
Frederick, Frederick County, Maryland

Ira E., 46
Jennie Thomas, 46
John Jacob, 36
Jonathan, 29
Reginald A., 71
Thaddeus McCauley, 33
Thaddeus McCauley, Jr., 67
Thomas Sherwood, 26
Bittinger
  Anne, 70
Black
  Barbara, 18
Blair
  Annie Elizabeth, 32
  Charles F. F., 50
  Henry, 34
Blumenauer
  Albert Leroy, 70
  Ann Catharine, 35
  Charles D., 43
  Dorothy M. Good, 61
  Edward K., Sr., 68
  George, 12, 34
  George Daniel, 69
  George W., 13
  Georgia, 46
  Gertrude Catharine, 25
  Grace, 13
  John N., 61
  John W. N., 39
  Julia Ann, 45, 64
  Margaret Ann, 35
  Mrs. Frederick, 19
  Nicholas, 15
  Nicholas J., 42
  Sallie Virginia, 65
Blumenouer
  Catharine, 23
  John N., 29
  Lewis Michael, 29
  Mary Katherine, 28
Blumenour
  Cordelia, 20
Bockins
  Eva, 6
Bockius
  Barbara, 2
Boetler
  Augustus L., 30
  Henry, 9
  Laura, 15

  Lucy, 23
  Ruth, 27
Bohley
  Sarah, 9
Boileau
  David Russell, 59
  Mary Elizabeth, 56
Boone
  Alma Willetta, 71
  Amy Sophia, 60
  Patrick Ray, 53
  Russell Loraine, 69
Bopst
  Edna Ruth, 20
  Joshua D., 36
Borckhardt
  Mary, 4
Boteler
  Margaret E., 42
  Silas, 35
Bowers
  James A., 53
  Alma Staley, 67
  Harriet M., 49
  Reine Grove, 61
Bowman
  John H., 51
Boyer
  Betty R., 71
  Emma Jane, 59
  Marion Davis, 61
  Mildred V., 71
  Rhoda Pauline, 69
  William Edward, Jr., 63
Bragonier
  Ann, 12
Brandenburg
  Amanda C., 40
  Jeannie May, 35
  Josiah Henry, 63
  Lewis H., 58
  Virginia Smith, 56
Brandenburger
  William Henry, 6
Brane
  Grandison G., 24
Brashears
  J. Henry, 13
Bready
  E. Tobias, 40

Breisz
  John, 8
  Mary Elizabeth, 7
Brengle
  B. F., 19
  Charles A., 10
  Charles E., 41
  Curtis, 13
  David M., 30
  Earle W., 26
  Eliza, 12
  Elizabeth, 42
  Florence C., 19
  Francis, 30
  Franklin Christ, 22
  George W., 37
  J. Nicholas, 29
  Jennie, 44
  Laura E., 32
  Lawrence J., 10
  Lewis A., 13
  Louisa, 19
  Maria, 23
  Nicholas John, 14
  Rebecca, 16
  Samuel Thomas, 47
  William Avery, 35
  William H., 19
Briedy
  John, 7
  Mary, 7, 8
Brine
  Christina, 5
Brish
  Annie V., 42
  Bessie J., 14
  Colegate Hanschew, 59
  Devillo Colgate, 55
  Harry H., 49
  J. Murray, 50
  Louis Edgar, 37
  Margaret S., 36
  Minnie H., 53
  William H., 14
  William W., 52
Brommett
  Ellen, 11
Brooks
  Eleanor, 13
  Harriet A., 29

Deaths and Burials of Evangelical Reformed
United Church of Christ
Frederick, Frederick County, Maryland

Brown
   Elizabeth Rebecca, 60
   Grace Virginia, 69
   James W., 50
   Jeannette, 33
   Lillian Olive, 66
   William Victor, 34
Brownlow
   Edna Estelle, 61
Bruchey
   Anna Mary, 59
   David Lee, 70
   Richard A., 50
   Richard T., Jr., 50
   Richard Thomas, 71
Bruder
   Henry, 2
Bruestle
   Mildred B., 70
Bruner
   Ann R., 19
   Ann Sophia, 22
   Elizabeth, 22
   George H., 25
   John H., 13
   Joshua, 21
   Lewis, 26
   Susan M., 12
Brunner
   Ann Sophia, 32
   Daniel, 2
   Elizabeth, 5
   Franklin E., 49
   George H., 40
   Henry, 17
   Isaac, 13
   James, 10
   Margaret J., 32
   Mary, 43
   Mary E., 18
   Milton O., 47
   Peter, 10
   Stephan, 2
   Susan, 16
   Theodore, 42
Brust
   Ann Florence, 26
   August F., 41
   August Trago, 60
   Carl Edward, 39
   Caroline B., 21
   Clara, 43
   Conrad, 32
   John Albert, 23
   John N., 48
   Louisa, 29
   Margaret N., 67
   Millard M., 61
   Robert Marion, 64
   Virginia, 17
Bucheimer
   Caroline E., 40
Buchheimer
   Catherine, 45
Buckey
   Edward, 43
   Isabella W., 13
   Mary R., 52
   William A., 53
   William Augustus, 37
Buckingham
   Hattye B., 53
Bucky
   Anna Mary, 8
   Math., 5
Buell
   Carlotta Pratt, 64
Buesing
   Mattie, 56
Bugos
   Robert Joseph, Sr., 68
Burger
   Anna M., 53
   Anna Margaretha, 31
   Anna Rosetta, 58
   Bertha Mae Wilhide, 63
   Catharine Irene, 32
   Charles E., 48
   Charles Henry, Sr., 55
   Elsie Marie, 22
   Ethel May, 22
   Lewis Bennett, 55
   Marcia M., 57
   Mary Smith, 61
   Nettie Irene, 41
   William A., 39
   William H., 32
   William Leslie, 62
   William Leslie, Jr., 68
Burke
   Jacob L., 19
Burkett
   Doris Virginia, 54
   Harry Vernon, Jr., 63
   Harry Vernon, Sr., 64
   Hester, 38
   Margaret M., 65
Burkhart
   Ezra C. J., 28
   Virginia, 10
Burucker
   John S., 27
Bürucker
   Sophia, 22
Bushong
   Drusilla H., 55
Bussard
   Clarence Lease, 70
   Walter Luther, 67
Butcher
   Baby Girl, 53
Butler
   Gennette E., 18
   Pearl, 41
Buxton
   Basil, 25
   Mary, 27
   Ruth Mussetta, 33
Byerly
   Catharine Elizabeth, 17
   Grace, 20
   Jacob, 15
   John, 21
   John Davis, 35
Cagle
   Mary Ellen, 60
Cain
   Flossie Elliott, 57
   Rose Main, 60
Campbell
   James, 7
   Mr., 5
Cample
   Mr., 7
Cannon
   Charles Burton, 61
Carey
   Ruth Shipley, 69
Carlin
   Ann Cecelia, 36
   Frank B., 15

Deaths and Burials of Evangelical Reformed
United Church of Christ
Frederick, Frederick County, Maryland

Carlson
    Dr. C. Edwin, Sr., 67
Carmack
    Salome, 12
Carnahan
    Barbara Ann, 39
Carny
    Mary, 8
Carson
    Alonzo, 21
Carter
    Franklynn Louise, 65
Carty
    Hellie Walker, 61
    Joseph W. L., 58
    Minnie D., 48
Cashour
    Charles W. F., 44
    Fannie Kemp, 40
    Kate H., 21
    Martha, 23
Cassin
    John, 30
    Nannie A., 18
Castle
    Georgianna M., 25
    Harriet D., 38
    John Jarboe, 16
    Thomas F., 38
Chambers
    Clara, 39
    George M., 43
Chaney
    Sarah Elizabeth, 36
Chatman
    Harry, 53
Chenkmeyer
    Mary Elizabeth, 6
Chew
    Adam Richard, 35
    Benjamin Franklin, 33
    Charles Edward, 39
    Charles Thomas Smith, 15
    Christine Roelke, 34
    Ida L., 42
    Joseph F., 25
    Mary Ann, 19
    Mary Jane, 32
    Maud May, 16
    Samuel, 34
    Thomas, 45

    William, 21
Chipley
    Edward B., 47
    Katherine, 46
Christ
    Jacob, 4
    Michael, 2
    Philip, 2
Clabaugh
    Bradley, 30
Clapp
    Bessie M., 55
    Robert Douglass, 32
    Robert Earle, Jr., 71
    Robert Earle, Sr., 61
Clark
    Dorothy O'Neal, 62
Clarke
    Charles S., 39
    Gen. James C., 29
    Susan, 29
    Wendell B., 39
Clary
    Adelaide M., 54
Clem
    Henrietta, 15
    Rhoda, 14
Cline
    Marlowe Melvin, 71
Clingan
    Frank G., 39
    Harry William, 14
    Lewis S., 38
    Maria, 24
    Marie L., 46
    Minerva Elizabeth, 38
Coblentz
    Edward Franklin, 26
    John Harman Ezra, 56
    Mary Helen, 69
    Oscar B., 52
Cockrell
    Edward W., Sr., 69
Cole
    Ida M., 45
    Julia Ann, 30
    Lamartine, 23
    Williiam G., 11
Colleflower
    Sarah C. B., 36

Colliflower
    Ann E., 24
    William F., 15
Collmus
    Dwight, 72
Collum
    Sanie, 12
Comfort
    Lucy L., 31
    Rev. H. I., 19
    Willian H., 51
    Willie Anna, 37
Condon
    Albert W., 48
Conner
    infant, 28
    Paul Stauffer, 30
Conrad
    Benice Ethel, 25
    Catherine A., 45
Conrod
    David Russell, 26
    John Robert, 17
Cook
    William, 70
Coons
    Harold Niver, 63
Corbet
    Charles Frank, 58
Corby
    Ursula Hutton, 71
Corey
    Paris, 12
Corun
    Myra Corine, 59
Cost
    Cyrus, 38
    Lloyd Albert, 38
Cover
    Susan, 11
    Thomas Franklin, 18
Cox
    Mary Rebekah Z., 63
Cramer
    Anna Barbara, 21
    Bertram S., 51
    Charles Edward, 61
    Dani Elizabeth, 61
    Dorothy R., 68
    Ella K., 50
    Ethan A., 29

Deaths and Burials of Evangelical Reformed
United Church of Christ
Frederick, Frederick County, Maryland

Ethan Alan, 64
Ezra Lewis, 28
Franklin Edward, 29
George L., 40
George T., 56
George W., 23
Harry M., 49
Henrietta, 25, 50
James Houck, 56
Katherine Loretta, 33
Kirk Donald, Sr., 66
Leslie, 55
Lucy C., 65
Lula Ent, 35
Lulu Ent, 45
Mary O., 21
Mary Reynolds, 21
Noah E., 44
Ruth B. Thomas, 60
Susan P., 46
Susan R., 28
William McClellan, 13
Crampton
   Claude Leroy, 62
   Dora Crone, 62
   Dorothy Marie, 69
   Luther Boyer, Sr., 60
Creed
   Marion, 68
Cronice
   Isaac, 17
   John Calvin, 32
Cronise
   Adele, 52
   Charles L., 34
   Clara Adelia, 21
   E. Margaretta, 39
   John F., 38
   Joseph, 25
   Margaret R., 24
Crum
   Catharine, 2
   Elizabeth, 3
   Emory C., 44
   Ethel Myers, 65
   Evelyn Virginia Gaver, 69
   Henry H., 40
   Irving H., 46
   Isaac, 11
   Jennie Phoebe, 59
   Kathryn Powles, 60

LeRoy Irvin "Pete", Jr., 68
Mary, 7
Pheobe A., 52
Raymond Rosen, 32
Susan, 6, 23
William, 4, 7
Crummitt
   Edna Mae, 66
   William E., Jr., 68
Crutchley
   Milton Clay, 42
Culler
   Albert Franklin, 56
   Annie E., 46
   Bertha Roderick, 53
   Edna Margaret, 70
   Ella Elizabeth, 64
   Harold Albert, 67
   John J., 43
   Kathryn Rebecca, 55
   Ralph Edward, 61
   Roy C., 71
   Thomas P., 53
Custer
   Margaret E., 23
Cutsail
   Horace Edgar, 55
   Inda Trapnell, 53
   J. Alfred, 71
   Susan, 12
Dabler
   Anna Susan, 7
Daniels
   Mary Elizabeth, 54
Danner
   Cicero, 19
   Thomas A., 27
Darner
   Alice, 71
Daub
   Barbara, 5
   George, 7
   Susan, 5
Davenport
   Sadie Pauline, 60
Davis
   Annie E., 22
   Arthur Eugene, 15
   Emily Ruth Myers, 61
   Frank T., 25
   Isabelle, 38

J. Francis, 43
Lucinda, 35
Mary Louise, 70
Rose Elizabeth, 32
Walter J., 59
William D., 11
Dean
   John, 5
Degrange
   Anna Mary, 9
   Daniel W. F., 30
Dehaven
   Andrew, 3
Dehoff
   Annie M., 19
Deisz
   Michael, 2
   Nicholas, 8
Delaplaine
   Eleanor Frances, 48
   Janie Quynn, 65
   William T., 60
   William T., III, 50
Delashmutt
   Alvida Browning, 62
   Alvida T., 47
   Arthur, 47
   Charlotte T., 58
   Edward T. H., 31
   Elias, 42
   Elias E., 16
   Mildred L., 50
   Sarah Elizabeth, 61
   Susan R., 33
   William R., 49
Delauder
   Bruce, 70
   Helen Eppley, 69
deLillo
   Virginia Carty, 67
Derner
   Anna Mary, 4
Derr
   Adelaide, 20
   Aida Grace, 53
   Alice V., 41
   Anna H., 33
   Betty Irene Klein, 62
   Catharine, 16
   Charles W., 16
   Daniel, 16

Deaths and Burials of Evangelical Reformed
United Church of Christ
Frederick, Frederick County, Maryland

Dr. John S., 57
Elizabeth, 16
Emma J., 13
Eugene L., 39
Ezra Z., 46
Fannie G., 18
Florence M., 47
Frances, 48
Frances V., 27
George C., 27
Hiram A., 42
Jeannette Rose Humphreys, 59
John A., 64
John S., Jr., 64
Julia L., 47
Mary Lugenbeel, 31
R. Earl, 52
Will May, 62
William H., 26
Dertzbaugh
  Carol Ann, 54
  Catharine E., 32
  Charles J., 46
  Cornelia, 47
  Emma I., 44
  Frank M., Sr., 64
  Frank Marion, 71
  George William, 12
  Harry B, 57
  John W., 27
  Katherine K., 57
  Lewis R., 64
  Mabel P., 58
  William Henry, 40
  William Lee, 38
Dertzebach
  Mary Magdalen, 3
Detrick
  Charles L., 10
DeVine
  Earl W., 38
Dibuss
  Elizabeth, 5
Diehl
  Frederick W. Edward, 32
  Laura G., 44
  Philip August, 16
  Roland Lee, 55
Dieterich
  Anna Mary, 58

Dill
  Joshua Ada, 36
  Lavinia Virginia, 36
  Mary Ellen, 50
Dinterman
  Lester Clarence, 68
Dittmar
  Maud W., 54
Dixon
  Ann Mary, 37
  Clarence B., 49
  Cora Virginia, 16
  Julia A. C., 25
  Laura Virginia, 23
  Louis Franklin, 53
  Matilda Rebecca, 17
  Sophia, 16
  Thomas O., 24
Doerr
  Anna Catharine, 2
  George, 4
Doffler
  George, 2
Dofler
  Anna Catharine, 3
Doll
  Anna Mary, 7
  Arthur Holtz, 63
  Charles D., 46
  Charlotte Wolff, 33
  Florence I., 48
  Hannah Margaret, 35
  Jacob, 2
  John L., 25
  Mary Lucretia, 36
  Melville Ezra, 35
  Samuel Valentine, 37
Dorsey
  Arthur, 8
  Barbara L., 68
  Elizabeth, 21
  George Alfred, 64
  Russell L., 66
Downing
  Robert L., 50
Draxel
  George Frederick, 6
Driszler
  William, 9
Droneburg
  Ethel H., 47

  Gloria Jean, 59
  Guy Herbert, 60
  John Thomas, Sr., 70
  Joseph, 25
Dudrow
  Joseph S., 26
Dull
  Henry G., 28
Dunn
  Charles McFarland, 56
Dunott
  Catharine Forne, 34
  Elizabeth, 38
Dutrow
  Ada R., 46
  Adele Nelson, 34
  Dr. Howard V., 57
  Elizabeth Lee, 65
  Grayson David, 59
  Joseph L., 11
  Kate, 28
  Katharine E., 66
  Katie L., 50
  Mary Irene, 59
  Mrs. Howard, 57
  Reba Mary, 59
  Rena Grace, 62
  Richard, 69
  Richard C., 65
  Richard S. J., 43
  Ruth Patterson, 64
  Samuel, 31
  Samuel P., 44
  Virgie May, 56
Duval
  William H. E., 25
Duvall
  Albert Justus, 12
  Belle E., 44
  Christiana R., 11
  James E., 43
  Margaret A., 48
  Mary R., 20
  Rosa V., 45
  T. Guy, 56
  Walter Harry, 61
  William T., 49
Duwall
  Mrs., 7
Dyer
  Katye R., 56

Deaths and Burials of Evangelical Reformed
United Church of Christ
Frederick, Frederick County, Maryland

Madaline A., 68
Rachel, 11
Ebbert
    Gustavus Adolph, 19
    John, 25
Eberhard
    Eva Elizabeth, 7
Eberly
    John Adam, 5
Ebert
    Elizabeth, 21
    Elmer Clarence, 14
    Fannie L., 15
    Frank Hill, 14
    M. Lucretia, 11
    Mary Elizabeth, 37
    Octavius A., 19
    Samuel B., 13
Eckhart
    Anna Margaret, 2
Eckstein
    C. Thomas, 48
    Charles Louis, 15
    Elizabeth, 22
Eder
    Mary, 6
Edmonds
    Eyster W., 40
    Honor Burnice, 23
    Loritto Pauline, 23
    no first name, 43
Ehbrecht
    Elizabeth, 9
Ehhalt
    Elizabeth, 8
Ehly
    Elizabeth, 4
Eichelberger
    Francis Marion, 45
    Lily C., 44
    Mrs. Grayson, 17
Eicholtz
    Mildred Catherine S., 64
Elias
    George, 7
Elkin
    Bertha V. Jones Smith, 69
    Walter LeRoy, 62
Ellis
    Bertha May, 28
    Daniel, 15
    Mary, 10
Elton
    Ellen Reid, 67
Ely
    Ella, 17
    James Arthur Garfield, 15
Engel
    Catharine, 8
Engelbrecht
    Bessie E., 38
Engels
    Mary Catharine, 4
    Peter, 4
England
    Emma Newman, 61
    Nathan J., 54
Englar
    Alice, 21
    Myrtle Marie, 60
Engle
    Calvin L., 46
    Ezra M., 15
    Gladys W., 47
    Lewis Henry, 70
    Lewis Henry, Sr., 39
    Mary Elizabeth, 60
    Roanna Stull, 38
Englebrecht
    Elizabeth, 23
    George J., 22
English
    James J., 13
    Jane R., 26
Epley
    infant, 13
Eppley
    Anna Mary, 58
    Francis, Jr., 51
    Jennie Mae, 71
    Samuel, 57
    Samuel Herbert, 60
    Virgie Grace, 55
Epps
    infant twins, 50
Eschbach
    Mary Susan, 35, 47
Eschleman
    Orpha Susan Showe, 69
Eshleman
    Elmer I., 68
Esterly
    Ann Rebecca, 15
    Fannie Virginia, 71
Esworthy
    Robert H., 53
Etzler
    Norma Wachter, 65
    Walter Paul, 54
Eyler
    Benjamin Franklin, 39
    Ella Roberta, 70
    Harry Edmond, 29
    Mary Ella, 63
Eyster
    Rev. Dr. Frederick Daniel, 58
Fahrney
    J. Welty, 53
    Mary Ella, 56
    Roenna, 70
Falconer
    Carol, 49
    Dale, 47
    Howard H., 64
    Lucille W., 64
Farrin
    Anne, 7
Faubel
    Elizabeth, 1
    Mary, 9
Fauble
    David, 17
    John, 15
    Laurence, 54
    Margaret R., 16
    Mary Ann, 22
    Mattie E., 19
Feaga
    Charles, 55
    Emma M., 46
    Ida F., 38
    John J., 47
    Lillie Hester, 17
    Lydia A., 50
    Susanna Maria, 12
Feete
    Hattie Ella Elizabeth, 28
    Kate A., 37
    William C., 39
Fehling
    Henry, 5, 6

Deaths and Burials of Evangelical Reformed
United Church of Christ
Frederick, Frederick County, Maryland

Fesperman
  Rev. Frank L., 64
Fetteroff
  Nannie G. Shriner, 54
Filby
  Mollie I., 66
Finney
  Robert Eugene, 12
Finny
  Julia Lee, 16
Firestone
  Rebecca, 35
Fisher
  Herman J., 24
  James, 52
  James Roger, 58
  Mary E., 48
  Mary Starr, 65
  Moses, 44
Fitez
  William Edward, 29
Flautt
  Gilmore R., 52
  Jennie Catherine, 44
  Lewis C., 43
  Walter, 63
Fleck
  Elizabeth, 4
Fleming
  Harriet, 21
  J. Alfred, 24
  Mary A., 21
  Nicholas Hughes, 34
  William W., 41
Flemming
  Joseph P., 10
  Matilda, 18
Fletcher
  James Wood, 57
Floyd
  Addie Winona, 41
Fogle
  Lillian F., 57
  Rhoda Mary, 69
Foland
  Anna M. E., 28
  Anne Elizabeth, 34
  Delia Martha, 35
  Edward, 36
  Helen Gertrude, 34
  John Michael, 53

Folsom
  Ann Elizabeth, 24
Forberger
  Katherine Gally, 34
Foreman
  Maurice Eugene, 54
Forney
  Abbe Rebecca, 18
  Ada Estelle, 56
  Arthur J., 66
  Samuel J., 36
  Walter Samuel, 60
Forrest
  Lucretia A., 22
  Minnie J., 15
  Sarah C., 25
  William McComas, 24
Fout
  Ann Rebecca, 32
  Charles, 39
  Elizabeth, 27
  John H., 16
  Margaret Elizabeth, 70
  Susan, 16
Fox
  Charles H. O., 23
  Harry O., 17
  Jacob, 10
  Sarah Catharine, 30
Fravel
  Rev. Noah H., 59
Frazier
  Clifford A., 41
  Matilda E., 30
  Stanley F., 45
Friederich
  Jacob, 8
Fritchey
  Martha, 13
Frosh
  Jacob, 1
Frushour
  Harold U., 60
  Katherine, 69
Fry
  Austin Thomas, 61
  Harold Edward, 62
Fuchs
  Margaret, 8
  Mary Julianna, 2

Gainer
  Giles Oliver, 67
Gaither
  Helen Engle, 63
  Millard David, 54
Galbraith
  G. L., 13
Gallagher
  Thelma Elizabeth, 65
Gannon
  Carol Lynn, 66
  Charles Franklin, 55
  Charlotte Ellen, 38
  Cora Irene, 62
  Lewis B., 50
  Lewis B. "Goose", 64
Garber
  Isabella, 40
  Lillian Jane, 53
  Solomon, 34
  Virgie J., 30
Gardiner
  Henry Tabler, 34
  Jesse, 72
Gardner
  Ethel V., 67
  Olga Lee, 39
  Samuel F., Jr., 67
Garrett
  Ella J., 44
  Franklin Edward, 59
  Harry Norman, 37
  Helen D., 61
  Sadie May, 62
  Willard N., 48, 66
  William D., 53
Gaver
  Pierce Horatio, 63
Gebhardt
  Peter, 2
Geisbert
  Calvin M., Jr., 66
  Nannie M., 41
  Ruth Perry, 69
  Samuel Stephen, 54
  William H., 44
Geisey
  Franklin K., 57
Geisinger
  Charlotte, 43

Deaths and Burials of Evangelical Reformed
United Church of Christ
Frederick, Frederick County, Maryland

Geisser
   Melchior, 7
Gephart
   Charles William, 51
   Louisa Virginia, 37
Gerecht
   Anna, 5
Gerlach
   Charlotte, 2
   Christian, 40
   Dora E., 41
   Mary Dora, 33
   Mollie A. G., 10
Germayer
   Elizabeth, 3
Gesser
   Frank Edward, 16
Getzedanner
   Ann, 3
   Catharine, 6, 9
   George, 3, 9
   Jacob, 3
   Samuel, 8
Getzendanner
   Ann E., 15
   Annie G. H., 40
   Catharine A., 16
   Christian, 17
   Edward T., 25
   F. Marion, 32
   John, 1
   John J., 10
   Joseph, 5
   Laura V., 36
   Margaret A., 18
   Martha V., 12
   Mary E., 23
   Mary Elizabeth, 42
   Michael, 7
   Milton Eugene, 33
Gilbert
   Charles, 40
   George Mortimer, 11
   Harry C., 10
   infant, 12
   Sarah A., 22
   Stewart Meredith, 25
   William L., 51
Gillis
   Cecelia Mary, 72

Gills
   Peter, 3
Gilman
   Anna, 51
Gilmet
   James Kerr, 53
Ginger
   Frank, 12
Githerman
   Helen M., 70
Gittinger
   A. Kate, 47
   Anna M. C., 23
   Anna R., 18
   Annie Laurie, 10
   Catharine, 26
   Clara M., 41
   Daisy Irene, 28
   Edward A., 41
   Edward A., Jr., 47
   Eleanor Hannah, 35
   Emelia A., 51
   Eugene Irving, 23
   Evelyn Virginia, 34
   George, 18
   George M., 50
   George Metzger, 37
   George W., 37
   Henry Mehrl, 40
   J. Albert, 45
   James Cyrus, 22
   John Edward, 31
   Laura C., 41
   Maggie, 41
   Maria Louisa, 10
   Mary Catharine, 37
   Mary Eleanor, 36
   Mary M., 29
   Samuel J., 45
   Zach. James, 30
Glaze
   Anne M., 48
   Elizabeth, 16
   Margaret Ann, 22
   Maria V., 19
   Nevin Hamilton, 18
   Samuel F., 24
   Sarah A., 33
   Worthington O., 46
Glessner
   Alice Adora, 52

   George W., 26
   Harry F., 46
   Harry L., 30
   James Schley, 36
   Jennie L., 29
   Jesse Marie, 27
   Mary Ellen, 31
   Millard M., 44
   Richard Ross, 40
   Thomas K. H., 35
   William, 18
   William T., 30
Gombe
   David, 2
Gomber
   John, 36
   Margaret F., 50
Gonso
   Susan, 17
   William H., 18
Gonzo
   Ariana, 48
Goodmanson
   Mary, 20
Gosnell
   Helen Rebecca Crum, 70
   Herbert E., 52
   Orie L., 59
   Roy R., Sr., 62
Gottseelig
   -------, 1
Gottselig
   Widow, 6
Graf
   Elizabeth, 9
Grafft
   Margaret, 5
Graham
   Richard Webster, 71
   Roy Webster, 62
   Vallie Q., 63
   Velma Grace, 71
Grahe
   John A., 51
Graser
   Annie E., 57
   Florence Elizabeth, 51
   John William, 53
Grazer
   Mary M., 35

Deaths and Burials of Evangelical Reformed
United Church of Christ
Frederick, Frederick County, Maryland

Greeman
  Cora Diller, 57
Green
  Howard Lee, 32
Greenwald
  Isaac W., 55
Griffith
  Raymond W., 69
Grim
  Ann Elizabeth, 3
Grindle
  Josie, 52
Gring
  Emma A., 44
  Vida Rebecca, 17
  William Aug., 20
Griny
  Naomi Catherine, 60
Grove
  Clayton Eugene, 18
  Cora, 53
  David, 30
  George W., 25
  Jemima B., 31
  John D., 36
  Maria, 9
  Philip Mathias, 62
  Reuben D., 12
  Vallie R., 47
Grumbine
  Cora M., 50
  Eleanor May, 21
  Lester R., 40
  Marshall S., 52
  Stewart Daniel, 31
Gunneau
  Betty Ruth, 67
Gurlach
  Ann Catharine, 18
  Christian, 17
  Elizabeth, 17
  Jacob, 14
  Lewis Clarence, 17
Hafer
  Ada M., 29
  Catherine, 33
  Ella V., 48
  Samuel, 32
Haffner
  Jane, 64

Häfner
  Elizabeth, 5
Hafner
  Henrietta, 18
  Julius F., 20
  Margaret, 4
  Sallie Blanch, 20
Hagan
  Charles McCauley, 36
  Margaret, 12
  Rose Catharine, 41
Hagerman
  Henry, 37
Hahn
  Catherine Virginia, 69
  Charles Earl, 60
  Charles S., 46
  Elmira Staley, 65
  Rose Agnes, 53
  Walter J., 66
  Walter Staley, 56
Hall
  Harry C., 44
Hallar
  Annie C., 41
  Eliza A., 44
  Eliza M., 17
  Grant L., 19
  Jessie, 51
  Nicholas T., 20
  Percy William, 18
  Silas L., 19
Haller
  Ann L., 10
  Anna M., 42
  Charles Edgar, 37
  Charles Edward, 31
  Charles W., 24
  Eliza M., 18
  Harry N., 31
  Harry T., 31
  Lucretia W., 50
  Margaret, 20
  Mary Genivieve, 29
  Nannie L., 26
  Nellie May, 24
  Robert Edward, 28
  Ruth Elizabeth, 58
  Ruth Evaline Lewis, 46
  Thomas Johnson, 30
  William, 35

  William Snyder, 38
  William Bernard, 20
Hamilton
  Raymond, 59
Hammell
  Frederick Paul, 70
Hammond
  Charles Leonard, 67
  Fannie O., 51
Handshu
  Mary Catharine, 4
Hane
  Barbara Jane, 63
  Meredith, 70
  Ruth Ellen, 67
Hankey
  John Henry, Sr., 53
  Myrtle B., 45
Hanschew
  Catharine S., 22
  Fritchie, 31
  Harriet C., 16
  Martha, 31
Hansen
  Helen Virginia, 68
Hanshew
  Daniel S., 39
  Eleanor, 43
  Emily, 36
  George Edward, 27
  H. Lee, 50
Harbaugh
  Helen Frances, 63
  Roland W., 67
Harding
  Clara R., 44
  Everest C., 48
Hardt
  Sarah J., 24
Hargate
  Clara Emma, 13
  Douglass Harry, 11
  Harry M., 13
  Margaret Ann S., 15
Hargett
  Anna M., 38
  Charles N., 30
  Douglass H., 32
  Earlston L., 39
  Emma M., 44
  Eva Rebecca, 43

Deaths and Burials of Evangelical Reformed
United Church of Christ
Frederick, Frederick County, Maryland

Harry, 57
Maud Riggs, 63
Richard Schaeffer, 63
Harley
  Anna Elizabeth, 35
  G. W. Tauman, 21
  Minnie E., 41
Harner
  Lola R., 45
Harp
  Bessie Dell Zentz, 59
  Maud Elizabeth, 56
Harrington
  Harvey A., 62
  Harvey A., Sr., 48
  Mary Lila, 64
  Robert C., 66
  Ruth Dixon, 69
Harris
  Claire M., 57
  S. Fenton, 65
Harrison
  James Victor, 45
Harriss
  Charles G. Knill, 60
  Ruth Noami Hagan, 58
Harry
  Mary Catharine, 40
  William H., 37
Hartman
  Christian, 2
Harwetel
  Emma J., 40
Hauck
  Henry, 8
  Jacob, 3
  Peter, 7
Hauer
  Ann Catharine, 17
  Anna Belle, 47
  Bradley Fritchey, 28
  Charles Nicholas, 28
  Fritchie H., 46
  George N., 10
  George Nicholas, 28
  Jennie May, 27
  John Henry, 31
  Lewis, 8
  Lucretia, 25
  Mary L., 34
  Nicholas, 8

  Nicholas Daniel, 34
  Susan, 27
  Susan Elizabeth, 43
Haugh
  Charles Thomas, 70
  Margaret E., 61
Hausser
  Mary, 3
Hawman
  Margaret, 10
Hawthorne
  Margaret Virginia, 38
Head
  Catharine, 10
  Mary, 28
Heagey
  Jesse F. R., 45
Heck
  Elizabeth, 22
  Hiram Webster, 54
  John, 12
Heckathorne
  Alice, 24
Hedge
  Charles, 6
Hedges
  Amanda S., 26
  Catharine, 12
  Christina, 8
  Cora Blanche, 30
  Elizabeth, 7
  George, 6
  Helen Hendrix, 29
  John A., 11
  Lycurgus E., 22
  Mary E., 24
  Mary Elizabeth, 68
Heffner
  Heidi Lynn, 66
  Maggie E., 45
  Vernon Eugene, Jr., 62
  William, 53
Heim
  Anna, 21
Heiner
  Dr. Peter E., 52
Heintz
  Elizabeth, 3
  William, 4
Heitshue
  Susan, 18

Hemp
  Ann Margaret, 4
  Balthasar, 4
  M. Magdalen, 6
Henderson
  Mildred K., 64
Herbert
  Henry H., 62
  Margaret E., 42
  Nora Ethel, 66
  Sylvia R., 65
Hergesheimer
  Sophia, 28
Herget
  Catharine, 1
Herm
  Anna Mary, 2
Herman
  Thomas Jefferson, 20
Hermann
  Charles M., 39
  Edward A. G., 63
  Elizabeth, 49
  Emma B., 49
Herndon
  Annie, 26
Herring
  Caroline, 18
  Henry, 8
Hershperger
  Bettie, 15
Hersperger
  Ella Kea, 67
  Helen Scholl, 35
  John Benjamin, 16
  Tilghman T., 30
  W. Scholl, 48
Herwig
  Clara E., 54
  Henry August, 56
  Theodore, 49
Hess
  Elizabeth A., 59
Hight
  Caroline, 26
Higinbotham
  Frank Weadon, 67
Hildebrand
  Anna Mary, 8
  Blanche Estelle, 61
  Frank T., 24

Deaths and Burials of Evangelical Reformed United Church of Christ
Frederick, Frederick County, Maryland

George, 39
Hattie May, 45
Isadora V., 39
John, 10
L. Cecilia, 57
Laura V., 29
Lewis N., 28
Lewis Robert, 11
Lydia, 10
Lydia A., 20
Hildebrandt
  Jerome, 4
Hilt
  George Thomas, 12
Hiltner
  Christian, 46
Himbury
  J. B., 11
Himes
  Charles Hamilton, 59
Hinkle
  George, 18
Hintzig
  Elizabeth, 4
Hiteshew
  Alick, 13
  Capt. Philip L., 33
  Elizabeth, 11
  Fannie, 30
  Floy, 49
  Martans E., 41
Hobbs
  Charles S., 15
  James Fuller, 60
  John Robert, 37
  Mary Margaret, 12
  Paul Philip, 59
Hocker
  Lena Dodd, 65
  Robert P., 63
Hodge
  Mary L. V., 14
Hodges
  Elmer Ernest, 68
  Katherine, 63
Hodgson
  Mary Condon, 69
Hoffman
  Daniel, 3
  Mary, 2
  William, 1

Hoffmaster
  Emma Margaret, 67
  Meredith R., 63
Hoffmeier
  Edgar F., 61
  Hester LeVan, 65
  Rev. Henry W., 24
Hoke
  Mildred R., 62
Holbruner
  Edward E., 32
  Florence, 31
  Lewis C., 26
  Thomas, 32
  Thomas M., 17
Holbrunner
  Philip Sheridan, 32
Hollinger
  Harold Clyde, 69
Hollis
  Milton Ross, 58
  Nellie Beatrice Thomas, 63
Holter
  Charles R., 56
  Lawrence Fahrney, 65
Holtz
  Agnes, 17
  Anna Mary, 6
  Benedict, 3
  Blantina, 2
  Carrie C., 52
  Clarence C., 47
  Harriet Victoria, 36
  Jacob, 8
  John, 8, 24
  Mary Catharine, 13
Hood
  James M., 24
  Margaret Elizabeth Scholl, 34
Hooper
  Elmer B., 33
  George William, 57
  James, 33
  Mary Elizabeth, 22
  Mary Simmons, 51
  Sarah Blanche, 40
  William R., 68
Hoover
  Lillian R., 50

Hopwood
  William, 43
Horine
  Effie Mahoney, 55
  Luther M., 48
  Malinda, 43
  Willard "Bill", 65
Hoskins
  George, 13
  Mary A., 20
Hossler
  Frances L. Sutton, 63
Houck
  Catharine, 17
  Eleanor W., 60
  Elizabeth, 29
  Elizabeth G., 29
  Ella V., 41
  Emma Bentz, 34
  Ezra, 12, 44
  Henry, 19
  Henry J., 23
  James, 29
  Laura V., 30
  Margaret Elizabeth, 54
  Mary E., 15
  Matilda Simmons, 29
  Nan Johnson, 53
  Samuel, 11
  William, 29
  William H., 52
  William Harry, 62
  William James, 25
Howard
  Charles Sotheron, 33
  Charles Sothoron, 47
  Charles T. F., 31
  Donald Fleming, 59
  Francis D., 50
  Mary Louise, 34
Huber
  Elizabeth, 6
  Gertrude E., 23
  Leonhard, 8
  Mary, 6
Hueting
  Darwin Albert, 71
  Eric Scott, 53
  Eutha Wachter, 70
Huffer
  Alice E., 68

Deaths and Burials of Evangelical Reformed
United Church of Christ
Frederick, Frederick County, Maryland

* Charles Jacob, 66
Hughes
  Elinor Markey, 62
Hull
  Benjamin, 6
  John, 5
  Naomi, 5
Humphreys
  Anna Mary, 70
  Jesse B., 64
Hunkel
  Ann Catharine, 35
Hydorn
  Beryl Bidwell, 70
  Walter Rutherford, 65
Hyssong
  Michael A., 57
Jacobs
  Catharine S., 35
  Mary Virginia, 61
Jaeger
  Robert Edward, 60
  Robert Frederick, 63
James
  Catharine, 22
  Lewis Franklin, Sr., 53
  Sadie F., 59
Jantz
  Catharine, 4
  George, 1
Jarboe
  Margaret, 10
Jauzy
  Peter, 6
Jendes
  John, 9
Jenkins
  Amanda J., 26
Jenks
  William D., 11
Johnson
  Albert L., 51
  Alice Camille, 34
  Catharine N., 63
  Eugene Augustus, 37
  Ida M., 57
  Manzilla, 44
  Mary, 23
  Michael G., Sr., 68
Jones
  Clara M. C., 58
  Daisy Sophia, 14
  Edgar, 16
  Ethel Florence, 26
  Grace Virginia, 68
  Jane Rice, 46
  Martha M., 32
  Mary C., 12
Josz
  Anna Barbara, 2
  Mary, 9
Jung
  Anna Mary, 9
  Henry, 5
  Jacob, 8
Kantner
  George, 16
Kast
  Mary, 2
Kauffman
  Fannie M., 28
  George Walter, 25
Kaufman
  Ann R. C., 45
  George L., 40
  Jesse D., 43
  Mary Catharine, 20
  Violet, 40
  Willian Conrad, 55
Keedy
  Edwin R., 57
Keefer
  A. Kemp, 48
  Alice V., 31
  Ann Elizabeth, 24
  Annie M., 29
  Charles H., 11
  Edward P., 42
  Elizabeth, 11
  Francis M., 47
  Frederick, 18
  George, 22
  Harry Clay, 29
  Katharine S., 48
  Margaret Quynn, 37
Keeney
  Minerva Alice, 37
Kefauver
  Anna Lee, 58
  George Harvey, 36
  H. Edward, 39
  H. Milton, 41
  Harry Joshua, 54
  Laura V., 46
  Lillie S., 66
  Manville E., 56
  Ruth Willard, 62
Keith
  Charles T., 48
  Ellen B., 45
Keller
  Charles Henry, 24
  Clinton E., 65
  Elizabeth, 2
  John, 3, 6
  Lemuel David, 72
  Mary Margaret, 9
  Nellie Irene, 58
Kelletts
  Deborah, 14
Kemp
  Alvin Edward, 49
  Annie Nixdorff, 54
  C. Edwin, 46
  C. Thomas, 44
  Caroline Ethel Troxell, 61
  Charles Edwin, 32
  Charles Wesley, 11
  Columbia A., 27
  Effie May, 9
  Eleanor, 23
  Florence V., 48
  Julian E., 43
  Lewis George, 34
  Mary Ellen, 53
  Mary Matilda, 48
  Robert A., 49
  Robert A., II, 47
  Robert Birely, 23
  Ruanah R., 26
  Sarah Margaret Miller, 34
Kempf
  Elizabeth, 1
  Henry, 6-8
  Jacob, 4
  John, 1
Kennedy
  Ann Elizabeth, 10
  Daniel Francis, 32
  David, 16
  Mary A., 34
Kenyon
  Firm Clark, 56

Deaths and Burials of Evangelical Reformed
United Church of Christ
Frederick, Frederick County, Maryland

Keplinger
  Elizabeth, 7
Kern
  Elizabeth, 5
  Michael, 4
Kessler
  Ann E., 27
  George Bernhardt, 3
Kidd
  Grace Darlene, 37
Kiefer
  Ann Sophia, 34
Kieffer
  J. Spangler, 58
  Henri L. G., D.D., 60
  Margaret R., 54
Killian
  William H., 18
Kina
  Edith May, 22
King
  Columbus Roe, 17
  George Joseph, 36
  Grace G., 68
Kinsey
  Gwynn X., 66
  Robert P., 50
  Virgie Mae Crum, 61
Kintz
  Harry, 69
Klee
  Henry, 3
Klein
  John, 3
Kleinard
  Mary, 2
Kline
  Frederick, 11
  Harry, 54
  Lewis L., 59
Knauf
  Adam, 4, 7
Knauff
  Alcinda, 37
  Annie M., 27
  Charles E., 35
  Deborah M., 13
  George H., 29
Kneck
  Frederick B., 49

Knight
  Margaret L., 31
Knipple
  Jesse Franklin, 37
Knock
  Annie E., 28
  Charles F., 44
  Hannah T., 38
  Henry Frederick, 26
  James H., 40
  Pauline Zentz, 64
  William H., 36
Knodle
  Christiana L., 25
Koblenz
  John, 8
Koester
  Christina L., 19
  Mary, 15
Kohlenberg
  Edythe A., 48
Kohlenburg
  Rachel, 25
Kolb
  Betty R., 49
  Caroline V., 47
  David, 39
  David Denmead, 39
  Helen T., 65
  Mary Alice, 69
  Robert L., 58
  William Aug., 25
Koontz
  Fannie Myrtle, 22
  Frances A. V., 20
  Mary E., 33
Kramer
  Elizabeth, 6
  Esra, 6
  George, 6
  Lewis, 4, 7
  Ralph William, 22
Krantz
  Alice Elizabeth, 39
  Bessie C., 62
  Catharine Elizabeth, 13, 28
  Charles E., 48
  Edward C., 41
  Frederick, 21
  Frederick B., 49
  Laura V., 25

  Laura Virginia, 39
  Margaret Ann, 45
  Mary Catharine, 28
  Mary Martha, 42
  Nannie E., 45
  Ruth Helena, 41
  William H., 44
Krass
  Henry, 2
Kreh
  Florence Bertha, 24
  Louis F., 20
  William Jennings B., 26
Krepps
  Mary Agnes, 58
Krise
  Buchanan K., 21
Krum
  William, 2
Kuhn
  Charles Bertram, 65
  Della M., 52
  Elizabeth, 22
  Nellie Fleming, 37
  Sarah Rebecca, 63
Kuhns
  Catharine, 4
  Theobald, 4
Kunkel
  Aurelia Frances, 35
  Mary C., 41
  Philip Baker, 27
Lafeber
  Mary Salome, 7
Lakin
  Charlotte E., 59
  Daniel F., 21
  Francis Thomas, 34
  Mary F., 43
Lamar
  Caroline J., 12
  Kate, 18
  Robert G., 17
Lambert
  Georgette, 49
  Jacob J., 49
  John George, 31
  Mary A. R., 31
Lambright
  Annie E., 33

Deaths and Burials of Evangelical Reformed
United Church of Christ
Frederick, Frederick County, Maryland

Lampe
   Ada Elizabeth, 57
   Allen R., 46
   Anna Thomas, 60
   Caroline A., 11
   Christian L. C., 46
   Elizabeth Ross, 34
   Emma Augusta, 17
   Henry R., 46
   J. Henry, 33
   Mary Christine, 58
   Mary E., 48
   Nettie Lee, 44
   Rev. Lewis Theodore, 31
   William E., 53
Landers
   Washington F., 33
Lang
   Abraham, 6
   John Frederick, 63
Lansdale
   Annis Elizabeth, 51
Larkin
   Ella, 42
   Rose, 51
Lavanture
   Charlotte, 32
Lawson
   Charles A., 46
Layman
   Mary J., 36
Lease
   Amelia, 12
   Ella, 13
   George W., 13
   Ignatius E., 71
   infant, 10
   Jane Elizabeth, 13
   Luther Edward, 34
   Mahala, 28
   Minnie Elsa, 55
   Noah L., 14
Lebherz
   Grace Marie Worman, 58
Lehmer
   Philip, 2
Lehr
   Daniel, 9
Leilich
   Catharine E., 38

Lerch
   Charles, 15
   Frank, 38
   Henry, 20
   Ruth Naomi, 22
Leschhorn
   Ann Dorothy, 6
   John, 9
   Paul, 9
Leshhorn
   John, 2
LeVan
   Dr. Charles Wilburforce, 56
Levi
   Mary Magdalen, 7
Levig
   Mary Ann Barbara, 6
Levy
   Charles Perry, 34
   Roberta, 52
Lewis
   Alida A., 54
Lidie
   Fannie M., 23
   Mary Ann, 14
Lieblich
   Elizabeth, 5
Lindsay
   Laura J., 21
Lingenfelder
   Charles, 4
Lininger
   Fannie Elizabeth, 55
Link
   Addie V., 35
Linton
   Elizabeth, 34
   Joseph, 33
   Mary C., 57
   Mrs., 6
   Sarah Elizabeth, 32
Lipps
   Annie P., 45
   Bessie, 16
   Catharine, 26
   Catharine E., 24
   Eleanor M., 45
   Ethel, 20
   Fannie L. C., 47
   George Lewis, 43
   John A. C., 40

   Mary Elenora, 61
Little
   Marion C., 52
   Sarah Louise, 40
Lochner
   Mary Stone, 60
Lodge
   Frederic George, 69
Loehr
   Polly, 12
Loh
   Elizabeth, 1
   George Frederick, 1
Long
   Ralph Alvin, 29
   Roberta Carty, 66
Lorentz
   Catharine J., 28
   George Egbert, 62
   Gloria Mori, 71
Lough
   Charles W., 60
   Eleanor Fisher, 59
   George W., 28
   Katharine Virginia, 34
   Margaret A., 42
   Margaret Eleanor, 71
   Uriah A., 43
Lovejoy
   Sara C., 44
Lukhorst
   Lucas, 7
Lull
   Mary Esther, 52
Lumpkin
   Dorothy E., 66
Lutz
   George Edward, 12
Lyon
   Susanna M., 29
MacGill
   Charles, 41
MacGregor
   Margaret E., 55
MacKenzie
   C. E. Bernard, 65
   Kathryne Elizabeth, 64
Mackie
   Mrs., 7
Madery
   Jacob, 1

Deaths and Burials of Evangelical Reformed
United Church of Christ
Frederick, Frederick County, Maryland

Mades
  Daniel, 5
Magill
  Dr. Lloyd T., 32
Mahoney
  Mary Elizabeth, 56
Main
  Anna C., 39
  Annie Elizabeth, 26
  Catharine, 40
  Clara Z., 45
  Clinton E., 45
  David, 10
  David M., 28
  Eleanor S., 27
  Eli R., 15
  Elizabeth, 28
  Elizabeth Ellen, 24
  Ella S., 50
  Ethel Riene, 22
  Frederick W., 30
  John Lewis, 23
  Joshua Thomas, 36
  Lewis C., 34
  Lewis H., 30
  Mary Ann Magdalen, 21
  Mary R., 11
  Sophia B., 40
  William, 14
Mainhart
  Ann Elizabeth, 30
  Caroline, 38
Maisel
  Edward F., 66
  Ruth Thomas, 62
Mantz
  Ann U., 30
  Anna Lee, 54
  Annie Rebecca, 47
  Caspar, 2
  Charles, 13
  E. Peter, 42
  Emanuel, 18
  Frank, 54
  Henry, 47
  Leda Catherine, 64
  Lucy J., 36
  Lucy Jane, 12
  Maggie, 40
  Manzella Malinda, 31
  Mary Ann, 46

  Medora W., 38
  Mrs. William E., 27
  Nettie K. V., 55
  William, 19
Maples
  Annie Kemp, 66
  Margaret Quynn, 70
  Sam Wynne, Sr., 62
Marble
  Jesse H., 12
  Julia Ann B., 18
Marcks
  Miriam Lark, 58
Marendt
  Ella Mae, 67
  Robert Paul, 59
Markell
  George, 27
  Louis, 19, 26
  Mary A. E., 19
  Mary Kate, 45
  Sophia, 30
Markey
  Bettie, 14
  David J., 24
  Richard Simpson, 35
Marks
  Gladys Clerene, 67
  James Daniel, Sr., 60
Marman
  Sallie M., 41
Marsh
  Alonzo Pierce, 31
  Martha W., 45
  Nevelyn Kenneth, 30
Marshall
  William, 5
Martin
  Hallie, 54
  William C., 46
Martz
  Amy Elmira, 62
  Daisie Rebecca, 12
  Eleanor Catharine, 63
  Emma E., 49
  George David, 63
  Grace Susan, 62
  Harriet G., 71
  Hattie Irene, 65
  Helen Whitmore, 69
  John H., 46

  John W., Sr., 61
  Joseph D., 56
  Lewis Joseph, 69
  Mary, 52
  Phoebe C., 39
  Ruth E., 52
Mateny
  Elmer E., 46
  George W., 21
  Guy Clinton, 67
  Helen, 66
  May Ida Rebecca, 49
  Nellie May, 37
  Thomas Clinton, 36
Mathers
  Helen Ramsburgh, 67
  Hellen, 64
  William T., 57
May
  Carl C., 66
  Ernest William, Sr., 67
  Lillian M., 71
  Valentine, 3
Maybury
  Joseph, 9
Maynard
  Dr. James H., 24
  Lewis S., 13
McCardell
  A. LeRoy, 51
  Adrian C., 44
  Albert N., 59
  Alforetta R., 40
  Edgar S., 52
  Eleanor Clingan, 61
  Helen L., 46
  Pauline R., 60
McClane
  William, 4
McCormick
  Rosebelle Biser, 70
McDaniel
  Jane E., 32
  William A., 11
McDannel
  Elizabeth P., 43
  Mary Elizabeth, 23
McDannell
  Abraham Sowers, 26
McDevitt
  Christiana Louisa, 28

Deaths and Burials of Evangelical Reformed
United Church of Christ
Frederick, Frederick County, Maryland

Guy H., 50
McDonald
  Frank P., 27
  Georgiana Bostick, 37
  Harriett M., 31
  Mary Hauer, 18
McKeever
  Sally Y., 71
McKenzie
  James Fenwick, 36
McKinsey
  -------, 6
McLain
  Harry Oscar, 29
McLane
  Georgianna, 55
  Helen Stull, 30
  Margaret J., 39
  Robert C., 49
  Rufus Almer, 28
McMan
  Anna Mary, 23
McMurry
  Luther Vincent, 59
Mealey
  Florence H. E., 52
  Isaiah, 27
Mealy
  Rosanna Rebekah, 32
Measel
  Annie B., 10
  Willie Zacharias, 14
Measell
  Annie Belle, 57
  Catharine Elizabeth, 25
  Charles Thomas, 30
  Christianna, 26
  Clarence C., 16
  Edward B., 55
  Ellen R., 12
  Harry Victor, 14
  Susan R., 45
Mehrling
  Barbara, 28
  Elizabeth, 60
  Florence Katie, 11
  J. Maurice, 21
  John, 36
  Nellie Louisa, 22
  Susan, 26

Meisner
  Naomi, 33
Meister
  Anna Christie, 18
  Fred, 41
Mercer
  Mary Ellen, 54
Merckel
  Elizabeth, 9
Mergardt
  Charlotte, 31
Mertz
  George, 4
Metcalf
  Catharine, 32
Metz
  Ann Phoebe, 14
Metzger
  Christina, 9
  George, 14
  Sarah, 15
Meyer
  David, 4
  Elizabeth Matilda, 28
  Jacob, 4
  Mary J., 20
Michael
  Charles Irving, 60
  Charles L., 18
  Elizabeth M., 59
  John L., 41
  Mary Custard, 34
  William C., III, 53
Mike
  Miriam M., 41
Miller
  Ann G., 57
  Bernice, 16
  Birdie May, 58
  C. Henry, 33
  Cecelia K., 49
  Charles Marion, 24
  Christina, 36
  Conrad, 8
  Edgar Lambert, 10
  Edgar Little, 20
  Edith, 61
  Elizabeth Rebekah, 24
  Emma June, 44
  Ethel, 15
  Ettie, 22

  Fannie, 19
  Fannie Stull, 41
  Franklin D., 55
  George P., 39
  Ira L., 50
  John Q., 57
  Joseph Getzendanner, 37
  Linol Matthias, 31
  Marion Stull, 55
  Mary E., 26
  Mary Eva, 9
  Mary G., 41, 43
  Mary Irene, 24
  Nellie May, 56
  Nina, 27
  Oscar Henry, Jr., 40
  Paul Biser, 23
  Roberta, 46
  Simon S., 40
  William H., 27
  Zoe Irene, 14
Mills
  Esker, 72
  James Benjamin, 63
Milyard
  John W., 49
  Mary Ann, 57
  Minnie L., 58
  Robert Biehl, 36
Minor
  Lillian Belle, 56
  A. Maude, 58
Misner
  Martha Linton, 35
Miss
  Edward W., 60
Moberly
  Daisy E., 12
  Sallie S., 49
Moffatt
  Bertie, 27
Mohler
  Bettie, 12
  Mary Catharine, 15
Molesworth
  John William, III, 68
  Winifred M., 66
Montgomery
  Irma Lucille, 50
  Julia A., 66

Deaths and Burials of Evangelical Reformed
United Church of Christ
Frederick, Frederick County, Maryland

Moore
  Daisie Marie, 16
Morgan
  George, 4
  John W., 66
  Lenora Rudy, 66
  Michael, 1
Morgenstern
  John Engelbert, 6
  Widow, 7
Mori
  Eric Hans, Sr., 62
Morse
  Barbara, 29
Morton
  Roberta Dixon, 60
  William Dare, 68
Mossburg
  F. Doris L., 68
  Paul Michael, 71
Motter
  Gabe M., 42
  Guy Kunkel, Sr., 58
  Janet C. W., 43
  John C., 42
  Lewis E., 50
  Margaret R., 67
  Samuel Lewis, 55
  Samuel Lewis, Jr., 45
  Serene K., 44
Mowry
  Virgie M., 52
Mull
  Alice Virginia, 57
  Florence G. M., 45
Murphy
  A. Kate, 48
  Annie Mary, 36
  Cora Margaret, 58
  James D., 33
  James G., 44
  Philomen S., 12
  Richard W., 49
Murray
  Lee, 61
  Roscoe Covert, 62
Mussetter
  Emma Catharine, 14
Myer
  George Ernest, 56
  John, 31

Myers
  Arthur V., 68
  Catharine, 21
  Drew Allen, 66
  Edward Irvin, Sr., 65
  F. Ross, 68
  Garrison E., 49
  George W., 32
  George Worthington, 62
  Julia Roelkey, 65
  Kate Estelle, 33
  Sally Pearl Delphey, 66
  Thomas F., 48
Neidig
  Emma Barbara, 37
  Grace, 66
  William C., 49
Neighbours
  Anna L, 47
  Fleet R., 43
  Mary F., 68
Neihoff
  Susan, 11
Newman
  Francis Jacob, 56
  Grace Viola, 60
  Helen Elizabeth, 61
  Jacob M., 42
  Kate, 28
  Mary H., 54
Nicholas
  Eliza M., 25
Nichols
  C. Randolph, 17
  Catharine, 16
  Edward, 20
  Elizabeth, 13
  J. Lewis B., 30
  Jacob, 5
Nicodemus
  Anna Elizabeth, 59
  Robert Fulton, Sr., 58
Nicthman
  Jennie I., 40
Niecky
  Johanna Elenor, 2
Niner
  Daisy Victoria, 56
Nitzler
  Ellen Achey, 37

Noell
  Edna May Wolff, 60
  J. Guyon, 54
Norris
  Frank Albertis, 13
  Hallie V., 59
Notnagle
  Carrie B., 32
  Helen L., 40
  James Leonard, 61
  Mary Dittmar, 62
Null
  Carroll F., 50
  Joseph Arthur, 38, 63
  Joseph M., 39
  Kenneth Ruthford, 36
  Lillian Regina, 49
  Lillie Regina, 60
  Maggie S., 48
  Roy Calvin, 53
Nusbaum
  Catharine, 21
  Lydia Ann, 31
  Susan J., 31
Nuss
  M. Emory, 23
Nusz
  Emory G., 58
  Margaret Young, 69
  Mary V., 53
Obenderfer
  A. Augustus, 28
  Elizabeth, 44
  Eva Margretta, 42
  Frederick W., 47
  J. William, 52
  Nellie M., 48
  Susan Virginia, 35
Oberland
  Harry K., 31
Oberlander
  Louis, 19
  Roger J., 29
  William C., 64
Oberlauder
  Emma C., 49
  Frederick A., 52
  Lucille S., 53
Odell
  Hazel Harrison, 38

Deaths and Burials of Evangelical Reformed
United Church of Christ
Frederick, Frederick County, Maryland

Oden
  Bertha May, 66
Ogle
  George, 1
Oland
  Agnes Lee, 72
  Lucy Belle, 25
Ordeman
  Charlotte Sinn, 62
  Dr. G. Frederick, 56
Orndorff
  Katherine, 72
Ott
  child, 3
  Christina, 5
  John, 12
  Mary A., 12
  Thomas, 19
  William H., 25
Otto
  Frederick, 7
  William, 7
O'Donnell
  Mary S., 52
Page
  Calvin, 15
Paisley
  Fannie Hiteshew, 37
  Florence E., 67
  George A., 43
  Pauline R. V., 41
  Ray A., 67
  Wililetta, 49
Paltzer
  Catharine, 1
Pampell
  Grace Irene, 11
Parker
  Ronald Dixon, 71
Parkinson
  Lillie M., 50
Parsons
  Laura J., 33
Patterson
  Caroline H., 39
  Charles Edison, 10
Pearre
  Albert L., 50
  Nannie R., 49
  William Walter, 28

Pease
  Edward Leroy, 71
  Helen R., 70
  Sarah Dorothy, 65
Peck
  David B., 34
  Margaret C., 50
Percival
  Charles F., 18
Perry
  Katherine Mehrling, 51
  Louise Ent, 65
Peters
  Charles Albert, 13
Pettingall
  Eliza, 19
  Robert, 22
  Sarah, 41
Phebus
  Charles Motter, 28
  Daisy M., 62
  Ethel M., 65
  Harry Edgar, 63
  Larry Francis, 58
Phillips
  Mary I., 54
Phleeger
  S. Laura, 45
Picking
  Barbara, 19
  Lottie, 26
  Thomas, 17
Pilgram
  Margaret Keiffer, 71
Plunkett
  Thomas Martin, 52
Poley
  Mary, 3
Pompell
  Frederick, 10
Poole
  Adam, 21
  Anna Mary, 33
  George W., 51
  Hanson, 27
  Jane, 44
  John, 21
  MacKenzie Autumn, 69
  Meleko, 68
Price
  Edwin Reynolds, 59

  John E., 11
  Lillian Elizabeth Motter, 62
Pyfer
  Philip, 14
Quynn
  Allen G., 10
  Allen George, 62
  Casper, 44
  Charles W., 50
  D. Hauer, 48
  Emily C., 45
  Harriet, 21
  Harriet Eleanor, 43
  John T., 20
  Katherine S., 51
  Kitty S., 49
  Mary M., 25
  Rachel Motter, 67
Radcliff
  James Ralph, 62
  Myrtle M. Zentz, 62
Ragan
  Annie, 40
Ramsburg
  Alice E., 26
  Alice May, 63
  Allen Miller, 25
  Catharine, 19
  Catharine A. R., 14
  Clara Maynard, 18
  Clara Sophia, 59
  Cornelia V., 42
  Dennis C., 27
  Dennis Casper, 43
  Donald Fitez, 58
  Drusilla H., 32
  Edward F., 11
  Elias B., 46
  Elias B., Jr., 66
  Ethel V., 50
  Franklin W., 22
  Guy R., 50
  Harry Bernard, 24
  Henry B., 27
  J. Richard, 61
  James Maynard, 21
  Jessie T., 54
  John, 10
  John H. L., 43
  Josiah A., 42
  Lester E., 53

Deaths and Burials of Evangelical Reformed
United Church of Christ
Frederick, Frederick County, Maryland

Lillian V., 61
Loraine Kemp, 36
Lulu Teresa, 63
Margaret J., 21
Marion, 10
Mary A., 19
Mary Florence, 63
Mehrl H., Sr., 58
Mildred A., 67
Peter, 11
Roy Hench, 60
Russell Upton, 56
Samuel Maynard, 20
Walter J., 48
William H., 13, 42
Ramsburgh
  Henry B., 51
  John S., 40
  Lucie T., 49
  Mabel E., 67
  Mary Catharine, 45
  S. Laura, 47
Ranck
  Dorothy, 71
  James B., Sr., 69
Raver
  Rose A., 51
Ray
  infant, 20
  Maurice Butler, 63
  Nannie E., 12
Rebert
  Naomi S., 48
Redmond
  Lewis Benjamin, 37
Reeb
  Adam, 3
Reed
  Ethel May, 22
  George Kenneth, 24
Reeder
  Carmey Emmonds, 68
Reel
  Catharine M., 29
Reese
  Carrie May, 27
  Catharine, 17
  Charles S., 18
  Franklin B., 58
  Louisa, 15

Reihm
  Ann Catharine, 6
Reinhard
  Catherine, 1
Reischwein
  Catharine, 8
Reitenauer
  A., 1
Reitmay
  William, 4
Remsberg
  Dorothy Maude Derr, 65
  Edith A., 71
  Emory C., 44
  Emory Earl, 68
  George P., 26
  Gerald Grosh, 67
  Margaret E., 30
  Mary G., 27
  Paul D., 72
  Stephen, 1
  Viola Thomas, 53
Remsburg
  Albert Irving, 35
  Charles J., 47
  Fannie R., 39
Remsburgh
  Courtnay May, 36
Remsperger
  Elizabeth, 2
  Isaac, 9
Renner
  Ada May, 32
  Andrew, 35
  Clara Elizabeth, 19
  Florence Emma, 14
  William A., 14
Reutz
  Jan Bowers, 72
Reynolds
  Mangen Stanhope, 34
Rhoades
  Gideon Mantz, 33
Rhoads
  Austin E., 49
  George Oscar, 55
  Grace A., 46
  Grace L., 52
  Harriet E., 43
  Mary Evelyn, 68
  Mildred Thomas, 70

  Vernon M., 48
Rhoderick
  E. Franklin, 25
  Earl James, 70
  Hannah Beatrice, 41
  Helen Elizabeth, 70
  Lillian A., 64
  Mahlon, 13
  Mary A., 27
  Melvin Dorsey, 41
  Rebecca, 46
  Thomas Bernard, 40
  Wayne A., 70
  Williiam E., 14
Rhodes
  Ann Minerva, 23
  Calvin A., 23
  Cornelia A., 31
  Elizabeth Jane, 34
  Frances T., 31
  George Philip, 29
  John, 17
  Margaret E., 47
  Orion Bernard, 25
  Susan S., 20
  Vernon Maynard, Jr., 32
  William H., 23
Rice
  Ada May, 20
  Albert Thomas, 28
  Anna Othetta, 42
  Barbara J., 26
  C. Frank, 37
  Charles M., 11
  Dr. Louis A., 67
  Eliza Jane, 35
  Elizabeth M., 68
  Harry Dennis, 9
  Henrietta, 16
  Lewis A., 69
  Lewis R., 48
  Lillian Catharine, 33
  Margaret, 27
  Marion C., 40
  Mary Elizabeth, 21
  Mary Louisa, 21
  Pauline G., 62
  Perry, 17
  Ruger Rollins, 55
  Susan Addie, 42
  Susan Font, 35

Deaths and Burials of Evangelical Reformed
United Church of Christ
Frederick, Frederick County, Maryland

Susan Matilda, 30
Thomas P., 45
William Henry, 23
William P., 2
Richards
   Minnie D., 45
   Wallace W., 43
Richmond
   Terry, 70
Richter
   Catharine, 7
Rickert
   Rebecca, 7
Ricketts
   Blanche, 25
   Daniel Zachariah, 18
   Harry Edward, 31
   Mary Nannie T., 10
Riddlemoser
   Alice E., 38
   Lewis W., 35
Ridgley
   Alvie Lewis, 71
   John H., 18
Ried
   Dorothy, 5
   Elizabeth, 9
   John, Sr., 6
Riehl
   Addie Louisa, 56
   Charles Jacob, 33
   Margaret, 8
Riggs
   Mary Hobbs, 20
   Susan A., 47
Rigney
   John H., 22
   Medora, 13
Rimer
   William Oscar, 52
Rinehart
   F. Evelyn, 68
   Rev. Bernard O., 60
   Russell J., 67
Ritschy
   Drue Hekiner Lipps, 34
Ritter
   Alfred, 33
   Edward Allen, 18
Robinson
   Elizabeth A., 14

James William, 38
Roderick
   Samuel Hallar, 37
Roderuck
   Roscoe E., 70
Rodgers
   Josephine, 29
Rodrick
   Margaret G., 48
Roelke
   Arthur Grover, 37
   Ginevera, 43
   Margaret Walker, 14
   Monroe Franklin, 16
Roelkey
   Celeste M., 51
   Elroy L., 43
   John W., 41
   Margaret, 57
Roelky
   Charles C. A., 29
   John, 26
   Lena, 30
   Lucy M., 10
   Mary Jane, 26
   Sarah A., 29
   Susannah, 26
Rogers
   Katherine Kieffer, 55
Rohr
   Daniel, 8, 15
   John, 4
   Margaret, 4
   Susan, 15
Rohrbach
   Ida R., 49
   Jacob, 51
   Martin N., 28
Rohrback
   Alice, 67
   Alice M., 55
   Allen, 30
   Ellen M., 13
   Gustavus M., 58
Romero
   Dorothy Ruth, 66
Rosenberger
   Frank Authur, 59
Roth
   Amos A., 20
   Barbara, 3

Donald A., 15
Dorothy Abrecht, 65
Jacob, 3
John, 1
Laura J., 35
Margaret, 1
Routzahn
   Albert B., 45
   Charles Emory, 37
   Charles O., 57
   Erma Lavada, 67
   Ida L., 49
   Laura G., 53
Rowe
   Julia Elaine, 43
   Margaret Lucretia, 36
   Mary Ellen, 32
   Mary L., 51
   Nettie Adelia, 32
   William C., 36
Rudy
   Annie E., 39
Ruland
   Kate, 31
Runckel
   Susanna Catharine Malvina, 9
Runkles
   Frances P., 47
Rupley
   Frederick William, 9
Rupp
   Ida J., 54
Sanders
   Lucy Estelle Derr, 62
   Thomas Lee, 54
Santee
   Charles A., 46
   Rebecca R., 51
Saunders
   Sophia E., 43
   Vina Grace, 55
   Walter Warren, 56
Schaefer
   Adam, 3, 5
   Anna, 52
   Edna M., 57
   Elizabeth, 3, 6
   Jacob, 2, 5
   John, 5
   Julianna, 6

Deaths and Burials of Evangelical Reformed
United Church of Christ
Frederick, Frederick County, Maryland

Magdalen, 7
Margaret, 5
Peter, 3
Susan, 6
Schaeffer
   Charles Edward, 34
   David Luther, 29
   Eliza Ann, 34
   Long Rhoads, 37
   Paul, 33
Schaffer
   Jonathan A., 26
Schamly
   Anna Mary, 8
Schaun
   Sarah, 8
Schell
   George E., 45
   Grace Elizabeth, 32
   John Edward, Jr., 64
   Mathias B., 36
   Serena Motter, 64
Schenkmayer
   John, 5
Schindler
   Cordelia E., 25
Schley
   Agnes, 52
   Ann Rebecca, 25
   Capt. Trench, 10
   Fairfax M. D., 29
   James M., 16
   Jennie Schley, 39
   John Reading, 38
   Lewis Fairfax, 22
   Lewis H., 11
   Lewis Weltzheimer, 11
   Lilian Kunkle, 59
   Mary Margaret, 68
   Rebecca Steiner, 22
   Sophia M., 21
   Steiner, 33
   Thomas, 1
Schmid
   Elsie W., 70
Schmidt
   Cora May, 51
   Jacob H., 48
   Laura R., 47
   Mazie C., 45

Schmit
   Agnes, 2
   Jacob, 5
Schneider
   A. Margaret, 7
   Conrad, 3
   Jacob, 8
   John, 8
   Susan, 1
Schnook
   Daniel, 7
Schober
   Anna, 8
Scholl
   Dennis, 16
   Louis V., 14
   Margaret, 17
Schreyer
   Elizabeth, 7
Schroeder
   Frederick, 17
   George Adam, 35
   George T., Sr., 60
   George Thomas, 71
   Lucy Medora, 55
   Mary A., 44
Schryack
   Eva Mary, 4
Schultz
   Caroline Amelia, 35
   Elizabeth, 2
   George, 10
   George J., 23
   Mary H., 39
   Theodore, 16
Schwartz
   John, 1
   John Valentine, 8
Seaman
   Margaret A., 19
Sechrist
   Sarah, 11
Seibert
   Anna Sophia, 12
Sellard
   Lillian G., 54
Shafer
   Abbie Maria, 58
   Earlston F., 50, 52
   Emma, 68
   Grace Virginia, 70

   James Elliott, Sr., 67
   Lester Ezra, 55
   Peter, 15
Shaffer
   Nellie R., 54
Shank
   Edward H., 18
Shankle
   Lola Alberta, 55
   Philip H., 37
Shapro
   Evelyn Grose, 64
   Frank M., 51
Shatto
   Paul Frederick, 66
Shaw
   Breckinridge, 44
   Joseph M., 50
   Mary Ruthella W., 65
   Pfc. Joseph M., 52
Shawbaker
   Annie M., 20
   Jacob Garfield, 64
   Jessie June, 64
Shawen
   Christianna, 13
   Grafton, 15
   Sarah A., 32
Shearer
   Amelia, 28
   Florence M., 49
   George David, 70
   Walter E., 48
Shelton
   John Edward, 37
   Lewis Donovan, 34
Shephard
   Eleanor, 25
Sheppard
   Charles Guy, Sr., 64
   Emma R., 36
   John K., 25
Sherer
   Daniel, 25
Shindler
   Iona J., 20
Shipley
   Blanche Catharine, 14
   Carrie D., 59
   Charles F., 52
   Charles Nimrod, 14

Deaths and Burials of Evangelical Reformed
United Church of Christ
Frederick, Frederick County, Maryland

Ernest H., 59
Francis Key, 14
Franklin Nathan, 61
Frederick, 15
G. Raymond, 65
George William, 56
J. Franklin, 44
M. Mae, 52
Mary Ketler, 35
Ruth Johanna, 67
Shober
  Henry, 2
Shoemaker
  Edna Freeman, 72
  Henry R., Sr., 65
Shook
  Barbara Ann, 32
  Edgar Haifew, 9
  Lewis A., 34
  Susan R., 19
  Susanna, 19
Shriner
  Alice Eader, 35
  Edward A., 28
  Edward D., Sr., 44
  Edward Derr, Jr., 65
  George W. B., 27
  Mary Phoebe, 26
  Virginia Musser, 61
Shriver
  Louisa E., 10
Shue
  Sarah, 14
  Viola Gwendolyn, 66
Shull
  Grayson F., 51
Shultz
  Catharine M., 20
  Mary Margaret, 32
  Sophia, 10
Sier
  Edith Gertrude, 55
  Jesse Benson, 52
Silance
  J. Vernon, 38
Simmon
  Balthasar, 7
  Margaret, 8
Simmons
  Capt. Charles E., 24
  George A., 33

Georgiana, 35
Louis, 46
Martha Elizabeth, 51
Martha M., 27
S. Cyrus, 11
Sinn
  C. Edward, 47
  Eva B., 46
  Mary E., 50
  Myra Elizabeth, 67
  Parmelia F., 17
  Walter E., 57
Slaethe
  Peter, 5
Slagle
  George C., Sr., 59
  Margaret Gertrude B., 63
  Mary Pearl "Patsy", 63
  Robert Sincell "Brue", 70
Slayman
  Charles Henry, Jr., 68
  Margaretta Fromke, 72
Sleber
  Anthony Jay, Jr., 68
Slick
  George F., 38
Smith
  Barbara Ann, 53
  Caroline Ross, 21
  Christiana, 29
  Daniel, 11
  Donald R., 39
  Dorothy E., 55
  Dorsey H., 20
  Eleanor, 17
  Emma, 48
  F. Lester, 50
  George, 5
  George Edward, 42
  Granville M., 49
  Jeannette J. S., 15
  John, 20
  Katie, 11
  Margaret Louisa, 20
  Mary, 18
  Mary A., 26
  Mary Ann Rebecca, 38
  Mary E. Bruner, 17
  Mildred Biser, 67
  Raymond, 49
  William Henry, 60

William S., 43
Snook
  Hallie F., 50
Snyder
  Christian Hegler, 34
  E. Jane, 27
  Elizabeth, 29
  Lucy Wolfe, 56
  May K., 53
Sofrit
  Helen M., 65
Spannseiler
  Andrew, 7
  Elizabeth, 8
Sparrow
  Helen M., 50
Spohn
  John, 8
Sponseller
  infant, 17
Springer
  Charles, 5
Stahler
  Margaret, 72
Staley
  Addie Elizabeth, 54
  Agnes, 12
  Alfred William, 9
  Altah Irene, 19
  Amanda Cordelia May, 11
  Anna E., 11
  Arlene Estelle Grove, 69
  Bertha C., 46
  Catherine Philabena, 59
  Charles A., 49
  Clara J., 38
  Cora Phoebe, 14
  Cornelius A., 15
  David Levi, 16
  Emma Grace, 59
  Ezra, 14
  Fleet B., 46
  George Albert, 16
  Glenna May, 58
  Grayson H., 60
  Hester Ann, 9
  I. Mary, 69
  Ida M., 14
  Ira Biser, 54
  Irving Edgar, 64
  Jane Elizabeth, 22

Deaths and Burials of Evangelical Reformed
United Church of Christ
Frederick, Frederick County, Maryland

 John H., Sr., 68
 Jonathan Aug., 24
 Kate E., 11
 Laura, 24
 Lurene A., 57
 Mae Estelle, 61
 Margaret Burger, 60
 May Jane, 18
 Mollie May, 61
 Orvis Marion, 69
 Paul Eugene, 68
 Shirley Brandes, 69
 William T., 47
Staples
 Katherine, 48
Starr
 Earl J., 71
 Ida R., 30
 Ira Nelson, 30
 June Estelle, 65
 Mary K., 40
 Mary Rosalie, 12
 Rebecca S., 12
Staub
 Fannie, 39
Stauder
 Christian, 3
Stauffer
 Anna Rebecca, 15
 Bessie M. Kaufman, 63
 Betty Lee, 60
 D. Murray, 44
 Daniel Valentine, 36
 David Murray, Jr., 36
 Guy V., 15
 Willie Anna, 39
Steckel
 Elizabeth, 6
 Mary Ann, 2
 Sybilla, 4
 Valentine, 6
Steele
 Mary Louise Tritapoe, 68
Stehly
 Ann Barbara, 4
 Anna Barbara, 2
 Elizabeth, 5
 Melchior, 2
Steiner
 Anna Mary, 9
 Catharine Elizabeth, 3
 Georgianna, 36
 John, 8
 John A., 28
 Lewis H., 22
 Louise Irene, 32
 Magdalen, 3
 Marietta, 29
 Mary, 19
 Mary A., 24
 Mary Ellen, 19
 Ralph Denning Smith, 11
 William, 3
Steven
 Marion P., 13
Stewart
 Bernard Roy, 62
 Harriet Loretta Z., 68
Stickel
 R. Dean, 57
Stimmel
 Eva, 3
 John, 6
 Peter, 6
Stine
 Ethel M., 56
 Mary Alice, 57
 Pierce Charles, Sr., 66
 William Sylvester, 57
Stitely
 Florence M., 34
Stober
 Dorothy, 7
Stockman
 Franklin E., 46
 Marion L., 46
 Marshall Henry, Sr., 55
 May Catherine, 56
 William E., 48
Stoener
 Almedia Susan, 32
Stoll
 Christopher, 2
Stone
 Ann Maria, 25
 Georgia V., 20
 Lydia A. E., 14
 Maude Estelle, 28
 Orfie E., 17
Stonebraker
 Daniel K., 32
Stoner
 Edna Maud, 20
 Harry A., 49
 Lemmiezine, 57
Storm
 Alice O., 42
 Anna Mary, 9
 Betty Culler, 70
 Frank Winter, 14
 Jacob, 5
 Johanna M. Magdalen, 8
 Sperry L., 66
Strailman
 Martha, 19
 Sarah, 10
Strauff
 Della M., 42
Stroup
 Elizabeth, 49
 Harry Milton, 53
Stull
 Adam, 25
 Charles, 52
 David P., 61
 Effie Gertrude, 30
 Elizabeth, 18
 Elizabeth Bussard, 70
 G. Bernard, 71
 George David, 57
 George L., 36
 Joshua, 10
 Mamie Estelle, 54
 Mary Ann, 38
 Mary Margaret, 55
 Rose Bavaria, 37
 Sarah Sophia, 19
 Susan Virginia, 43
 Susanna, 12
 William H., 33
Stup
 Charles E., 67
 Elijah Curtis, 11
 Elizabeth, 10
 Harvey T., 12
 Jonathan, 37
 Mary Ann, 42
 Sophia Ann, 41
Sturgis
 Anna Eliza, 14
Saunders
 Caroline E., 36

Deaths and Burials of Evangelical Reformed
United Church of Christ
Frederick, Frederick County, Maryland

Sulcer
   Emma K., 47
Suman
   Mary E., 23
Summers
   baby, 54
Suter
   Laura Virginia, 38
Swadener
   Anna Bertha, 51
   Henry Clinton, 54
Swain
   Laura Virginia, 62
Sweigert
   Jane, 23
Swope
   Florence May, 47
   Mary Elizabeth, 61
Tabler
   Kate S., 40
   William Benjamin, 11
Talbott
   Lillian Baker, 22
Tanner
   Lydia Isabel, 71
Taylor
   Florence Barrick, 39
   Mabel Lucy, 21
Thomas
   Anna May, 56
   C. Newton, 52
   Calvin Augustus, 35
   Caroline S., 22
   Catharine Harriet, 37
   Catherine Alice, 65
   Cephas M., 43
   Charlotte E., 10
   Christian, 10, 21
   Christina, 5
   Clarence C. C., 64
   Clarence S., Jr., 66
   Clinton C., 48
   Curtis William, 69
   David O., 10
   David Otho, 41
   Dr. Edward P., Sr., 57
   Dr. S. Frank, 32
   Edith M., 45
   Effie S. Hargett, 59
   Elizabeth, 24
   Elizabeth C., 36
   Elizabeth Ellen, 9
   Emily V., 45
   Ethel Sarah, 18
   Francis Granville, 34
   Gabriel, 4, 5
   George F., 38
   Grace A., 65
   Helen, 38
   Henry C., 19
   Henry Leven, 20
   Hiram G., 53
   Hiram Irving, 71
   Ira Newton, 35
   Jesse E., 29
   Jessie Lee Diller, 65
   John, 6
   John B., 23
   John D., 43
   John G., 28
   John Peter, 6
   K. Virginia, 42
   Lauretta, 39
   Lewis Michael, 14
   Louisa P., 44
   Louise, 38
   Louise G., 66
   Maria Virginia, 42
   Mary, 27
   Mary Cordelia Boyer, 61
   Mary Edith, 57
   Mary Eleanor, 13
   Mildred Lee Wenner, 71
   Ralph J., 61
   Rilla V., 68
   Ruth Dixon, 62
   Samuel D., 38
   Samuel Donald, 29
   Sarah E., 39
   Sarah Ellen, 40
   Susan Elizabeth, 56
   Susan L., 51
   Susan M., 27
   Valentine, 6
   Walter Graham, 33
   William H., Jr., 70
   William H., Sr., 57
   William M., 15
   William Mantz, 20
   Zacharias G., 30
Tice
   Nannie B., 35
Tinney
   Lillian R., 62
Titlow
   Adie Ely, 14
Titlow
   George W., 24
   Lewis Scholl, 12
Tobery
   Edna Irene, 68
Topper
   Margaret E., 31
Trago
   Eveline, 13
   William, 12
Traut
   Mathew, 4
   Michael, 2
   Valentine, 4
Trimmer
   Harry Clay, 19
   Mary Elizabeth Lease, 29
   Samuel, 30
Troxell
   Charles P., 46
   Helen Staley, 69
   Robert Allen, 67
Truett
   Mabel G., 40
Trundle
   Bessie B., 58
Tshudi
   Barbara, 2
Tull
   Eleanor M., 59
Tustin
   Mr., 6
   Mrs., 6
Tyler
   Catharine M., 16
Tyson
   Katharine A., 46
   Katharine Aubert, 37
   Margaret, 31
   Nathan S., 24
Umbach
   William, 8
Umberger
   Roy Eugene, 16
Umstead
   Bernice S., 66

Deaths and Burials of Evangelical Reformed
United Church of Christ
Frederick, Frederick County, Maryland

Unger
  Sophia Elizabeth, 42
Urban
  Carrie Y., 42
Van
  Grace DeLashmutt, 58
VanDevanter
  Lillian M., 46
VanFossen
  Carrie B., 49
Vann
  Dan MacIntyre, 58
VanSwearingen
  Charles, 66
Veist
  Mary Salome, 4
Virts
  Charlotte Inez, 53
Vollweiler
  Jacob, 3
Wachter
  Steiner R., 48
  Catharine Ann, 15
  Catharine E. M., 15
  Charles E., 23
  Cheryl Anne, 61
  Christina Sophia, 55
  Elmer E., 71
  George N., 59
  Grayson Phillip, 64
  Helen G., 71
  Helen Krepps, 38
  Helen Rhoads, 61
  Lewis, 31
  Lois Kathryn, 60
  Phoebe, 40
  Ralph F., 50
  Susan Elizabeth, 19
  William Noah, 37
  William Noah, Jr., 67
Walker
  Annie M., 45
  James E., 30
Wallen
  David, 3
  William, 5
Walling
  Ruth, 17
Wallis
  Albert R., 53
  Fannie Elizabeth, 54

Walter
  Mary Kathryn, 55
  R. W., 57
Waltz
  Margaret, 56
Warner
  Ruth Elizabeth, 23
Waters
  Ann Eliza, 18
  F. Gordon, 43
  Richard C., 35
Ways
  Margaret H., 20
  William H., Sr., 20
  William Henry, 16
Weber
  Jacob, 3
  Philip, 7
  William, 4
Weigle
  Anne Elizabeth Korn, 70
Weil
  John George, 9
Welsch
  Jean, 71
Wenger
  Msgt John H., 55
Werking
  Dove E., 50
Werntz
  Florine, 70
  Rev. W. Garner, 69
Wertheimer
  Mildred Lee, 24
Whalen
  John W., 17
Whaley
  Isabelle Frances, 34
  Sophia, 14
Wharthen
  May Jane, 27
Whisner
  Catharine Elizabeth, 33
  Minnie Z., 30
  S. Guy, 37
White
  Alice A., 47
  Dorothy Sier, 63
  Roscoe Conklin, 33
Whitter
  Susan E., 24

Wiest
  Catharine, 6
  Eva Catharine, 7
Wigle
  Polly, 11
Wilcoxen
  Anna Mary, 33
  Annie V., 31
  George E., 40
  Rebecca, 51
  Urner, 33
Wilcoxon
  Andrew Jackson, 23
  Clarence Eugene, 13
  Harry Jackson, 11
  John, 15
  Rufus H., 17
Wiles
  Alvie C., 64
  Charles "Hambone", Sr., 68
  Ella Louise, 38
  George Daniel, Jr., 54
  Ida M., 42
  Pfc. James Edward, 52
  Steven Ray, 58
Wilkinson
  Jean Collmus, 69
  T. D., 69
Willard
  J. Lee, 58
  Jane Russell Meade, 68
  Mary E. S., 54
  Roger H., 66
Williams
  Alma V., 55
  Eleanor, 22
  John H., 25
Wills
  Alice V., 40
  Charles, 11
  Cpl. Victor L., 54
  no first name, 41
Wilson
  Charles, 10
  Henry Leo, Sr., 55
Windsor
  James, 40
Winebrener
  Annie L., 44
Winebrenner
  Arie, 49

Deaths and Burials of Evangelical Reformed
United Church of Christ
Frederick, Frederick County, Maryland

Laura A., 51
Winkelman
　Paul, 37
　Wilhemina, 38
Winpigler
　Robert Earl, 64
Winter
　Frederick, 12
Winters
　Caroline Fleming, 61
Wintz
　George, 1
　Margaret, 1
Wirtenbecher
　-------, 1
　Adam, 9
Wise
　Ellen R., 24
　Florence M., 41
Wissinger
　Catharine, 4
Witmer
　Mary Elizabeth, 5
Witter
　Joseph Henry, 21
Witterich
　Dorothy, 9
Wolf
　Peter, 4
Wolfe
　Adam, 9
　Alice V., 41
　Alice Virginia, 37
　Charles Edward, 28
　Elizabeth Ryon, 17
　Elsie May, 53
　Enoch Pratt, 17
　George H., 17
　Guy F., 49
　Janet Hinks, 43
　Mary A., 43
　Rose May, 51
　Thomas M., 21
　Thomas Melville, 26
Wolff
　Amelia Catherine, 56
　Henry, 8
　Margaret, 6
Wollenschlager
　Nicholas, 3

Wood
　Grace B., 31
Woodward
　Margaret, 2
Worman
　Amanda J., 41
　Charles W. D., 47
　Emma J., 49
　Emma K., 55
　George M., 42
　Mary Elizabeth, 32
　Mary Willetta, 56
　Scott, 52
Yinger
　Charles Lewis, 13
　Harry Eugene, 37
Yingling
　Nora Kefauver, 52
Yost
　Amelia, 47
　Catharine, 27
　George, 30
　Mary, 47
　Minnie Elizabeth, 36
Young
　Alvey Doub, 60
　Alvey Doub, Jr., 57
　Annie K., 38
　Austin U., 57
　Charles Brown, 58
　Joseph, 57
　Julia Latham Derr, 72
　Leah Hamilton Lark, 67
　Manzella, 41
　Mary Ann, 21
Zacharias
　Catharine Z., 24
　George Merle, 33
　Jane, 31
Zeigler
　Amy Rebecca, 59
　Caroline C., 45
　Charles C., 43
　George Z., 58
　Rosanna, 24
Zeiler
　Ann Sophia, 30
　Clarence, 17
　Emma M., 13
Zellers
　Charles C., 10

　Flora Emma, 22
Zentz
　Jennie M. C., 48
　Newton M., 41
Ziegler
　Henry Edward, 24
　Susan Chandler, 54
Zieler
　Charles E., 34
Zimmerman
　Alberta F., 44
　Alfred Glaze, 58
　Barbara Alice, 14
　Bernard F., 31
　Caroline R., 30
　Charles E., 48
　Charles Herbert, 58
　Clara, 43
　Clayton Maynard, 56
　Dorothy Jean, 70
　Elizabeth H., 62
　Elsie R., 50
　Florence M., 48
　George, Sr., 6
　Georgia W., 51
　Harry Franklin, 44
　Harry "Bud", 70
　Harvey S., 47
　Helen G., 66
　Hester C., 42
　Horace, 29
　infant, 50
　Irving Franklin, 61
　Isabele E., 63
　Jacob, 16
　Jessie M., 51
　John, 3
　Laura K., 40
　Laura M., 47
　Lola Bell, 54
　Madeline M., 65
　Margaret M., 63
　Maria A., 47
　Marion, 42
　Mary D., 21
　Mary E., 19
　Mary Margaret, 55
　Mazeppa A., 53
　Merle Henry, 27
　Myra Beatty, 56
　Nettie E., 42

Deaths and Burials of Evangelical Reformed
United Church of Christ
Frederick, Frederick County, Maryland

    R. Clinton, 47
    Raymond R., 66
    Robert Fleming, 20
    Ruth, 27
    S. Joseph, 56
    Spencer G.H., Sr., 44
    Susan, 1
    Thomas H., 66
    Walton Roelky, 31
    William Henry, Jr., 69
    William Henry, Sr., 69
    William Marion, 55
Zumstein
    Catherine, 33
    Louis D., 13

www.ingramcontent.com/pod-product-compliance
Lightning Source LLC
Chambersburg PA
CBHW071153090426
42736CB00012B/2315